Dr Kathleen Rankin, née Lilley (1928–2018), was a graduate of Queen's University, Belfast where she completed her Ph.D. on the In-service Education of Teachers with particular reference to science. For many years she was involved with the organisation of both Chemistry and Biology courses for teachers at the Queen's University Teachers' Centre. In addition she was a graduate of Trinity College, University of Dublin where she obtained an M.Litt. in Education. Dr Rankin was the daughter of the late Herbert R. Lilley, a well known linen designer, and from retirement as a lecturer in Lisburn Institute, she was involved with Living Linen, an organisation associated with the gathering of information on the Irish Linen industry in the twentieth century.

Kathleen Rankin published several books on a range of subjects, mostly concerning Irish linen. They include *Linen Houses of the Lagan Valley, the story of their families*, and on the same theme, *Linen Houses of the Bann Valley, the story of their families*.

Kathleen Rankin was appointed MBE in the 2010 New Year's Honours List.

Quai des Menetriers, Bruges, 1912
Herbert R. Lilley
From a Private Collection

The
LINEN HOUSES
of the
BANN VALLEY

The story of their families

KATHLEEN RANKIN

ULSTER HISTORICAL
FOUNDATION

Dedicated

to

Living Linen

*which has done so much to ensure that
Irish linen heritage is not forgotten*

First published in 2007
by the Ulster Historical Foundation
www.ancestryireland.com

Except as otherwise permitted under the Copyright, Designs and Patents Act 1988, this publication may only be reproduced, stored or transmitted in any form or by any means with the prior permission in writing of the publisher or, in the case of reprographic reproduction, in accordance with the terms of a licence issued by The Copyright Licensing Agency. Enquiries concerning reproduction outside those terms should be sent to the publisher.

© Kathleen Rankin, 2007

Reprinted by Lightning Source, 2023
Design and production, Dunbar Design

ISBN 978-1-913993-44-3

CONTENTS

ACKNOWLEDGEMENTS	x
LIST OF ABBREVIATIONS	xi
PREFACE	xii
INTRODUCTION	xiv

1
CASTLEWELLAN

Murland Family Tree		2
The Murland Family of Annsborough		4
Murland	Annsborough House, Castlewellan	8
Murland	Ardnabannon, Castlewellan	11
Murland	Wood Lodge, Castlewellan	14
Murland	Woodlawn, Castlewellan	16
Murland	Greenvale, Castlewellan	18

2
KATESBRIDGE, TULLYCONNAUGHT, BALLIEVEY and BALLYDOWN

Lowry	Linen Hill, Katesbridge	22
The Mulligan Family of Tullyconnaught		23
Mulligan	Millbank House, Tullyconnaught	24
Mulligan	Parkmount, Tullyconnaught	26
Mulligan	Roselawn, Ballydown	28
Crawford	Ballievey House, Ballievey	29
Crawford Family Tree		33

3
TULLYHENAN near BANBRIDGE

The Lindsay Family of Tullyhenan 36
The Lindsay Family Tree 38

Lindsay   Tullyhenan House, Banbridge   39
Lindsay   Moorlands, Banbridge   41
Lindsay   Ashfield House, Dromore   43
Lindsay   Ballydown, Banbridge   45

4
BANBRIDGE

McClelland   Belmont House, Banbridge   50
Walker   Solitude House, Banbridge   52
Robinson   Rockville, Banbridge   54

The Ferguson Family of Banbridge 56
Ferguson Family Tree 60

Ferguson   Edenderry House, Banbridge   61
Ferguson   Clonaslee, Banbridge   63
Ferguson   Iveagh House, Banbridge   65
Ferguson   Aghaderg Glebe House, Loughbrickland   67
Ferguson   Warrain, Banbridge   69

The Cowdy Family of Banbridge 71
Cowdy Family Tree 74

Cowdy   Millmount House, Banbridge   75
Cowdy   Edenderry Lodge, Banbridge   77
Cowdy   Dunida House, Banbridge   79
Cowdy   Summer Island, Loughgall   81

The Smyth Family of Banbridge 84
Smyth Family Tree 87

Smyth   Brookfield House, Banbridge   88
Smyth   Milltown House, Lenaderg   90
Smyth   Bellfield, Lenaderg   92
Smyth   Lenaderg House, Lenaderg   94
Dunbar   Huntly House, Banbridge   96

Dunbar Family Tree 98

5
GILFORD

Law	Hazelbank, Lawrencetown	102
Law	Glenbanna House, Lawrencetown	104

The Uprichard Family of Springvale Bleach Works — 105
Uprichard Family Tree — 108

Uprichard	Fairview House, Lurgan	110
Uprichard	Bannvale House, Gilford	111
Uprichard	Lawrencetown House, Gilford	113
Bell	Tullylish House, Gilford	115
Haughton	Banford House, Tullylish	118
Haughton	Mount Pleasant, Tullylish	121
McMaster	Dunbarton House, Gilford	123

McMaster Family Tree — 127

Dickson	Gilford Castle, Gilford	128
Dickson	Elmfield Castle, Gilford	130
Watson	Stramore House, Gilford	133
Watson	Lakeview, Lurgan	135
Watson	Beechpark, Lurgan	137

The Sinton Family of Tandragee — 139
Sinton Family Tree — 140

Sinton	Ballyards Castle, Milford	141
Sinton	Banford House, Tullylish	144
Sinton	Woodbank, Gilford	146

6
MOYALLON

The Richardson Family of Moyallon — 152

Richardson	Moyallon House, Gilford	154
Richardson	Old Drumlyn, Portadown	157
Richardson	Drumlyn, Portadown	159
Richardson	The Woodhouse, Bessbrook	161
Richardson	Mount Caulfield House, Bessbrook	164

7
LURGAN

The Bell Family of Lurgan		168
Family Tree of Samuel A. Bell of Lurgan		170
Bell	Bellvue, Lurgan	171
Bell	Solitude, Lurgan	173
McGeagh	Derry Lodge, Lurgan	175
The Johnston Family of Lurgan		177
Johnston	Fallowfield, Lurgan	180
Johnston	The Demesne, Lurgan	182
Johnston	Annadale, Lurgan	184

8
PORTADOWN

Acheson	Bannview House, Portadown	188
Dawson	Corcrain House, Portadown	190
Hamilton Robb	Edenderry House, Portadown	192
The Spence and Bryson Families of Portadown		194
Bryson	Gleneden, Portadown	196
Bryson	Rathowen, Portadown	198
The Greeves Family of Portadown		200
Owden Greeves	Tavanagh House, Portadown	202
T. Jackson Greeves	Fairacre, Portadown	204
W. E. Greeves	Ardeevin, Portadown	206
Shillington	Altavilla, Portadown	208

9
TANDRAGEE and ARMAGH

Turtle	Mullavilla House, Tandragee	212
McCrum	Manor House, Milford	214
Compton	Umgola House, Armagh	218
Compton	Glenanne House, Glenanne	220
Proctor	Tullydowey House, Blackwatertown	222

10
DUNGANNON

Dickson	Milltown House, Dungannon	228
The Dickson Family Tree		232
Stevenson	Aloha, Dungannon 233	
The Greer and the Greeves Families of County Tyrone		236
Greer	Rhone Hill, Dungannon	239
Greer	Tullylagan Manor, Dungannon	241
Greeves	Fernshaw, Dungannon	243
Acheson	Castlecaulfield House, Castlecaufield	246
BIBLIOGRAPHY		249
INDEX		253

ACKNOWLEDGEMENTS

A book of this nature requires an input of knowledge from a considerable number of sources.

I would like to take this opportunity to thank the many people who have helped to make this work possible, in particular the members of a small committee, John R. Cowdy, Robert J. McKinstry, Peter J. Rankin and J. Fred Rankin who gave helpful knowledge and advice. I am deeply indebted to the owners of the many houses who have allowed photographs to be taken and also, in some cases, provided family photographs. They often contributed information concerning the history of their houses, and this has been of great assistance. My thanks are also due to Jason Diamond, Banbridge Heritage and Genealogy Services, who provided helpful information on Banbridge families, and some photographs of houses and portraits of their owners. In particular, I would also like to thank Dr Jonathan P. Hamill who read the script and made suggestions for which I am very grateful.

Where possible modern photographs of the houses have been used and, on occasion, an older photograph included for comparison. Unfortunately a number of the 'Linen Houses' no longer exist, and photographs have had to be sourced from former owners or local museums and libraries. This book endeavours, wherever possible, to give some idea of the lifestyle of the people who lived in the 'Linen Houses'. Many of their descendants are still alive and my thanks are due in very great measure to them for photographs of houses and their residents. I am grateful to the following for photographs: Dr Robert A. Logan, John R. Cowdy, Dr H.A. Lyons, Norman G.D. Ferguson, Paul McCandless, Miss Rosalind M. Hadden, Jim Lyttle, John Morton, Jerry Murland, John Girling, Thomas A. Dickson, Mrs Rosemary C. Dickson, Stanley Ferguson, Richard D. Bell, Joe A. Johnston, Mrs Esther Carswell, Ms Marilyn Braun, Canon J.R.B. McDonald, Mr & Mrs N. Carswell, J.W. Jackson, Margaret Gamble, Mrs N. Milliken, Peter N. Acheson, Mrs Muriel Palmer, Mrs Rena Brien, Barry Finlay.

Acknowledgement must also be made to the various institutions that assisted with archive material and photographic research, and that have kindly given permission for photographs to be reproduced from their collections: the Public Record Office of Northern Ireland (PRONI), the Historic Monuments and Buildings Branch of the Department of the Environment for Northern Ireland (HMBB), the Trustees of the National Museums and Galleries of Northern Ireland: Ulster Museum (UM) and Ulster Folk and Transport Museum (UFTM), Craigavon Museum, the Irish & Local Studies Library, Armagh, the Controller of Her Majesty's Stationery Office on behalf of the Ordnance Survey of Northern Ireland.

ACKNOWLEDGEMENTS

Lastly, I owe a very great debt to my husband, Fred, who entered into the project with great enthusiasm, and is responsible for the majority of the photographs in this book. With the inclusion of many illustrations it became clear that sponsorship support was required from outside bodies. I am extremely grateful to those listed for their generous contributions:

The Esmé Mitchell Trust
The Miss Elizabeth Ellison Charitable Trust
Banbridge District Council
Belfast Natural History and Philosophical Society
Ulster Garden Villages Limited
Craigavon Borough Council
Environment and Heritage Service, Department of the Environment

ABBREVIATIONS

BNL	*Belfast Newsletter*
BT	*Belfast Telegraph*
ILC & LM	Irish Linen Centre & Lisburn Museum
LL	Living Linen
MBR	Monuments and Buildings Record of Northern Ireland
PRONI	Public Record Office of Northern Ireland
NMGNI UFTM	Ulster Folk & Transport Museum
NMGNI UM	Ulster Museum
JFR	J.F. Rankin, Esq.

PREFACE

The Living Linen Project was set up in 1995 in order to record as an Oral Archive the knowledge of the linen industry still available within a nucleus of people who were formerly working in the industry in Ulster. Over the period 1870 to 1970 the north east of Ireland was the world's leading linen producing area. Ulster manufacturers produced three quarters of the United Kingdom's output, specialising in the medium and fine end of the market. Concern has been expressed regarding the fact that despite the linen industry underpinning the local economy no comprehensive history of the industry over three centuries has been written. Nevertheless, considerable historical studies on the Irish linen industry in the eighteenth and nineteenth centuries have been published, but very little has been done in the last one hundred years to emphasise the world wide nature of this trade in that period.

A very important feature of the linen industry in Ireland has been the resilience of the small or medium size private family firm. Although in the aftermath of the First World War, the difficulties of trade in the 1930s, and the Second World War, many of these companies were forced to close, a considerable number survived into the 1970s. However, by the close of the twentieth century there had been a very great reduction in numbers with less than twenty companies continuing to operate. Therefore, with the Irish linen trade in very steep decline, there appeared to be an urgent necessity to gather information while it was still available. The Living Linen project, in Phase I, was set up to gather knowledge quickly, which was held by many of the former owners and managers of the industry, since there was a wealth of information not put in writing. Nevertheless, there was also oral knowledge which could be recorded, from the representatives of the linen trade who travelled world wide and from pockets of highly skilled people living in manufacturing areas. This second group of recordings, with the work supported financially by the Heritage Lottery Fund from 1999 to 2002, constituted Phase II of the project and all Living Linen recordings were placed in the Ulster Folk & Transport Museum, Cultra, County Down.

Initially, in Phase I, various Living Linen committee members made, in the main, recordings of the owners and managers of the old linen industry. With others, I had the privilege of invitations to homes of linen merchants where, in some cases, records of their lifestyle, including portraits and photographs, going back over many years, were held. Many of the linen merchants built new properties or improved existing ones with the large growth of the linen industry in the nineteenth century in the Upper Bann Valley, and particularly around the

PREFACE

stretch of the river from Banbridge to Portadown. It therefore appeared appropriate to compile a book concerned with a historical and architectural study of these houses as with the companion volume for the Lagan Valley. Although this book makes use of information and photographs gathered in the Living Linen project, it has had to draw on the considerable records of the Public Record Office of Northern Ireland, the Linen Hall Library, Belfast, the Ulster Folk & Transport Museum, and the Craigavon Museum, County Armagh.

INTRODUCTION

The River Bann is the longest river in Northern Ireland, flowing for eighty miles from the south of the country north to the sea, but also being a river of two halves. The Upper Bann rises in the Mourne Mountains in south Down and flows into Lough Neagh just north of Craigavon, while the Lower Bann continues from the northern end of Lough Neagh eventually entering the ocean north of Coleraine between Portstewart and Castlerock. The water power of the Upper Bann was a significant factor leading to the early establishment of the linen industry in the rich farmland around Banbridge, continuing on to Lawrencetown and Gilford. Portadown also had a considerable linen industry, along with the famed excellence of early hand weaving around Lurgan which is unique as a linen making town , standing on the low interfluve between the River Bann and the River Lagan.

Conrad Gill, 1923, in his book on *The Rise of the Ulster Linen Industry*, states,

> In the first place, the bleachgreens all lay along the lines of rivers: on the lower course of the Lagan, especially between Lisburn and Belfast; on the upper Bann, in the neighbourhood of Banbridge, Moyallon, and Lurgan; on the lower Bann, about Coleraine; and on the River Roe at Limavady.

The water of the Upper Bann was relatively soft and free of discolouration as it flowed through Katesbridge, Banbridge, Gilford and on to Moyallon, but after this point the river flowed through peat bogs near Portadown which imparted a brown colour, and was a disadvantage in the bleaching of linen yarn or cloth. The bleach mills around Banbridge were dependant on a regular supply of water but very often, in summer, the level of water in the Bann fell. This is well illustrated in the *Ordnance Survey Memoirs*, 1834, for the parish of Tullylish:

> Notwithstanding the various dykes and weirs raised by the owners of the different mills there is so scanty a supply of water (in summer) that they are sometimes unable to work more than eight hours of the twenty-four.

Continuity of the water supply was essential both in the manufacture of linen and in bleaching, therefore, in 1836, the Bann Reservoir Company was set up to provide a more abundant and regular supply of water in the River Bann. A survey was made by a distinguished engineer, Sir William Fairburn of Manchester, who recommended the construction of three reservoirs, although eventually only two were constructed. The Lough Island Reavy and Corbet Lough reservoirs increased the volume of water on the Upper Bann five fold, and ensured a continuous supply of water to the mills.

INTRODUCTION

Lewis, writing in 1837, comments on the enterprise of the linen merchants of Banbridge who had commenced manufacturing on an extensive scale and were already trading with America. He also states that in 1772, around Banbridge, there were no less than 26 bleach greens on the River Bann, with the trade being principally carried on at Gilford. However, by 1837, Banbridge had become one of the most important inland manufacturing towns in Ireland with linen of every description being manufactured and bleached in the surrounding area. This led to greater employment in these districts and changes, both industrial and commercial, were quite rapid. In the nineteenth century, with a steadily increasing demand on the part of bleachers for the direct supply of cloth, weavers gradually settled in larger and larger numbers in the neighbourhood of bleach greens. Again, Gill, 1923, states that the census returns show time after time, a bleach yard, the owner's house, and a little community of bleach yard workers and weavers settled round them. The bleacher's house was of singular importance and in many cases a modest eighteenth century house was replaced in the nineteenth century with a much more impressive building, reflecting the opulent lifestyle of the linen barons. Although the linen industry has folded, many of these houses still remain and there are particularly important houses between Banbridge and Moyallon.

In Ireland, during the eighteenth century, the spinning of linen yarn was carried out by women in their cottages, which were scattered throughout the countryside. Irish linen developed and specialised in the production of extremely fine yarns, which were woven into damasks and cambrics, unmatched in quality world wide. However, in England, within twenty years of the successful mechanisation of the spinning of cotton yarn a beginning had been made with the power spinning of flax. John Marshall of Leeds and his associates opened the first spinning mill in 1790 as a result of the inventions of John Kendrew and Thomas Porthouse of Darlington. From Yorkshire power spinning of flax was taken up in the linen manufacturing districts of the east of Scotland where it soon became an important industry. The English and Scottish industries manufactured mainly coarse linens, for which the yarn produced by the primitive mill spindles was considered satisfactory. In Ireland, the linen industry remained almost untouched by these changes since it concentrated on fine cloth made from locally produced yarns. However, by the beginning of the nineteenth century, outside the traditional centres of the Ulster industry in Lurgan, Portadown, Banbridge, and Lisburn, the cottage spinning of yarn and weaving of cloth did begin to decrease and considerable quantities of flax were exported from Ulster to Britain for dry spinning. In 1825 James Kay of Preston invented a wet spinning process in that he discovered that a thorough soaking in cold water made flax fibres more slippery so that they could be drawn by machinery into a really fine yarn.

In County Down some of the earliest attempts were made at spinning by power, stimulated by a subsidy from the Linen Board, (1711–1828), and small spinning mills existed for a few years at Comber, at Kilmore near Crossgar, and at Templegowran, near Newry. These were dry spinning mills, and the yarn, which they produced, was not suitable for manufacturing fine cloth, but the introduction of wet spinning meant that a manufacturer need no longer rely on hand spun yarn. Irish manufacturers quickly adopted wet spinning since there were many employers who could afford the capital required for working the new process. They were helped by grants from the Linen Board, given on the advice of a Parliamentary Committee of 1825, and the first of the County Down manufacturers to adopt the wet spinning process was James Murland, of Annsborough, near Castlewellan.

According to Green, 1963, wet power spinning was responsible for the most profound changes which had so far taken place in the Irish linen industry, resulting in a concentration of spinning, manufacturing, and bleaching on the River Bann. Samuel Law, a bleacher, built the first spinning mill on the Upper Bann at Hazelbank, about 1834, but somewhat earlier, in 1810, Hugh Dunbar had begun making linen thread at Huntly, near Banbridge, the business also being taken up by William A. Stewart of Edenderry, and by Brice Smyth of Brookfield. A major development took place in 1834 when Hugh Dunbar, of Huntly, decided to erect a wet spinning mill, driven by steam power, at Gilford. As capital was required for the project he was joined by John Walsh McMaster, and later by James Dickson. Eventually, the Dunbar McMaster five storey spinning mill opened in 1838, and was the largest industrial undertaking on the River Bann.

As the linen industry developed, a group of closely related Quaker families became engaged in it all along the Upper Bann between Moyallon and Lawrencetown. These included the Richardsons, Wakefields, Christys, Uprichards, and the Nicholsons. Alexander Christy settled in the townland of Moyallon in 1675, and the family is reputed to have introduced linen bleaching into the Upper Bann Valley. James Christy, a grandson of Alexander, established a small chemical works at Moyallon in 1786 to produce sulphuric acid for the bleaching trade. However, in the latter part of the eighteenth century Moyallon bleach green belonged to Joseph Wakefield, who had married Hannah, daughter of Thomas Christy of Moyallon. Wakefield had originally come from Westmoreland to learn the linen business with Joseph Richardson of Stramore.

As the Upper Bann leaves Moyallon it flows into the northern area of County Armagh and passing through Portadown reaches Lough Neagh not far from the River Blackwater. This river divides County Armagh from County Tyrone for upwards of 30 miles and is joined by the River Callan just south of Charlemont. Gribbon, 1969, writing about the Rivers Blackwater and Callan, states:

> In their upper reaches these streams were, in the 19th century, more thickly studded with mills than any others in the province, mills connected with the linen industry predominating.

Blackwatertown, in County Tyrone, four miles north west of the city of Armagh,

INTRODUCTION

was the site of the Jackson & Eyre bleach green, however, McEvoy, 1802, notes that they had two more bleach greens adjoining, in the County of Armagh. Some years later, Lewis, 1837, reported that the principal trade of Dungannon, County Tyrone, and neighbourhood was the manufacture and bleaching of linen.

In north Armagh around Lurgan, and also in south east Tyrone there was a considerable number of Quaker settlers who helped to establish the linen industry. Henry Greer, who came to Ireland from Northumberland in 1653, settled at Redford, near Grange, County Tyrone, and became an early member of the Society of Friends. One of his sons, James Greer (1653–1718), married in 1678 into the Rea family of Lisacurran near Lurgan, and their four sons became very wealthy linen drapers. At this time a number of the Greer families lived in the area between Dungannon and Moy, and were highly esteemed linen merchants, so much so that the grandson of Henry, John Greer of The Grange, County Tyrone, in the late eighteenth century, became Inspector General of the Linen Trade in Ulster. Descendants of one branch of the family, who changed their name to Greeves, continued in the nineteenth century their involvement with the mechanised linen industry, when the brothers John and Thomas Malcomson Greeves set up, in 1862, J. & T.M. Greeves & Co., flax spinners, Forth River Mills, Belfast. Coming into the twentieth century, two sons of John Greeves (1831–1917), started the Portadown Weaving Company which was situated at the lower end of Thomas Street in Portadown, close to the Annagh River, which flowed from the western side of Portadown into the River Bann on the east.

Many of these enterprising linen manufacturers and bleachers built homes for themselves close to their work place in the eighteenth, nineteenth and twentieth centuries. Although almost all linen manufacture in Northern Ireland has ceased a considerable number of the linen houses remain. This book aims to provide an illustrated and informed commentary on the major linen families and the magnificent houses they lived in along the Upper Bann Valley. Areas included are those associated with South Down, Banbridge, Gilford, Lurgan, Portadown, Tandragee, Armagh and Dungannon, with a study of seventy nine houses. The images – exterior views of the actual houses, interior scenes of the stately rooms and portraits of their owners, many selected from private collections of the families themselves – present glimpses of a bygone age. In the areas of Lurgan and Portadown considerable difficulty arises due to the creation of Craigavon and the subsequent demolition of many important houses, nevertheless every effort has been made to find old photographs which are relevant to its linen history. The format of the book is similar to The Linen Houses of the Lagan Valley, with short family histories and family trees for major linen families, which have, of necessity, been limited to the male members of a family, who have, for several generations, been involved in some aspect of the linen industry.

The identification of these houses, some of which are very old, with the entrepreneurs of the Irish linen industry, will also serve to show the importance of that industry to the growth of Ulster over a period of three hundred years.

1
CASTLEWELLAN

HINCKS PRINT PLATE IV
representing the Beetling, Scutching and Hackling the Flax

WILLIAM HINCKS 1783

THE MURLAND FAMILY
OF ANNSBOROUGH

MURLAND

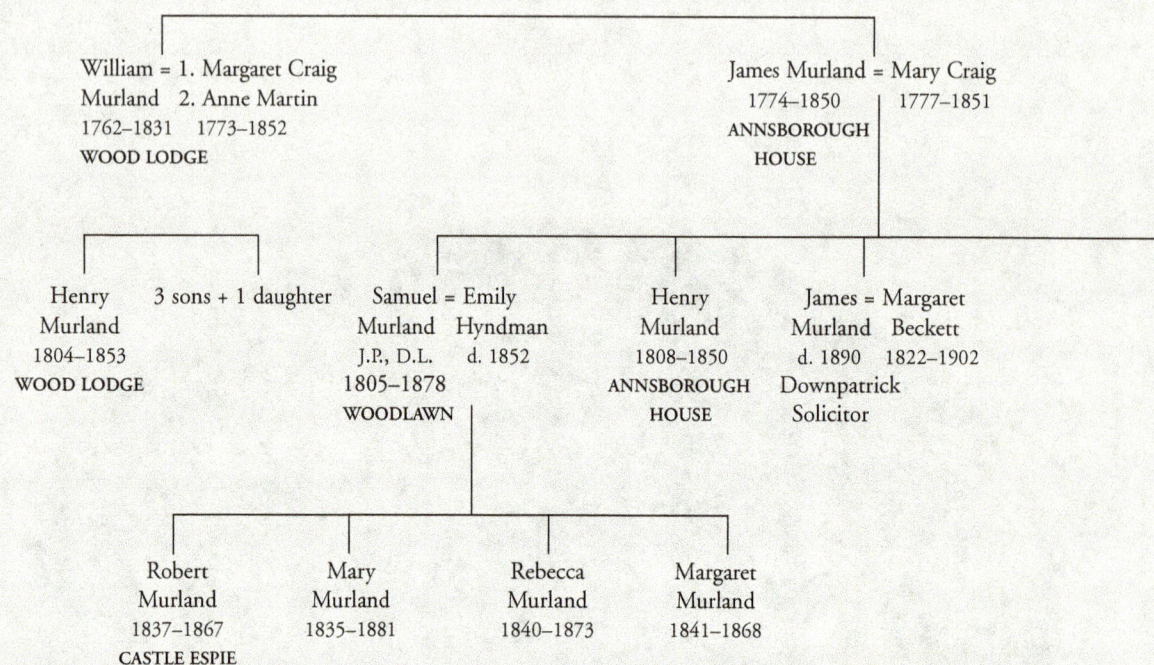

William Murland = Portaferry, Co. Down
d. 1800

William Murland = 1. Margaret Craig
1762–1831   2. Anne Martin
             1773–1852
WOOD LODGE

James Murland = Mary Craig
1774–1850   1777–1851
ANNSBOROUGH HOUSE

Henry Murland
1804–1853
WOOD LODGE

3 sons + 1 daughter

Samuel Murland = Emily Hyndman
J.P., D.L.   d. 1852
1805–1878
WOODLAWN

Henry Murland
1808–1850
ANNSBOROUGH HOUSE

James Murland = Margaret Beckett
d. 1890   1822–1902
Downpatrick
Solicitor

Robert Murland
1837–1867
CASTLE ESPIE

Mary Murland
1835–1881

Rebecca Murland
1840–1873

Margaret Murland
1841–1868

ARDNABANNON PARTY

Top left: Evelyn and Florence Murland

Middle back row: William Forster Uprichard

Second from right back: Charles Murland

Front centre: Warren Murland

Extreme right: Emile Uprichard

Front second right: Forster Uprichard

Centre: Beatrice Murland

COURTESY JERRY MURLAND

FAMILY TREE

```
                    ┌──────────────────────┬──────────────────────┐
              William              Charles = Jane          3 daughters, Elizabeth, Margaret and Jane
              Murland              Murland   Dobbin
              1815–1848            1820–1887 d. 1890
              ANNSBOROUGH          ARDNABANNON  eldest daughter of
              HOUSE                HOUSE        Clotworthy Dobbin of Belfast
```

James M. = Ellen B. Murland Davison 1845–1876 1846–1939 **WOOD LODGE**	Clotworthy = Sarah Ferguson Warren 1853–1895 Murland J.P. eldest daughter of 1847–1903 Thomas Ferguson **ARDNABANNON** Edenderry, Banbridge **HOUSE**	William = Sarah Henry Fenton Murland d.1934 1850–1888 **GREENVALE** **HOUSE** 2 sons

| Charles
Murland
1870–1922 | Helen
Margaret
Murland | James = Beatrice
Warren Eliza
Murland Hastings
1870–1943 1875–1956
ARDNABANNON
HOUSE | Thomas = Ellen
Stanley Dulcie
Murland
1877–1912
solicitor | Clotworthy = Susan
Warren   Mary
Murland   Ewing
b.1879
GREENVALE
HOUSE | 2 sons
+ 2 daughters |

James Robert = Beatrice Amy
William   Burke
Murland
b. 1909

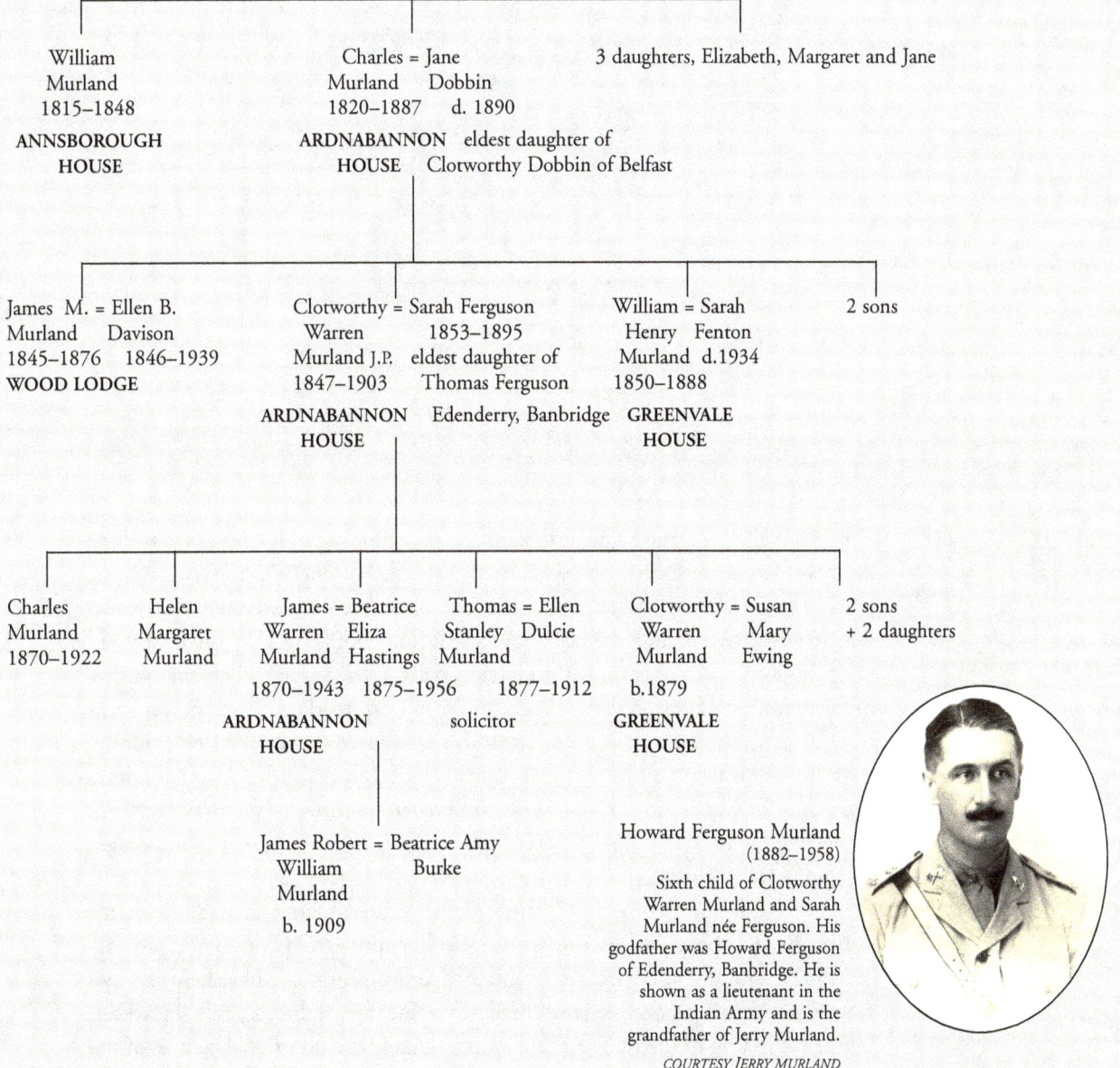

Howard Ferguson Murland
(1882–1958)
Sixth child of Clotworthy Warren Murland and Sarah Murland née Ferguson. His godfather was Howard Ferguson of Edenderry, Banbridge. He is shown as a lieutenant in the Indian Army and is the grandfather of Jerry Murland.

COURTESY JERRY MURLAND

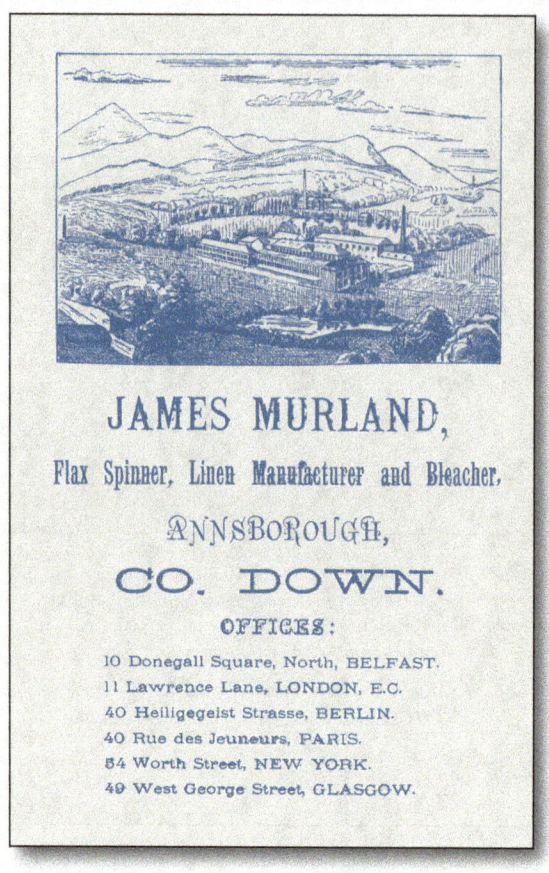

THE MURLAND FAMILY
OF ANNSBOROUGH

Hand bill reproduced from George Bassett, *County Down, 100 Years Ago*

In Ireland, during the eighteenth century, the spinning of linen yarn was done by women in their cottages, which were scattered throughout the countryside. Irish linen developed and specialised in the production of extremely fine yarns, which were woven into damasks and cambrics, unmatched in quality world wide. However, in England, within twenty years of the successful mechanisation of the spinning of cotton yarn a beginning had been made with the power spinning of flax. John Marshall of Leeds and his associates opened the first spinning mill in 1790 as a result of the inventions of John Kendrew and Thomas Porthouse of Darlington. From Yorkshire power spinning of flax was taken up in the linen manufacturing districts of the east of Scotland where it soon became an important industry.

The English and Scottish industries manufactured mainly coarse linens, for which the yarn produced by the primitive mill spindles was considered satisfactory. In Ireland, the linen industry remained almost untouched by these changes since it concentrated on fine cloth made from locally produced yarns. However, by the beginning of the nineteenth century, outside the traditional centres of the

Ulster industry in Lurgan, Portadown, Banbridge, and Lisburn the cottage spinning of yarn and weaving of cloth did begin to decay and considerable quantities of flax were exported from Ulster to Britain for dry spinning. In 1825 James Kay of Preston invented a wet spinning process in that he discovered that a thorough soaking in cold water made flax fibres more slippery so that they could be drawn by machinery into a really fine yarn.

In County Down some of the earliest attempts were made at spinning by power, stimulated by a subsidy from the Linen Board. Small spinning mills existed for a few years at Comber, at Kilmore near Crossgar, and at Templegowran, near Newry. These were dry spinning mills, and the yarn, which they produced, was not suitable for manufacturing fine cloth, but the introduction of wet spinning meant that a manufacturer need no longer rely on hand spun yarn. Irish manufacturers quickly adopted wet spinning since there were many employers who could afford the capital required for working the new process and they were helped by grants from the Linen Board, (1711–1828), given on the advice of a Parliamentary Committee of 1825. The first of the County Down manufacturers to adopt the wet spinning process was James Murland, of Annsborough, near Castlewellan.

William and James Murland, the sons of a Portaferry tanner, acquired bleach greens at Annsborough in 1800, lying at the foot of the steep hill which falls away from the village of Castlewellan. An ample water supply came from a stream fed by the lake in Lord Annesley's demesne and by 1816 the Murland brothers had two bleach yards capable of finishing between 7,000 and 8,000 pieces a year. James Murland, (c. 1774–1850), was the younger but clearly the more forceful of the two brothers and many stories survive among his descendants and the mill people which bear witness to the strength of his personality, along with stories of his travels in the United States as a dealer in linen cloth. The history of the beginnings of power spinning at Annsborough are far from clear, the traditional date being 1828, two years before the opening of the Mulhollands' steam power mill in York Street, Belfast. In fact the evidence for this date is corroborated by a board lettered 1828 which was found at Annsborough and came from the old mill, indeed it may be the date of the erection of the building or at least a part of it. A portion of an old spinning frame has also survived, dated 1820, which again points to a fairly early date. Finally, James Murland told the assistant commissioner of the hand loom weavers' enquiry in 1840 that he had been manufacturing for fourteen years, perhaps meaning that he began power spinning in 1826 or very soon after it.

Within a few years of commencing wet spinning the Murland business had grown to such an extent that another mill was required and it was built further west on the bleach greens where water power was available. Originally, William Murland's bleach green was at the top of the hill near his house Wood Lodge,

James W. Murland (1814–90) son of James Murland and his wife Mary née Craig of Annsborough House, who established Murlands, Solicitors, in Downpatrick, in 1832.

COURTESY OF MURLANDS SOLICITORS

Castlewellan. About half way down the hill was James Steele's house, then called, Green Vale, and his bleach green. However, James Murland's bleach green and house, Annsborough Cottage, were at the foot of the hill and this became the site for the original mill, standing close to the main road from Castlewellan to Clough. By 1840 there were three hundred workers in the mills and Murlands also gave employment to about seven hundred hand loom weavers, who worked in their homes. Yarn was given out twice a week both at Annsborough and at Kilkeel, the weavers' earnings averaging six to seven shillings a week. In 1836 the Murlands were bleaching an average of 20,000 pieces of cloth a year, most of which was for the American and West Indian markets.

Nevertheless, the greatest expansion of the Murland business came during the lifetime of Charles Murland, (1820–87), James's youngest son. During the American Civil War, (1861–65), supplies of material for the cotton industry were cut off and Murlands, like all the linen firms, enjoyed great prosperity. They had acquired James Steele's bleach green and house at Green Vale, on the western side of the mill, about 1850 and a new bleach works on this site in 1863. Two years later a block of warehouses, stores, and offices were built in front of the 'new mill'. In all, by 1886 there were two hundred and twenty nine acres of bleach greens at Annsborough, the two spinning mills, a power loom factory, and one hundred and thirty eight workers' houses, the works giving employment to one thousand people, two thirds of them women. McCall writing in 1870 gives some idea of the importance of Murlands to Castlewellan,

> At that time there had arisen a more than ordinary demand for warp yarns, prices were accordingly high and the cost of new material was much under the average of other yarns. Thus while the proprietors of the Castlewellan Mill were reaping enormous profits they had the honour of being the pioneers in establishing advantageously to themselves and also to the manufacturer that department of the linen trade which in the course of forty years has become most gigantic as well as the most important branch of Ulster industrial enterprise. As is usual however in such cases the prosperity that follows the erection of the tall chimney did not concentrate itself within the walls of Messrs. Murland's Counting House. All classes shared in the advantages of the trade – the people who found regular employment armed the spindles. The shopkeepers of the town and the farmers in the neighbourhood were largely benefited by the new system of Flax Spinning in consequence of the increased consumption of produce and also by the greater demand for raw material i.e. flax.

The drive and enthusiasm of Charles Murland transformed the firm into one which was known world wide and had offices in Belfast, London, Berlin, Paris, New York and Glasgow.

The Murlands also took an active part in the development of Dundrum harbour, having a steam packet built which ran a weekly passenger and cargo service to Whitehaven, and they had a leading share in the formation of the East Downshire Steamship Company. A traction engine ran twice a day between

Annsborough and Dundrum until 1906, when the rail link between Castlewellan and Newcastle was completed.

Charles Murland was succeeded by his son, Clotworthy Warren Murland, who had married in 1875, Sarah Ferguson, eldest daughter of Thomas Ferguson, Esq., JP, of Edenderry House, Banbridge. The Fergusons also manufactured linen and three years before Warren Murland's death in 1903 the Murland business was formed into a private limited company, in which four of the original seven shareholders and two of the directors were members of the Ferguson family. In the 1920s, James Murland, Ltd., like so many other linen firms, encountered insuperable difficulties and the old mill stopped work in July 1927, the new mill closing down three years later. However, the earlier size of the enterprise may be judged from a statement made in the late 1940s regarding just one part of the Murland business, by the editor of the *Textile and Cordage Quarterly*,

> The late Mr James Murland told us many years ago that the small original mill made a steady profit of £12,000 per year. When power reels were installed the operatives refused to work them and hand reels were used in Castlewellan Mill until it finally closed down.

Eventually, in 1937, James Murland, Ltd. was acquired by the Ulster Weaving Company, which retained the original name. At that time the Ulster Weaving Company was cloth bleaching at Linfield Road, Belfast, and the factory being very fully used, had begun to search for a larger bleach works. Prior to the Second World War, Mr Frank Maxwell had just completed an apprenticeship training in the linen industry with the Ulster Weaving Company and had intended to join his father in the Durham Street Weaving Company. However, Mr Graham Larmor, Managing Director of Ulster Weaving, asked him to stay on, to move to Annsborough as their manager and to restart James Murland, Ltd.

During the Second World War cotton was not imported into the United Kingdom, due to the emergency, and the armed forces had to rely on supplies of flax, which was used to manufacture both coarse and fine linen. From 1939 onwards the growth of flax in Ireland, both north and south, increased to a peak of over one hundred thousand acres in 1943, 1944 and 1945. The Ulster Weaving Company in conjunction with Jennymount Mills, owned by Philip Johnston & Co., Ltd., established a green flax factory at Annsborough and Mr Maxwell helped to get this up and running. At their best they processed about 1500 acres of green flax which was suitable for the coarser yarns, but it undoubtedly helped the war effort. By 1948 Ulster Weaving had installed many improvements at Murlands and the firm was doing very extensive business in the bleaching and finishing of linen.

At the start of the twenty first century, the company, now known as Ulster Weavers, and part of the John Hogg Group, continued to bleach at Annsborough. However, they have recently closed the plant.

Annsborough House,
Castlewellan

© CROWN COPYRIGHT HMSO

ANNSBOROUGH HOUSE
CASTLEWELLAN

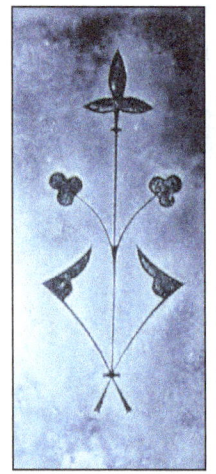

Murland family motif
JFR

Annsborough House lies at the bottom of the steep hill on the road from Castlewellan to Clough, in the village of Annsborough, and would appear to be the original residence of the two Murland brothers, William and James, who acquired bleach greens at Annsborough around 1800. William Murland established a new bleach green near the top of the hill and adjacent to Castlewellan, where he also built his house Wood Lodge. However, his younger brother James remained in Annsborough House close to the mills which were established for the spinning of linen yarn. The *Ordnance Survey Memoirs*, written in 1836, for the Parish of Kilmegan, County Down mention both the house of James Murland and the spinning mill, as does Samuel Lewis, 1837, who comments on the extensive manufacture of linen by Mr J. Murland and Mr Steele. James Murland died in 1850 and was succeeded in the linen business by four of his five sons, two of whom, Henry and William, continued to live in Annsborough

Clotworthy Warren Murland
COURTESY JERRY MURLAND

House. In the 1870s the house was occupied by Clotworthy Warren Murland, after his marriage to Sarah Ferguson of Banbridge, and after the death of his father, Charles Murland, he moved to Ardnabannon.

The original Annsborough House was built *c.* 1790 but it was extensively refurbished and extended between 1810 and 1820, but in the twenty first century still retains some of the original features. This is a two storey three bay roughcast house with slated gabled roof and sash windows edge-panelled glazed, with exterior shutters shown in an early photograph, but which have since been removed. The front door is sheltered by a Georgian classical porch featuring Ionic columns and which is topped by a small balustrade. Spacious accommodation of three reception rooms and six bedrooms is complimented by original marble fireplaces in some rooms, one of which contains the Murland family crest. Gardens surround the house with a large garden or potential paddock to the rear with a considerable range of outbuildings.

Murland fireplace
JFR

Ardnabannon House, Castlewellan

JFR

ARDNABANNON HOUSE
CASTLEWELLAN

Ardnabannon House was the home of Charles Murland (1820–87), youngest son of James Murland, who was chiefly responsible for the great expansion of the Murland business during the mid-nineteenth century. He married Jane Dobbin, eldest daughter of Clotworthy Dobbin of Belfast in 1844 and had five sons. In the early years of his marriage he lived in Annsborough Cottage which is close to the village of Annsborough but on the opposite side of the road from the linen factory and bleach green. However, Charles Murland commissioned the architect Thomas Turner in the late 1850s to build a new house on the site and this was completed about 1868 being named Ardnabannon House.

Ardnabannon House has been described in the Ulster Architectural Heritage Society's Listing of Castlewellan, 1975, as a solid early Victorian two storey house of pleasant pale buff brick with sandstone quoins and dressings and having a shallow hipped roof with a number of chimney stacks, which are slender with wide cornices topped by tall slim pots. The north entrance front is three bay, with a Victorian tripartite window on either side of a centre projecting porch with balustrade which has round headed windows on either side of the door with semi circular fanlight. On the first floor to the front are three segment headed windows with a shallow pediment over a centre projection. There is a canted bow on the north end of the west side of the house. In addition there are numerous buildings formerly used as stables and servants' quarters.

Dean, in *The Gate Lodges of Ulster,* 1994, states that the early Ordnance Survey map indicates a tiny square lodge pre-1834 at Annsborough Cottage built according to him by James Murland. However, this clearly became outdated

LINEN HOUSES OF THE BANN VALLEY

Staircase
JFR

since the present lodge looks to be mid-Victorian and was probably built by Charles Murland along with Ardnabannon House. The gate lodge is recorded as single storey three bay symmetrical with a gabled roof and having delicate moulded surrounds to openings and a corniced chimney stack in similar neo-classical vein. The lodge was later extended to four bay with an additional room but is recorded in 1994 as deserted.

Charles Murland was succeeded by his son, Clotworthy Warren Murland, JP, who married a daughter of the linen manufacturer Thomas Ferguson of Banbridge. He lived in Ardnabannon House until his death in 1903, but three years before his death the business was formed into a private limited company, in which four of the original seven shareholders and two of the directors were members of the Ferguson family. James Warren Murland succeeded his father in the business and in Ardnabannon House but after the First World War, the company, like so many linen firms encountered difficulties and by 1930 both the old mill and the new mill had closed. Finally, in 1937, James Murland, Ltd., was acquired by the Ulster Weaving Company who were seeking new bleaching premises, and after James Murland's death in 1943 Sir Graham Larmor and his family moved to Ardnabannon House.

James Murland with his wife Beatrice and his son Mick (James Robert William) at Ardbannon, 1920
COURTESY JERRY MURLAND

ARDNABANNON HOUSE, CASTLEWELLAN

In 1967 the house was purchased from Sir Graham Larmor by the Down County Education Committee, and converted to an Outdoor Pursuits Centre by the architects John Neil and Partners, opening in 1968. This was a particularly appropriate use for the house since in 1836 the Murland family, showing a keen interest in the benefit of education, founded a school at Annsborough. Ardnabannon was re-opened as Ardnabannon Outdoor Education Centre in 1994, by the South Eastern Education and Library Board, with an expansion of hosting capacity from thirty to seventy young people and leaders and is fully used.

Mr J.W. Murland's 'Soothing Glass', winner of £1,000 Victory Steeplechase at Manchester, 1 January, 1924. The jockey was Fred B. Rees.
PRONI D/3488/2

Wood Lodge
JFR

WOOD LODGE
CASTLEWELLAN

Charles Murland
(1870–1922) who was
brought up at Wood Lodge
COURTESY JERRY MURLAND

Wood Lodge is situated adjacent to Castlewellan on the road from Castlewellan to Annsborough and close to the top of the hill. This house is certainly pre-1835 and is an enlargement of an earlier eighteenth century house, the enlargement probably carried out by William Murland prior to his marriage to Margaret Craig in 1796. William Murland set up a bleach mill and bleach green near to his house. Wood Lodge has been described by Peter Rankin in the Ulster Architectural Hertige Society publication, *Mourne Area of South Down*, 1975, as a solid grey two storey house with groups of three Georgian glazed windows either side of the slightly projecting centre. The shallow roof, with a decorated moulded cornice, is hidden behind a low parapet leaving only the chimney stacks to be seen. A single storey Ionic portico has coupled Doric columns with a single round headed window above. There are assorted back returns and outbuildings which would have been associated with the considerable linen bleaching on site in the nineteenth century.

William Murland married firstly Margaret Craig, daughter of Samuel Craig of Carricknabb, but she died in 1800 and was buried at Clough with two infant sons leaving one daughter Ann. He married secondly Anne Martin, daughter of

Andrew Martin of Inch and had four sons, and after his father's death in 1831, the eldest Henry joined his uncle James in the family linen business, living in Wood Lodge until his death in 1853. However, William Murland's other three sons were not associated with the business.

Latterly, in 1937, after James Murland, Ltd., was acquired by the Ulster Weaving Co., Ltd., Mr Graham Larmor, later Sir Graham Larmor, and his family moved to Annsborough about 1940. According to the late Mr Peter Larmor they lived firstly at Wood Lodge but later, as a wartime situation, part of Manor House School, Armagh, was evacuated to Wood Lodge, they moved to live temporarily at Drumee House until finally moving to Ardnabannon House in the 1950s.

Doorway
JFR

The fountain in the garden at Wood Lodge
JFR

Woodlawn
JFR

WOODLAWN
CASTLEWELLAN

Woodlawn, now named Corrywood, is situated just off the road from Castlewellan to Annsborough, not far from Castlewellan and opposite Wood Lodge. This was the residence of Samuel Murland, JP, DL, eldest son of James Murland, and was probably purchased by him at the time of his marriage in 1835 to Emily Hyndman, daughter of Robert Hyndman of Holywood. Samuel Murland (1805–78) with his youngest brother Charles (1820–87), was involved in the greatest expansion of the Murland business in the 1850s and 1860s. He became High Sheriff of Down in 1858 and Deputy Lieutenant in 1872. Robert, Samuel's only son, withdrew from the Murland business and went to Castle Espie where he established a pottery and brickworks. Samuel Murland died in 1878 leaving Woodlawn to his unmarried daughter Mary for life, but she died a few years later in 1881.

Corrywood, which faces north over the Annsborough valley, is described by Peter Rankin in the Ulster Architectural Heritage Society publication, *Mourne Area of South Down*, 1975, as:

> A substantial stuccoed house of late Regency/early Victorian appearance: in fact the present house, formerly known as Woodlawn, existed pre 1835 but was

WOODLAWN, CASTLEWELLAN

considerably enlarged to its present size between 1835 and 1859. The house is four-bay, two-storey, right-hand bay projecting slightly and with a shallow bow, and all the windows are tripartite with plate glass. Corrywood has a low pitched hipped roof and there are low chimney stacks with tall pots. There are two three-storey towers à la Osborne attached to each side elevation, with paired round-headed windows on the first and second floors under low pitched pyramidal roofs.

Woodlawn was advertised for auction in March 1882 as part of the estate of Samuel Murland, deceased, and the Descriptive Particulars include the following:

> The House and Out-offices are of elegant, modern and substantial structure, having been recently re-built by the late Mr Murland at great cost ... The House contains Great Hall, large and small Drawing-room, large Dining-room, Library, Morning-room, Billiard-room, 8 large Bed-rooms, Lavatory, Water Closet, Bath-room, Writing Office, Kitchen, Servants' Hall, range of Attic rooms, Dairy, Pantries, and other extensive and necessary accommodation.

Doorcase
JFR

The description of Woodlawn also mentions an extensive and well cultivated walled-in fruit and vegetable garden, with two vineries, one greenhouse, one peach house, one plant store and melon and cucumber pits. For the period Woodlawn would appear to have had very generous accommodation with not only gas lighting but also a supply of pure spring water laid in pipes throughout the house.

A gate lodge to Woodlawn was built by Samuel Murland *c.* 1840 and was, according to Dean, 1994, originally a single storey three bay standard cottage below a hipped roof. The lodge has been extended many times, now having many canted bay windows. Dean expresses the view that much of this work may have coincided with the transformation of the house into an Italianate villa and its being renamed Corrywood. Nevertheless, when the house was advertised for auction in 1882, the name of the property was Woodlawn.

Corrywood is now a residential home set in densely planted grounds.

The gate lodge to Woodlawn
JFR

Greenvale House
JFR

GREENVALE HOUSE
CASTLEWELLAN

In the early 1800s James Steele established his bleach green and house, and then called Green Vale, half way down the hill on the road from Castlewellan to Annsborough. William Murland's bleach green at the top of the hill and near to Castlewellan was adjacent to James Steele's bleach works. However, about 1850, after James Steele's death in 1845 the Murlands acquired his bleach green and house at Green Vale, on the western side of their linen mill, and a new bleach works was built on this site in 1863.

Greenvale House is an early nineteenth century five bay, two storey roughcast house with slated gabled roof and attic windows, set in well planted grounds, and enjoying a considerable view over the surrounding countryside. The windows of the house are Georgian glazed, sashed and silled with exterior shutters, and the door is slightly recessed and flanked by glazed sidelights and fanlight with simple classical detail. Internally, the house has a unique staircase, where,

The doorway to Greenvale House
JFR

at the entrance, the central staircase leads down to the basement, while two flights of stairs, on either side of the centre staircase, lead to the first floor.

William Henry Murland, (1850–88), third son of Charles Murland and Jane Dobbin, married on 18 June 1873, Sarah Fenton, daughter of William Fenton, founder of Fenton's Bank in Rochdale, and who lived at Dutton Hall. They firstly lived at Woodlawn but subsequently moved to Greenvale House after improvements to the house, and the building of a gate lodge which has subsequently been demolished. Bassett, in 1886, records Mr William Murland at Greenvale. In the early twentieth century Greenvale House was the home of Captain C. Warren Murland, who served in the First World War in the North Irish Horse.

Greenvale House is now in use as a care home.

The staircase in Greenvale House
JFR

Warren Murland on the steps of Greenvale House
COURTESY JERRY MURLAND

Florence and Evelyn Murland who lived with their brother Warren at Greenvale House
COURTESY JERRY MURLAND

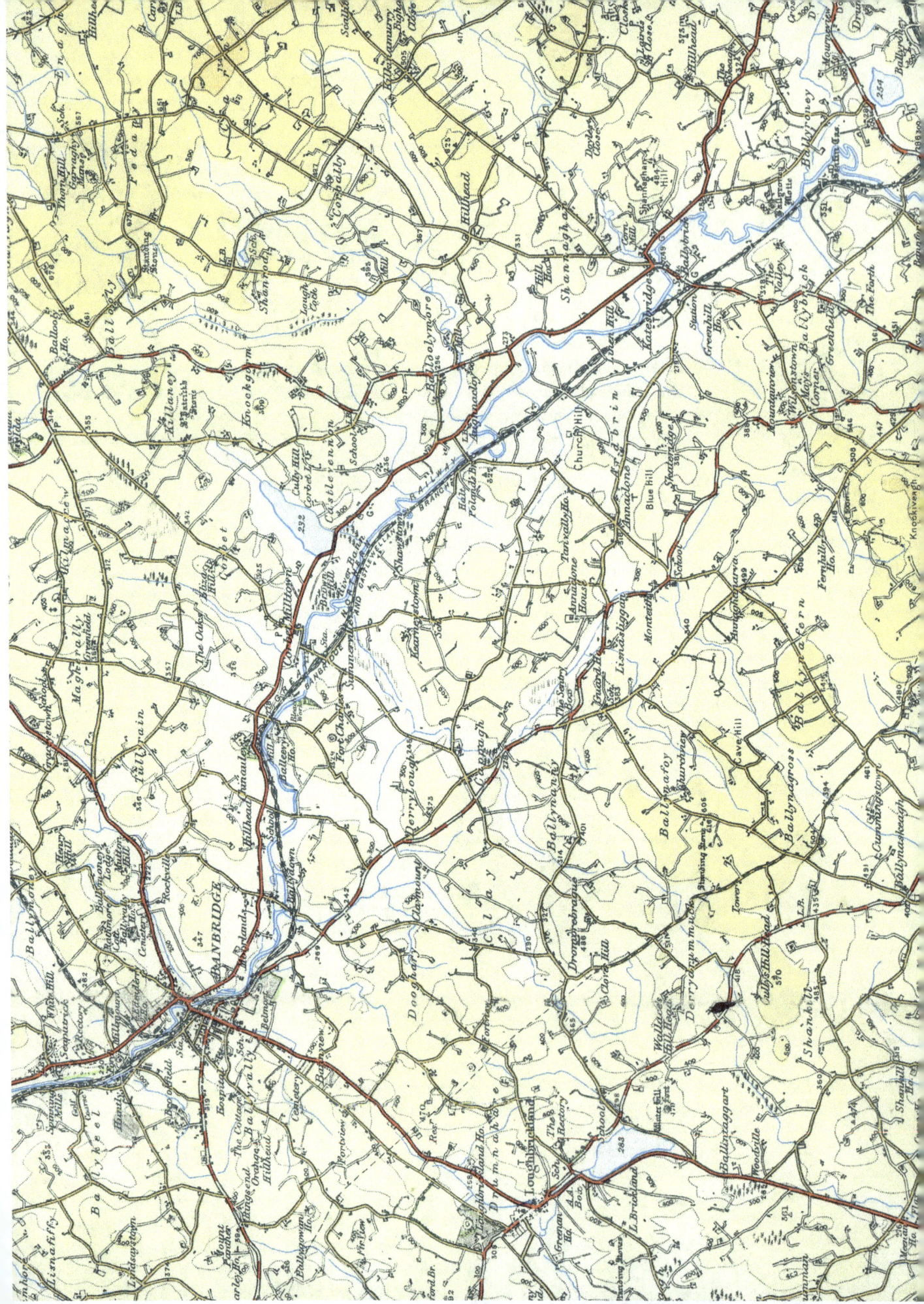

2
KATESBRIDGE, TULLYCONNAUGHT, BALLIEVEY, BALLYDOWN

HINCKS PRINT PLATE X
illustrating Linen Hill House on a Hill above a Bleach Green

WILLIAM HINCKS 1783

LINEN HILL
KATESBRIDGE

Linen Hill
JFR

Linen Hill is considered to be the site of one of the earliest bleach works and linen houses on the River Bann, and it is also thought to be the house featured in William Hincks' engraving 'Perspective view of a bleach-green taken in the County of Down', dated 1783. However, as reported in the *Ordnance Survey Memoirs* of 1836, bleaching had already been given up and the buildings were being used for corn milling. At this point in time Linen Hill was the property of David and James Murphy, but it had originally belonged to the Lowry family in the eighteenth century. Alexander Lowry, the last of the family and also the most famous, was a prominent United Irishman who fled to Hamburg in 1797, but was eventually allowed to return. Linen Hill became the property of the Murphy family after his death.

Linen Hill is situated about mid-way between the towns of Banbridge and Castlewellan. The house is two storey, five bay, gabled with slated roof and remains very similar to the Hincks' engraving, which has been described in *Illustrations of the Irish Linen Industry in 1783*.

> A substantial Georgian-style dwelling house stands on the hill slope behind the bleach mill. It is gabled with symmetrical façade, lower windows of twelve panes in four rows of three, upper windows of nine panes in three rows of three, an entrance flanked by pillars or pilasters and surmounted by a fanlight the head of which is accommodated in a gablet springing from the eaves. There is a chimney stack on each gable.

The pediment and fanlight above the window of the middle bay have gone and, around 1936, the door was set back about two feet, the fanlight being removed. Modern replacement windows similar to the original windows have been installed but otherwise Linen Hill remains unchanged.

THE MULLIGAN FAMILY
OF TULLYCONNAUGHT

The *Ordnance Survey Memoirs* of 1834 mention in a 'Table of Mills' for the Parish of Seapatrick, two sites with water wheels, wood and iron machinery, and two double beetling engines at Tullyconnaught, belonging to Messrs John and George Mulligan. In the late eighteenth and early nineteenth century various members of the Mulligan family appear to have set up bleaching works on the River Bann adjacent to the Corbet Lough at Tullyconnaught. The Linen Board Report for 1817 contains details of the tour of their Secretary, James Corry, through Ulster in 1816 when he stated that Banbridge was the largest linen market town in County Down. A number of the members of the Mulligan family feature in records of linen bought for bleaching, not only in Banbridge, but also in Armagh, and John Mulligan is mentioned as a registered bleacher. Richard Linn in his *A History of Banbridge*, 1935, writes,

> In the development of the linen trade of the Bann towards the end of the eighteenth century the families of Mulligan, Crawford, Lindsay and Hayes were pre-eminent. The Mulligans were long established up the river in the Corbet district.

In order to ensure that a regular flow of water was available throughout the year, the linen merchants formed the Bann Reservoir Company in 1836, building two storage lakes at Lough Island Reavy and at Corbet Lough. Water was brought to the lake by canal from the Bann, and then released back into the river by a second canal when it was required for industrial purposes by the linen industry.

Corbet Lough
JFR

MILLBANK HOUSE
TULLYCONNAUGHT

Millbank House
JFR

Millbank House is one of the houses of the Mulligan family and was built overlooking the mill race on the River Bann and one of the beetling mills at Tullyconnaught. However, the present house was erected on the site of a previous Mulligan residence, which had belonged to James Charles Mulligan, since it is of a much later period and the family were in business at this site in the late eighteenth century. Charles Mulligan (1726–1806) may have been the first member of the family to set up as a linen draper and bleacher at Millbank. His son, James Charles Mulligan is mentioned in the 1809 Vestry Minutes of the old parish church of Seapatrick (Banbridge) and in succeeding years he took a prominent part in the plans for a new Church of Ireland church in Banbridge. The new house was built in 1907, having a date stone above the front door, and is on the site of the earlier Millbank House since the old foundation stonework remains in the basement of the present building. Adjacent to the house are many of the old buildings which housed the beetling engines. In the twentieth century Millbank was owned by the Ballievey Bleaching Company but the mill at the site ceased to operate in the 1930s when new beetling equipment was installed in the main factory.

MILLBANK HOUSE, TULLYCONNAUGHT

Millbank House, which is about three miles out of Banbridge on the southern side of the River Bann, has been built in the style of the Arts and Craft Movement and the architect may have been Hobart. The house is two storey with the ground floor in red brick and the first floor harled and whitewashed, with windows of differing sizes. To the front there are bay windows to the left of a single storey porch which has the door on the side with a recessed porthole window on the front. The roof is gabled with deep eaves and string courses run level with the sills of the ground floor windows and with the top of the single storey porch.

Millbank House is close to Mulligan's bridge, which crosses the River Bann, and according to the *Ordnance Survey Memoirs* of 1834 for the Parish of Seapatrick was built in 1826. The memoirs record that the bridge is built of granite and whinstone procured in the neighbourhood and consists of three elliptical arches. Across the River Bann and within sight of Millbank House is Parkmount, another house associated with the Mulligan family.

Mulligan's Bridge
JFR

PARKMOUNT
TULLYCONNAUGHT

Parkmount
JFR

Parkmount, situated about two miles from Banbridge on the Castlewellan Road, was the residence of John Mulligan who was also a linen draper and mentioned in records as a registered bleacher in the Corbet area. The house is on the opposite side of the River Bann from Millbank House but not far from it. In notes compiled in 1912 by Dr John Campbell on the death of John Francis Mulligan (solicitor) he states:

> Daniel Mulligan, who was of Irish descent, lived in Scotland and was twice married. The maiden name of his second wife was Isobel Glen. Upward of two hundred years ago Daniel Mulligan and Isobel, his wife, left Scotland and settled in Tullyconnaught in the neighbourhood of Banbridge. Their grandson, John Mulligan, was married to Miss Gamble, niece of Dr Gamble who lived near Belfast.

John Mulligan, died at Parkmount in 1845 leaving the house to his eldest son, Gilbert who was married to Martha Nicholson, daughter of John Nicholson of

PARKMOUNT, TULLYCONNAUGHT

Donacloney. Gilbert Mulligan and his wife continued to live at Parkmount until his death in 1869.

The rear of Parkmount could date back to the beginning of the nineteenth century and may have originally been a rectangular two storey plan house built of rubble masonry and having a chimney stack. The front of the house, which is quoined, cement rendered and painted white, would appear to have been added at a later date making a three bay two storey building. On each side of the doorway are two semi circular bays rising to the full height of the house with the bays having three sash windows on each floor. Above the door is a segmental fanlight with spider-web glazing and the whole is sheltered by a porch which is supported by Corinthian columns. The roof is shallow and slated with chimney stacks at either end, and to the front has a dentilled cornice and moulded parapet.

In more recent times Parkmount was the home of Edward Lamont, of the Ballymena linen company Samuel Lamont & Sons, Ltd., who lived at the house while he was director in charge of the Ballievey Bleaching Company.

Doorcase
JFR

ROSELAWN

BALLYDOWN

Roselawn
JFR

Roselawn is situated about a mile from Banbridge on the Castlewellan Road and close to the northern side of the River Bann. This was the home of George Mulligan, brother of John of Parkmount, and they jointly owned bleach works at Tullyear and beetling mills at Tullyconnaught. They participated in life in Banbridge and in the Seapatrick church records of 1825 Mr George Mulligan is named as Rector's churchwarden. George Mulligan died in his 47th year at Roselawn in 1845.

Roselawn, now known as Ballydown House, is a two storey cement faced house which is well covered in Virginia Creeper, with three central bays placed between two sets of bow windows at either end of the house. There is a shallow gabled slated roof with very shallow eaves and moulded cornice, along with three sets of chimney pots. The doorway is on the side of a front porch on the middle bay. Roselawn appears to be an early nineteenth century house, which at the rear has Georgian style windows. To the front of the house the windows are two paned with sills.

In 1866 William Malcomson & Co., of Portlaw, County Waterford, built a yarn bleach works at Tullyear with a date stone on the building. This was eventually taken over by their manager, James McWilliam, who ran the Banbridge Bleaching Company and, after his death, in 1884, Messrs James Anderson & Co., continued to bleach linen yarn at Tullyear. Linn records that in 1935 Roselawn was the home of T.N. Anderson and it was later lived in by James A. Beck, one of the main chemical suppliers to the linen trade.

Ballydown House (Roselawn) continues to be well cared for by its present owners.

BALLIEVEY HOUSE
BALLIEVEY

Ballievey House is situated just off the Banbridge to Castlewellan road on the southern side of the River Bann and not far from Corbet. The *Ordnance Survey Memoirs* of 1834 for the Parish of Seapatrick, County Down, state:

> There are many mills and bleach greens in the parish, all situated on the River Bann. Beginning at the east end of the parish, where the river enters, there is a corn mill and bleaching one, either side immediately above the Corbet bridge, which latter is a new stone bridge of 3 arches built by the county in the year 1826. About half a mile further down, and on the south side of the river where there is a good wooden bridge, are the bleach green and mills of the Messrs Crawford of Ballievey House.

There had been a bleach works and a beetling mill at this site from the mid-eighteenth century and in 1763 there was a newspaper notice of a robbery from the bleach green of Gilbert Crawford at Ballievey. However, on the hillside above the former beetling mill is Ballievey House, which is believed to have been built in

Ballievey House
JFR

1784 as this date is carved in an upstairs room. Ballievey House is one of four similar houses known as Bleachers' Houses as they were all built about the same time, the others being, Newforge House, Magheralin, Sheepbridge House near Newry and Bishopscourt, Dromore which has been demolished.

George Crawford, son of Gilbert Crawford, married Elizabeth Bradshaw in 1769 and settled at Ballievey, carrying on a very successful business and eventually building Ballievey House. Their daughter Margaret married William Hayes, who set up a bleach works on land at Edenderry, and built Millmount House *c.* 1796. George Crawford's second daughter Catherine married John Lindsay of Tullyhenan in 1808 thus bringing together two important linen families and creating the firm of Crawford and Lindsay, which took over the Ballydown Weaving Co., and bleach works, in 1822 and continued in business until *c.* 1919.

Sale of Ballievey House, 31 July 1827
Belfast News Letter

Walter Crawford succeeded to Ballievey House in 1817 and continued the bleaching business but in 1827 he put everything up for sale in order to emigrate to Canada. The advertisement for the sale is interesting in that it shows the extent of the business.

> The Bleaching Mills, which are in the best possible repair, are capable of finishing from 12 to 13,000 Pieces of Linen annually, and are also capable of being much extended. A new Water Wheel of the very best description, besides other new Machinery, have been also lately erected on said premises.

Nevertheless, ten years later the house was in the possession of George and Thomas Crawford who ran the bleach works at Ballievey in conjunction with those at Ballydown.

Ballievey House, which is five bay and Georgian glazed, consists of a semi basement and three floors built of rubble masonry and harled externally with a platband separating the ground floor from the upper storeys. The house appears to have been enlarged at the back by a two storey addition, in the early part of the nineteenth century. The slated and hipped roofs have moulded eaves and cornices, and the windows are sashed and silled. Dr W. Haughton Crowe, former headmaster of Banbridge Academy, has given a description of Ballievey House on the day in the early 1940s when he and his wife were first shown over the house and decided to buy it.

Opposite:
Entrance to Ballievey House with Mr H.C. Hatrick, Professor E.R.R. Green, and Mrs Crowe
© CROWN COPYRIGHT HMSO

> A completely unspoilt Georgian country house, it stood on top of a high terrace overlooking the Hall Green and the valley of the Bann leading up to

Doorway to Ballievey House
JFR

Banbridge. Its perfect Palladian doorway was surrounded by its many-windowed, ivy covered façade. Inside was a fine hall with Adams design archways, and a wide stairway with its exquisite mahogany banister curving gracefully upwards. Below stairs was a great flagged kitchen with an old-fashioned range; and there were all the other appurtenances of a house of the period: buttery with ceiling hooks for hams; wash house, speaking tube, and old wire bells that made a wonderful jangle throughout the house. Outside there was a courtyard surrounded by farm buildings, another yard with steward's house and more farm buildings.

On either side of the hall were the spacious living rooms; the one on the right with an added bow window of greenish Waterford glass looked out toward a jungle of holly trees, a great copper beech, rhododendrons and laurels, and beyond – trees, trees, trees as far as the eye could see. At the back of the stairway there was a minimal bath-room, with a bath calculated to scrape the backside off you, and a small lavatory with a round window like the porthole of a ship. Behind the left hand living room there was another smaller room fitted out as a modern chemical laboratory. Each of the two floors upstairs had three large bedrooms and two small rooms, one of which, the upper one was a useless attic.

Dr Crowe and his wife remained at Ballievey House until his retirement from Banbridge Academy when his daughter and her husband took over the care of the property.

Entrance hall to Ballievey House
© *CROWN COPYRIGHT HMSO*

CRAWFORD FAMILY TREE

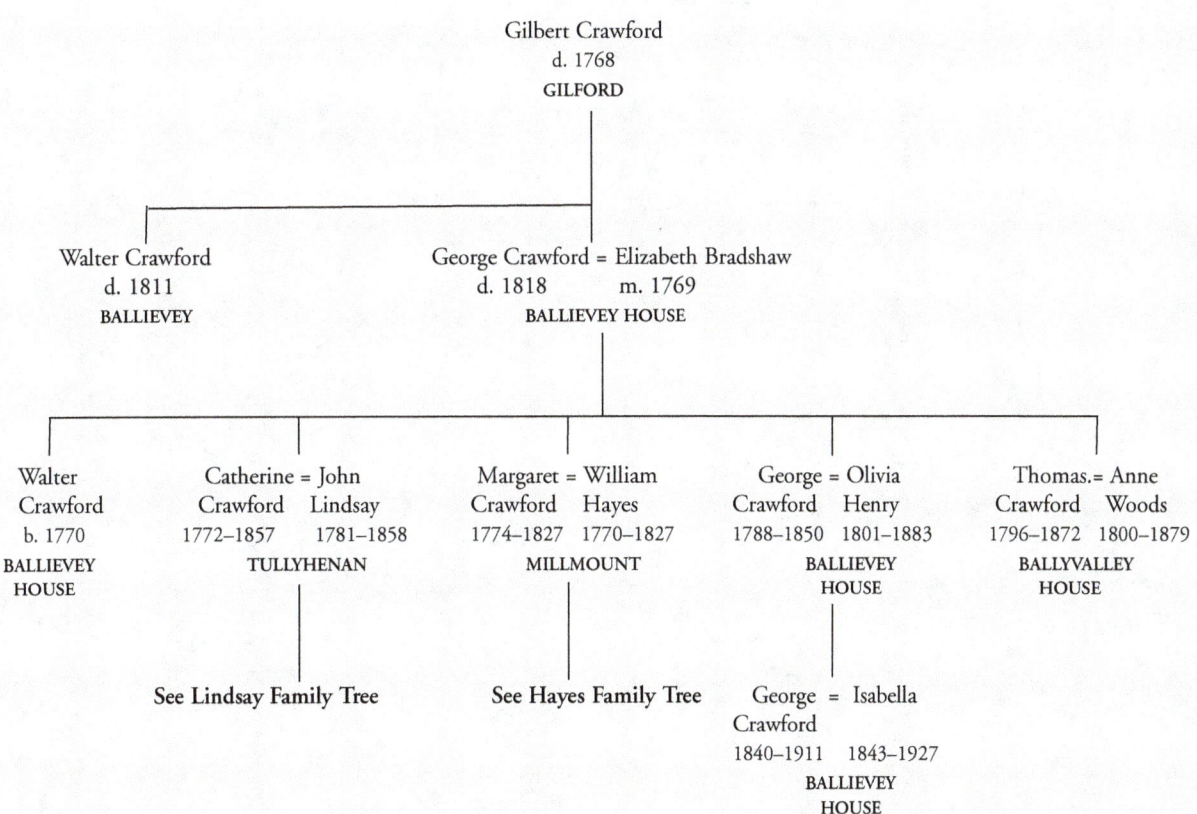

3
TULLYHENAN
NEAR BANBRIDGE

HINCKS PRINT PLATE I
illustrating a view near Scarva representing
Ploughing, Sowing the flax Seed and Harrowing

WILLIAM HINCK 1783

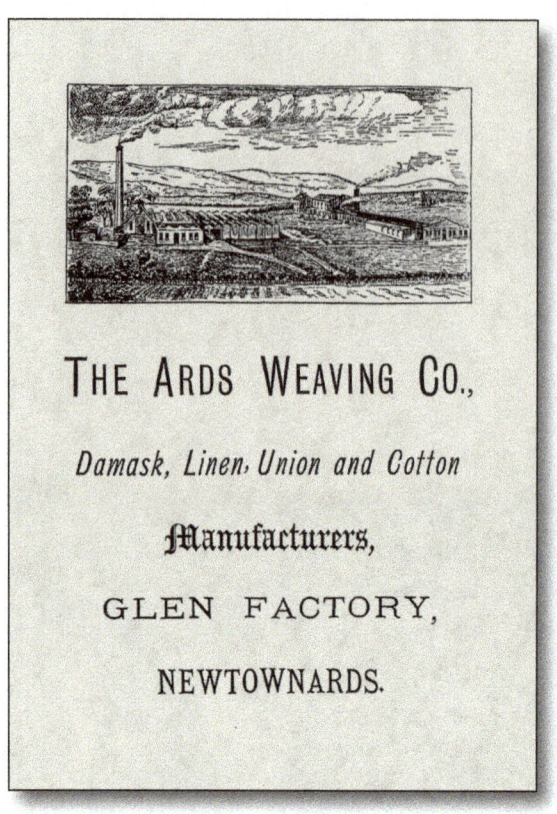

THE LINDSAY FAMILY
OF TULLYHENAN

The first of this branch of the Lindsay family came from Scotland with General Munro in 1642 to help the Irish Protestants after the massacre of 1641 and they settled at a farm in Tullyhenan. Records exist showing that a son of the first Lindsay had an interview with King William III in June 1690 when he was encamped with his army on his way to the River Boyne. He sold cattle and provisions to the troops for which he was paid by an order for £300 on the Belfast Custom House. The first named member of the family, David Lindsay, would at this time have been about ten years old.

In the development of the linen industry of the Bann towards the end of the eighteenth century the Lindsay family played a notable part. David Lindsay's son John set up the Hilltown branch of the family while his son David continued at Tullyhenan founding the family from which sprang the Moorlands and Ashfield branches of the Lindsays. The family is connected with many other well known linen families such as the Crawfords, Mulligans, and Hunters. John Lindsay of Tullyhenan married George Crawford's daughter Catherine of Ballievey in 1808 bringing together the Lindsay and Crawford families and creating the firm of

'Crawford and Lindsay' which in 1822 took over the Ballydown bleach works. John Lindsay was very successful in the linen business and he became a local director of the Provincial Bank. His son, George Crawford Lindsay, who was involved in the business, lived at Moorlands, near the Ballydown works while his son John, also in the business, succeeded him in Tullyhenan. Bassett, 1886, states:

> At Ballydown, Messrs. Crawford and Lindsays' linen factory and bleach works, gives employment to about 400 people. Of this number 150 are at Ballydown, and the remainder are handloom weavers, living in Down and Armagh.

By the mid-nineteenth century power spinning was responsible for the most profound changes in the Irish linen industry with weavers losing their independence and being forced to seek work from a manufacturer. Large scale manufacturers appeared around Lisburn and the system spread from there to Dromore and Banbridge. David Lindsay (1795–1859) established a factory at Ashfield in 1828 for weaving by hand loom and in 1839 he employed 950 weavers in the manufacture of linens, unions, and cottons. The business continued into the early twentieth century with David Lindsay being succeeded by his son Maurice (1842–77) and his grandson David Maurice.

The Lindsays were also associated with the Ards Weaving Company which was established in 1882 in Newtownards for the manufacture of damasks, and linen and cotton cambrics. Bassett, 1886, states that Mr J. Crawford Lindsay was the managing partner, living in Newtownards, other members of the firm being Mr John Lindsay, Ballydown, Banbridge and Mr Walter Lindsay, Tullyhenan House, Banbridge. However, after the sale of Tullyhenan House, Mr Walter Lindsay lived at Ballydown, Banbridge.

LINDSAY FAMILY TREE

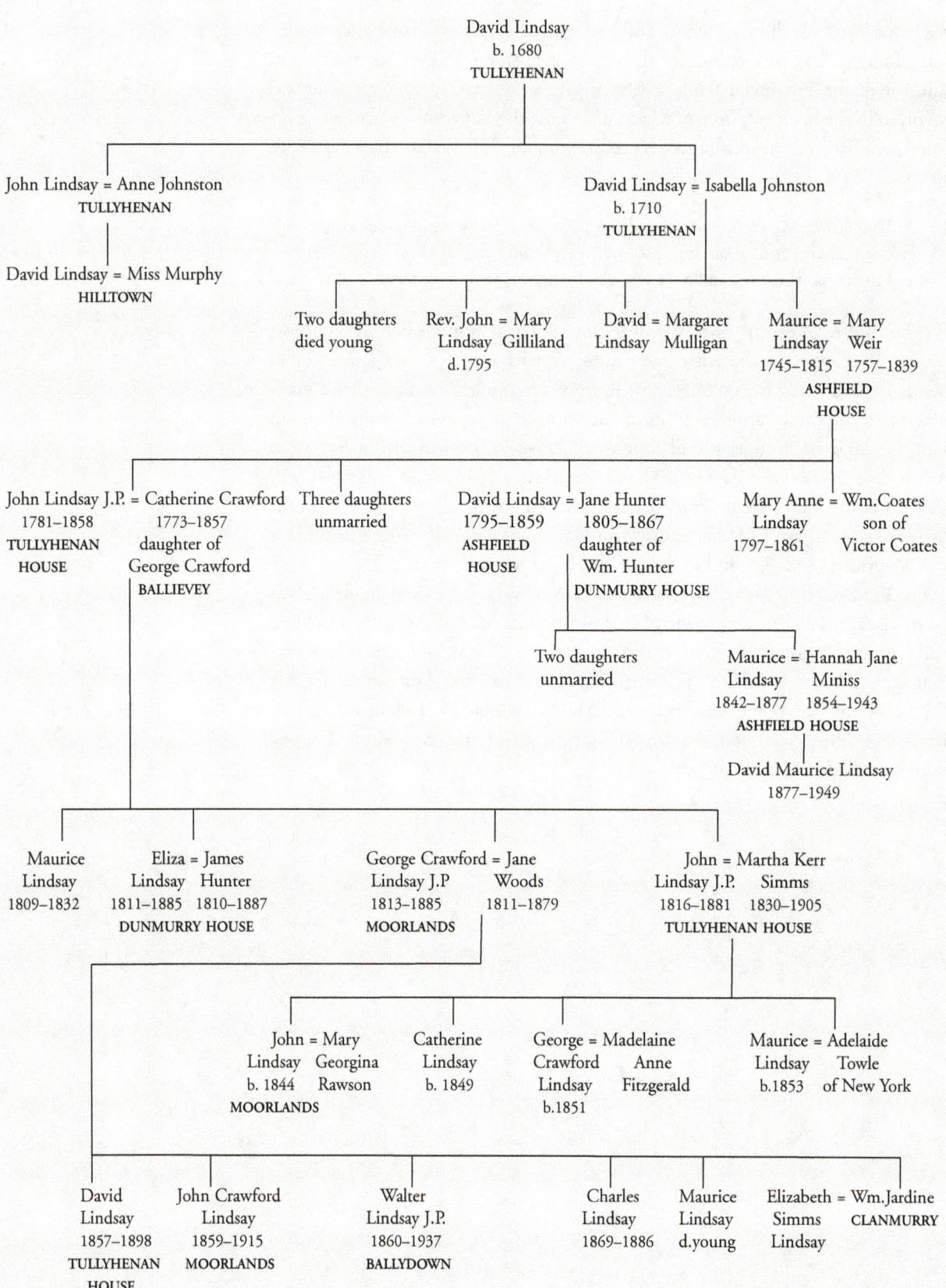

Tullyhenan House
JFR

TULLYHENAN HOUSE
BANBRIDGE

Tullyhenan House is situated almost mid-way between Dromore and Banbridge on the northern side of the dual carriageway and was the main seat of the Lindsay family for more than two hundred and fifty years. The Lindsays are reputed to have come to Ireland from Scotland with the army of General Munro in the 1640s and to have settled at Tullyhenan where they had a farm of considerable size. David Lindsay was born at Tullyhenan about 1680, and from his elder son John descended the Hilltown branch of the family while his younger son David founded the Moorlands and Ashfield branches. David Lindsay's grandson John (1781–1858) of Tullyhenan, married Catherine Crawford of Ballievey in 1808 connecting the Crawford and Lindsay families.

John Lindsay, linen manufacturer of Ballydown, commissioned the architect, Thomas Turner, to build the present Tullyhenan House in the 1850s. Thomas Turner, a Dublin trained architect, came to Belfast to work with Lanyon as his senior architectural assistant early in the 1840s and the two men worked together for about ten years. In 1852 he is recorded as an architect in practice on his own and in the same year he produced designs for Craigavad House, built for

Tullyhenan House staircase
JFR

Andrew Mulholland, on the shores of Belfast Lough. Although Turner was commissioned to design many public buildings in Ulster such as Stormont Castle, and Court Houses at Lurgan and Magherafelt, he is also recorded as responsible for numerous country houses including Tullyhenan House.

Tullyhenan House is a three bay, two storey house of classical design with the bottom storey of ashlar. There is a single storey projecting porch, with Doric columns, which reaches the decorated platband separating the two storeys. The windows on either side of the porch are of a greater height than those of the second storey and are supported on console brackets, a rosette below each. On the upper storey the windows are framed by small pilasters with rosettes on the capitals and above the windows. An elaborately moulded cornice hides the roof leaving only two chimney stacks visible.

Turner favoured a dignified classical style and one of the features of this was the use of three sets of heavy columns, at the entrance, at the back of the hall, and on the landing. The hall of the house is of great height, rising through a central well to the roof. At the front of Tullyhenan House are found the principal rooms; drawing room, dining room, hall and morning room, and upstairs, three large and three small bedrooms. At the back is an older section on a lower level and perhaps part of the earlier Tullyhenan House. This comprises downstairs the kitchen apartments and upstairs there is the bathroom and rooms which were at one time nurseries.

Turner also designed a gate lodge for Tullyhenan House but it has been demolished possibly at the time of the building of the Hillsborough to Banbridge dual carriageway.

Tullyhenan doorway
JFR

Tullyhenan House with water tower to the side

MOORLANDS
BANBRIDGE

Moorlands is situated just over a mile from Banbridge on the Castlewellan Road and on the northern side of both the road and the River Bann. The house was built *c.* 1840 by George Crawford Lindsay (1813–85), second son of John Lindsay of Tullyhenan House and Catherine Crawford of Ballievey. In 1822 the Crawford and Lindsay families took over the Ballydown Weaving Company, and bleaching works, which had been owned by William Hudson. The firm of Crawford and Lindsay was very successful and continued in business until *c.* 1918. According to Green, 1963, in 1884 it gave employment to four hundred people, including two hundred and fifty hand loom weavers, and there was a power loom factory at Newtownards and offices in London. Moorlands was built not far from the works at Ballydown.

Moorlands is a two storey, five bay house built in natural stone with granite quoins. The windows which are silled have a brick surround indented at the sides. The door is set in a single storey porch with side windows, which also have an indented brick surround, and the porch is quoined.

Moorlands
JFR

There is a hipped slated roof with moulded eaves and cornice supported on paired console brackets. Internally the period detail matches the simple elegance of the house, with the main reception hall having oak panelling, oak flooring, and a stone fireplace. The oak staircase rises to the first floor landing, above which it is lit by a leaded stained glass roof dome, and the accommodation comprises three reception rooms and five bedrooms.

Although the Ballydown works has closed and the Lindsays have long since left, Moorlands continues to be well looked after by its present owners.

Moorlands interior

ASHFIELD HOUSE
DROMORE

Ashfield House, situated in the townland of Killysorrell, is about two miles from Dromore and four miles from Banbridge. This is the oldest remaining Lindsay house, having been built by Maurice Lindsay (1745–1815) in the 1760s. David Lindsay (1795–1859), his son, established a manufacturing concern at Ashfield in 1828 for weaving heavy fabrics by hand loom, and in 1839 he employed 950 weavers in the manufacture of linens, unions, and cottons. These would all have been out workers weaving in their own homes using yarn provided by the Lindsays. There are extensive buildings on the site suitable for large scale linen manufacture and in 1878 there were also twenty one dwelling houses known as 'Ashfield Village'. After the death of David Lindsay in 1859 the business was carried on by his son Maurice but he unfortunately died aged thirty five years and Ashfield House, Ashfield Village and Lands were sold by auction on 26th March, 1878.

Ashfield House
JFR

Ashfield Mill
JFR

Ashfield House is an eighteenth century three bay, two storey house which is stuccoed and has a single storey projecting porch with a window similar to those on either side. The windows are sashed and silled with those on the ground floor taller than those on the first floor. The roof is slated with chimney pots at either end and there is considerable coverage of the walls by Virginia Creeper.

This very old and delightful house remains in occupation.

MARCH 2, 1878.

IMPORTANT SALE.

ASHFIELD HOUSE, ASHFIELD VILLAGE AND LANDS, (formerly the property of MAURICE LINDSAY, Esq., Deceased.)

TO BE SOLD BY PUBLIC AUCTION,
(under a Power of Sale contained in a Mortgage),

At the DOWNSHIRE ARMS HOTEL, BANBRIDGE,

On TUESDAY, the 26th day of MARCH, 1878,

At the hour of 2 o'clock, p.m.,

All that piece or parcel of Land, commonly called Ashfield, containing, by estimation, 20 acres Irish Plantation Measure, situate in the townland of KILSORELL, Parish of Dromore, Barony of Lower Iveagh, and County of Down, with the Dwelling-house, known as "Ashfield House," and extensive Office Houses, and Buildings thereon.

The Land is in the highest state of cultivation, thoroughly drained, well fenced and watered.

The Dwelling-house, which is nicely situated, and in every way suitable for a Gentleman's residence, is very commodious, 2 stories high, substantially built and slated, and in excellent order.

The Buildings in connection with the Dwelling-house are very extensive, and well adapted for carrying on the Linen Manufacturing business on a large scale; the late Owner having carried on this business therein, up to the time of his death.

On the above-mentioned Farm are situate those 21 Dwelling-houses, known as "Ashfield Village," which are nearly all occupied by solvent Tenants, and are estimated on a moderate computation as capable of producing a yearly rental of £242 1s 0d.

The Lands are estimated to let at £4 per acre, or £80 annually; and the Dwelling-house, Offices, and Manufacturing Concern, in connexion therewith, at £100 per annum.

The entire is held in Fee Farm, at the rent of £2 5s.

Estimated Annual Letting Value of Ashfield House and Concerns,	£100 0 0
Estimated Annual Letting of Lands,	80 0 0
Estimated Annual Letting Value of Houses in Village,	64 11 0
	£244 11 0
Net Amount, Deduct Annual Head Rent,	2 10 0
Estimated Annual Profit Rent,	£242 1 0

Ashfield House is situated about 2 miles from Dromore, 1 mile from Mullafernaghan, and 4 miles from Banbridge—all Railway Stations on the Great Northern Line.

For further particulars, as to Title, Terms of Sale, &c., apply to
HUGH GLASS, Esq., Solicitor for Administratrix, Banbridge.
WILLIAM CARSON, Solicitor for Mortgagees, Victoria Street, Belfast.

23rd February, 1878.

Auction notice in the *Banbridge Chronicle* of Ashfield House, 2 March, 1878

The house at Ballydown
JFR

BALLYDOWN
BANBRIDGE

A group of industrial buildings has existed at this site since the early eighteenth century and were firstly built as a corn mill. There are date stones at the north east corner of one building, one of which reads 'John Greer 1740' and the other 'William Hudson A.D. 1812', this building being identified by the *Ordnance Survey Memoirs* as the corn mill. In addition there was also a bleach mill, part of which had been built in 1800, on the site. In 1822 the Crawfords and their Lindsay cousins, in partnership, bought the business from William Hudson, who left Banbridge and went to Mount Caulfield in County Armagh to set up a linen mill spinning by power. Messrs Crawford & Lindsay had a very successful bleach green extending to forty acres and along with this they manufactured linens by hand loom, which were exported to the principal European and American markets.

Ballydown is on the Banbridge to Castlewellan road, a short distance from the town and close to the River Bann. The residence, which appears to have been connected to the business premises, was a two storey Georgian

Ballydown windmill
JFR

Death of Walter Lindsay, J.P.

THE regretted death on Tuesday, of Mr. Walter Lindsay, J.P., removes the last male representative of one of our oldest families, which goes back to the year 1680. The third of four sons of John Lindsay, J.P., Tullyhenan House, he was born on 28th August, 1860, and had long outlived his brothers, David, Crawford, and Charles. He was educated at the Royal Academical Institution, Belfast, and the Royal School, Armagh. Most of his long life was spent in his native place, where he looked after the local department of the famous Crawford and Lindsay linen business, and subsequently the bleaching concern of Uprichard & Lindsay, at Ballydown. He was also secretary to the Bann Reservoir Company. Fond of the

masonry building with granite quoins and brick surrounds to the sashed and silled windows. The door was set in a single storey porch with Doric columns surmounted by a semi circular fanlight of spider-web glazing and the front of the porch had a brick finish similar to the windows.

Mr Walter Lindsay was the last member of the family to live at Ballydown, and, although the building still existed at the beginning of the twenty first century, it has now been demolished.

Left: Death notice of Walter Lindsay in the *Banbridge Chronicle*, 19 June 1937

Below: A Hunting party from left: Howard Ferguson, Wilson Smyth, Walter Lindsay, Sir R. Liddell and C.S. Waller Watson

The River Bann at Ballievey near Banbridge

4
BANBRIDGE

HINCKS PRINT PLATE VIII
illustrating the Brown Linen Market at Banbridge

WILLIAM HINCKS 1783

BELMONT HOUSE
BANBRIDGE

Belmont House
JFR

Belmont House is situated on the eastern outskirts of Banbridge on the Rathfriland Road and is now used as a hotel. The house was built, according to a date stone in 1838, to a design by Thomas Jackson for Robert McClelland, whose family had been in the linen trade since the mid-eighteenth century. In 1865, Robert McClelland built the Banbridge Weaving Factory on the Rathfriland Road, just across the road from Belmont House and close to the River Bann. The *Ordnance Survey Memoirs* of 1834 list 'Andrew McCleland and Sons' as manufacturers of linen cloth in the town or vicinity of Banbridge. Robert McClelland's daughter Anna married John Smyth who lived at Milltown House, which had also been designed by Thomas Jackson. Belmont House remained in the occupancy of the McClelland family up to the 1900s when it was bought by William Anderson (Jumbo) Smyth on his marriage to Katherine McNeill, in 1901, and it remained in his possession until his death in 1927. William Smyth (1861–1927) was born at Brookfield House and was the eldest

BELMONT HOUSE, BANBRIDGE

son of William Smyth and Catherine Anderson, being a member of one of the most respected linen families in Banbridge.

Belmont House has been described in the publication *Banbridge* by the Ulster Architectural Heritage Society, 1969, as:

> A fine square two storey merchant's mansion of horizontally rusticated golden freestone with tetrastyle Ionic portico; an excellent example of the Greek revival style at its late best.

The house is three bay with an imposing single storey Ionic portico with fluted columns and the roof is hipped and slated with moulded eaves and cornice on paired console brackets. Unfortunately, the windows of the ground floor have had their glazing bars replaced with plate glass but those of the first floor retain theirs in the original form. A two bay, two storey extension has been added to the side of Belmont House which detracts from the classical appearance of the house.

William Anderson (Jumbo) Smyth and his wife Katherine, 1914

Belmont House was set in twenty acres of land with lawns, gardens and considerable grazing. Dean, in 1994, records a gate lodge which is deserted.

> A solid Neo-Classical design with central hipped roof porch flanked by Doric columns with equivalent pilasters as quoins. Single storey with a hipped roof, a frieze surrounds the building below the eaves.

There was also a chauffeur's house and a gardener's house, along with four cottages on the estate.

After the death of William Smyth, Belmont House was sold in February 1928 to the Finney family, but it has again been sold, and is now run as a hotel.

Belmont House during the visit of Sir Edward Carson, 1914

SOLITUDE HOUSE
BANBRIDGE

Solitude House
JFR

Solitude House is situated in the town of Banbridge on the Castlewellan Road and close to Church Square. The house was built *c.* 1840 for the Clibborns, a Quaker family who originally belonged to Moate, County Westmeath, and who owned a factory, a bleach green and a flour mill on the south side of the River Bann. Crowe, 1980, states that the factory was in existence from 1767 and that the factory appears to have occupied the Prospect Terrace site. In the late eighteenth century they belonged to James Clibborn, who traded under the name Clibborn & Co. James Clibborn's name appears in a list of residents in Banbridge and neighbourhood who signed a Petition to Parliament in favour of Catholic Emancipation in 1828. After his death James Clibborn was succeeded by Edward C. Clibborn who kept the company going and, at the Great Exhibition held in London, 1852, the first prize for diapers went to Clibborn & Co., of Banbridge. However, later in the 1850s the business was carried on under the name of Clibborn, Hill & Co., when a nephew was taken into partnership. In addition, the *Ordnance Survey Memoirs* of 1834 record Thomas

SOLITUDE HOUSE, BANBRIDGE

Clibborn having a bleaching works on the north side of the river.

Solitude House is a three bay, two storey over basement Georgian house, which is stuccoed and has quoins adorning the façade. A description of the house is given in *Linen Houses of Banbridge*, 1995:

> The fine Georgian doorway is reached by a flight of steps, a second flight on an axis with the doorway leading down to the garden. The windows on each side of the doorway are round-headed, sashed and simply recessed with a sill. The upper storey windows differ only from the others in that they are of a smaller height. The roof is hipped and slated with deep eaves and a dormer window rising between the chimneys.

The house was originally sited on an island between the River Bann and the mill race, with access by a road bridge, and a foot bridge which led to Bridge Street. In 1972 the foot bridge was washed away in floods during the occupancy of the Burnett family who had taken possession of Solitude House in 1919 and remains the family home.

In 1865 William Walker built a power loom factory on part of the site of the old Clibborn factory. William Walker was already in business with William Waugh of Hazelbank mill, and in 1866 Messrs William Walker & Co., employed three hundred people in the linen industry. After the death of William Walker the premises were bought out of chancery by Robinson and Hamilton, and subsequently John Robinson and John Cleaver formed the Belfast firm of Robinson & Cleaver Ltd., which took over the running of the factory and exported linen world wide.

ROCKVILLE
BANBRIDGE

Rockville
JFR

Rockville was built in 1901 on the site of the original Robinson house which appears to have been known as Rockview since this was the name on the Ordnance Survey first edition of 1834. The map shows a bleach green and boiling house at Rockview and the Ordnance Survey 1858 edition marks 'linen factory' at the site. Rockview was the home of William Robinson and his brother John had a cambric bleach works at Ballydown. John Robinson joined with John Cleaver of Belfast to found Robinson & Cleaver Ltd., Belfast, a well known linen retailer.

Rockville is situated on the east of Banbridge on the road leading from the dual carriageway into the town. Rockville is a three bay, two storey stuccoed house which was built adjoining an old farmhouse. The building is well described in the *Linen Houses of Banbridge*, 1995:

> The upper storey windows are deeply recessed while those of the lower storey are silled and set within breakfronts on each side of the single storey porch. An interesting feature on each breakfront is the small columns which rise the height of the windows, a detail reflected in the bevelled edges of the chimneys. The

ROCKVILLE, BANBRIDGE

breakfronts are topped by an entablature with a moulded cornice, level with the cornice of the porch. The porch itself, topped by a small balustrade stopping level with the string course, has windows on each side and fluted pilasters at each corner. The roof is hipped with moulded eaves and cornice supported on console brackets.

In the 1930s the then owner, Mrs Walsh, leased the property to John B. Cowdy, of the Banbridge bleaching company, Anthony Cowdy & Sons, Ltd. He married Miss Susan Stewart-Liberty of the renowned Liberty shop in London and they lived at Rockville from 1935 to 1939. Rockville, referred to by many as 'the Rock', remains a well maintained fine family home.

Advertisements for Robinson and Cleavers in the *Banbridge Chronicle*, 1878

THE FERGUSON FAMILY
OF BANBRIDGE

Thomas Ferguson

The history of Thomas Ferguson & Co., Ltd., and the Edenderry Works begins with Thomas Ferguson who was born at Clare, Waringstown in 1820. He was one of a family of five children of whom only two survived to adulthood. In addition, his mother died in 1826, and his father died in 1831, so that he and his brother John were left orphans. It is believed their guardian was the Rev. Dr Johnston of Tullylish Presbyterian Church, as they were both educated at Belfast Academy with William and Harry Johnston, his sons. When Thomas Ferguson left school he was apprenticed to Brice Smyth of Brookfield, Banbridge, who was a blind man but also an outstanding hand loom linen manufacturer. Others who went to serve their time with Brice Smyth were Henry Matier, a future linen manufacturer, and John Preston, later Sir John Preston, who eventually became a yarn merchant.

It is not known precisely when Thomas Ferguson left Brookfield and started up in business on his own but he told his son of journeying both to Dublin and Belfast with Brice Smyth, so he would have been well introduced to the ins and outs of the trade. In those days Dublin had a linen market and a linen hall as did Belfast. Naturally, starting at the time he did, which must have been in the early 1840s, he was a hand loom weaver and it is believed that he started his business in a house in the middle of Banbridge backing on to the River Bann, which gave him access to a supply of water for treating his yarn. However, this was the period of the introduction of power loom weaving, and from deeds it is known that the lease for the site of the future factory was acquired in 1855 from John Temple Reilly of Scarva. The Reilly family were large landowners around Banbridge, and it was quite an extensive property extending to both sides of the Lurgan Road out of Banbridge, but again with one side bounded by the River Bann.

By 1866 Thomas Ferguson had decided to go in for power loom weaving, and in that year the firm of Dickson Ferguson & Co., was formed through his partnership with two brothers-in-law, James and Benjamin Dickson. They had previously been involved as partners in Gilford Mill and in a company with Hugh Dunbar of Huntly in the firm of Dunbar Dickson & Co. The precise date of the building of the factory is not known except for a keystone above the entrance archway to the old engine room which had the date 1866 upon it. Another important factor for the company at this time was the advent of the railway because the factory was situated at the top of a hill with a yarn treatment works at the bottom of the hill beside the river. Power was derived from steam which was generated by coal delivered to a siding beside the works, as the railway line ran along what had been company property. Continual improvements were made in the weaving factory, which at first made hucks, and towelling, but the move into damask manufacture as the predominant product did not take place immediately.

In 1883 the Dicksons retired from business, and the company of Thomas Ferguson & Co., Ltd., was incorporated in 1884, with Thomas and his sons Howard and Norman being the first directors, with another son, Thomas as secretary. In later years three grandsons of the founder entered the company, later still two great-grandsons, and finally a great-great-grandson. By the end of the nineteenth century the era of electricity had arrived and the first generators were installed about 1891 to drive the machines replacing steam as an energy source. Thomas Ferguson died in 1900, in his eightieth year, but he already had three very able sons, Howard, Norman, and Thomas in the business. In the early years of the twentieth century the weaving of damask was introduced requiring some modifications in the factory. In response to the retail demands of the North American market the production of double damask was introduced and eventually by the 1930s Fergusons had become manufacturers of damask as opposed to towels and drying cloths, which were the main product of the company in the early days.

An important step was taken in the 1930s by Thomas Ferguson & Co., Ltd., when they set up the associated company Ballievey Bleaching Co., Ltd., on a fifty-fifty ownership basis with Samuel Lamont & Sons, Ltd. Ballievey Bleaching was involved in the majority of bleaching, finishing, and dyeing for these two companies and went on to secure contracts for similar work from other linen companies in the ensuing years. During the Second World War everything was controlled and the supply of flax limited so that the company, like many others, produced aeroplane cloth and other standard cloths under the Utility regime. Wartime restrictions continued into the early 1950s but the situation gradually eased and there was freedom to sell anywhere in the world. By then the management of Thomas Ferguson & Co., Ltd., had passed to Thomas and James, sons of Norman (1866–1960), and Stanley, son of Stanley (1863–1943), who had been a solicitor, and also a director of the Ulster Bank.

In 1945 the board of the company decided that automatic machinery should be installed to replace the old non-automatic then in use, and from 1948 to 1956 a complete re-equipment programme was undertaken. In the late 1950s the company was producing linen, cotton and rayon damask, being renowned for its 'Double Damask', a cloth defined by the number of warp and weft threads. At least sixty per cent of the production of the company went to North America: the United States and Canada selling damask in the retail trade to the very large department stores such as Marshall Field in Chicago, Altman, Bloomingdales, Maceys in New York and the T. Eaton Company in Canada.

There were therefore regular pilgrimages by management to North America, although they had an agent who resided in New York but travelled the country between visits by principals from Banbridge. In the 1950s, 60s and 70s there was a regular autumn visitation touring the customers in North America, by one of the family, Mr Tom, Mr Stanley or Mr James but latterly this visit was undertaken by Mr N.G.D. Ferguson, son of Mr Tom, or his cousin, Mr S.M. Ferguson. There was a modest trade in damask with Australia, a little went to South Africa and New Zealand, but essentially it was a Commonwealth based business, with no business in South America because that market was primarily for suitings and dress linens. As time passed the market focus shifted, and the United Kingdom and Europe became increasingly important, this being particularly true after the United Kingdom joined the European Union.

The company remained predominantly damask weavers up to the 1970s when they started to become more interested again in towels and towelling, and also in the direct user trade of hotels, airlines and railways.

The Ferguson family were generous in their support for the community in Banbridge and gave freely of their time and management expertise in the interests of education, notably Banbridge Academy. This is reflected in a passage in *Bridges to Banbridge*, 1980, written by Dr W. Haughton Crowe a former headmaster of Banbridge Academy.

Norman D. Ferguson
1866–1960

Both Mr Norman and Mr Tom Ferguson were men who not only made their living in the town; they also made a living for many; and they gave freely of their time and energies toward the social, sporting, cultural, and governmental life of Banbridge. My own contacts with them were largely concerned with the affairs of the Academy which at that time retained a good deal of its private character; and, though numbers were small, the business of its running was for that very reason the more difficult. In this sphere none could have been more helpful than the Fergusons; their business expertise and acumen were at all times, and in all circumstances, at our disposal.

In Tullylish Presbyterian Church there is a memorial tablet in the church porch which states:

In memory of Thomas Ferguson, Esq., Banbridge, who during his lifetime was a true friend of Tullylish Congregation, born April 27th 1820, died February 24th 1900. Erected by the congregation.

Members of the Ferguson family were also involved with the Iveagh Harriers and in 1881 Mr Thomas Ferguson was Master, and his eldest son Howard also became Master in 1902.

Latterly the linen trade became increasingly difficult in the 1970s and 1980s although Fergusons still found a niche with their 'Double Damask' at the very top end of the market where overseas producers could not compete. In 1988 the company was sold to William Franklin & Son (NI) Ltd., Scarva Road, Banbridge who retain the name of Ferguson's Irish Linen. Modern computer aided rapier looms were installed in the Scarva Road premises of Franklins, who have a high level of automation in the factory, with modern working practices. The company deals principally with up-market hotels and shipping companies, and at times supplying special orders to Buckingham Palace and the White House. However, the name of Thomas Ferguson & Co., Ltd., still exists, and this is a tribute to the reputation of quality and reliability built up over a century by the company.

Michael McGarigan's original elevations of the Market House, Banbridge held in the Public Record Office of Northern Ireland.

FERGUSON FAMILY TREE

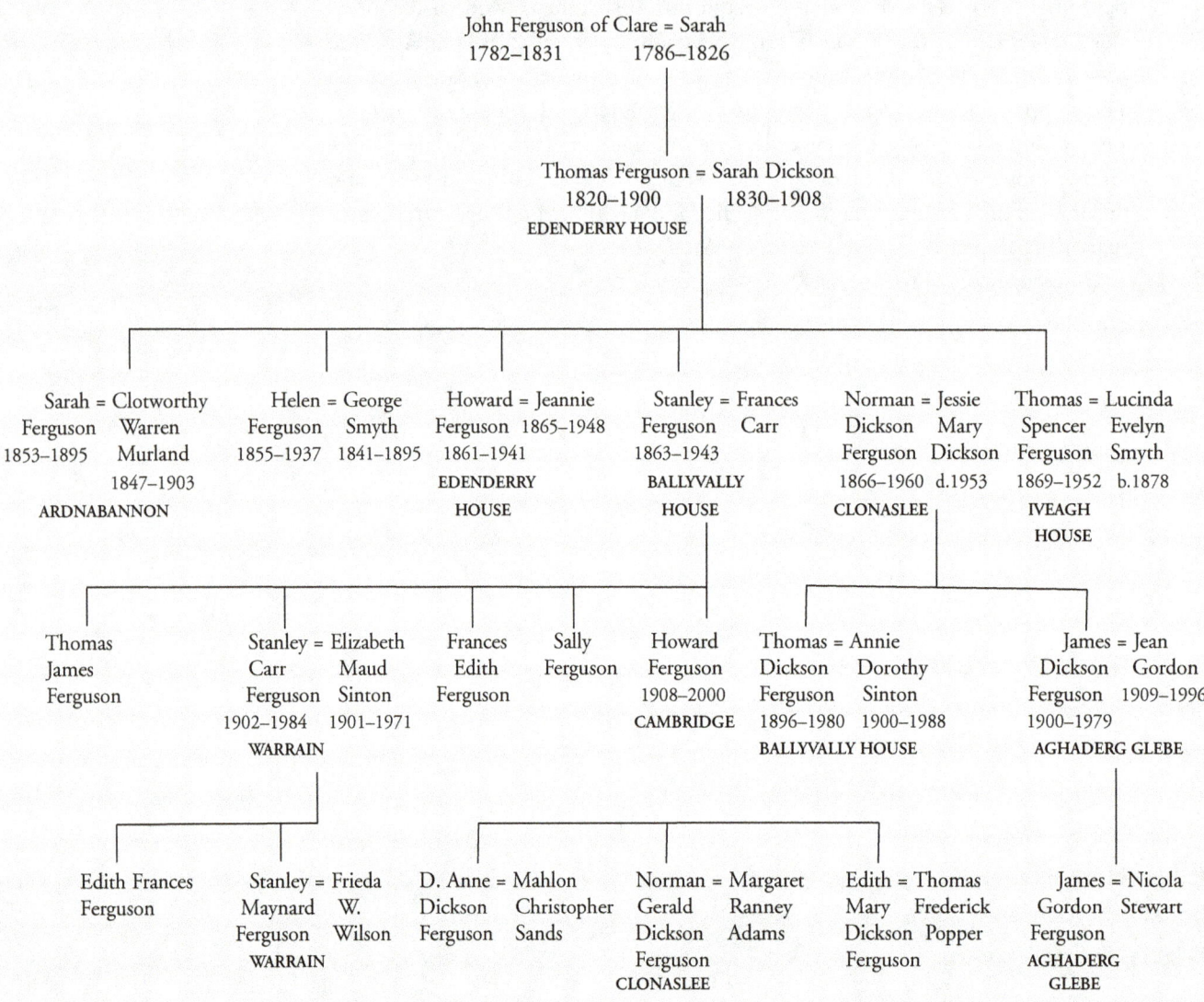

EDENDERRY HOUSE
BANBRIDGE

Edenderry House is situated a short distance from Banbridge on the Lurgan Road, and is now in use as a school – the main building of Banbridge Academy. The house is one of three houses built in the area and designed by William Spence of Glasgow, the other two being Elmfield Castle and Gilford Castle, respectively the properties of James and Benjamin Dickson. Edenderry House was built *c.* 1865 by Thomas Ferguson on land acquired in 1854 on a 999 year lease from the Reilly Estate of Scarva which also included land on the other side of the Lurgan Road where the power loom factory was built *c.* 1866. The house, set in grounds of forty acres, has a somewhat restrained Italianate style and is built of grey Portland stone and Scrabo sandstone with a portico balustraded around the top and supported on acanthus brackets, this effect being repeated above the two large ground floor windows on the front. Adjacent to the portico and rising above the roof is a small corbelled square turret, which projects from the front of the building.

Bassett, writing in 1886 about linen manufacture in Banbridge states:

> The Edenderry Linen Factory, of Messrs. Thomas Ferguson & Co., Ltd., occupies an elevation on the western side of the Bann, and with Edenderry House, the beautiful residence of Mr Thomas Ferguson, JP, managing director, forms one of the most conspicuous and pleasing features of the town, as seen from the railway station.

Edenderry House
COURTESY JERRY MURLAND

Banbridge Academy

Howard Ferguson

After the death of his parents, Edenderry House was inherited by Howard Ferguson, who lived there in great style, maintaining a considerable establishment to support his great love of the outdoor life, in particular riding to hounds. In his early years in the company Howard Ferguson was their representative in America where, through his efforts, the business connections became very extensive. Latterly, following the example of his father, he took an active part in the public affairs of Banbridge, not only as a magistrate, but also as chairman of the urban council.

After the death of Howard in 1941, Edenderry House, sometimes known as Ferguson's Castle, was inherited by James Dickson Ferguson, younger son of Howard's brother Norman. However, in 1947, the house was sold for the sum of £11,000 to the County Down Education Authority for the use of Banbridge Academy, as it remains at present, with extensions and new additional buildings.

Interior of Banbridge Academy

CLONASLEE
BANBRIDGE

Clonaslee is situated relatively close to Banbridge on the left hand side of the Lurgan Road leaving Banbridge, and just above the former site of the linen factory beside the River Bann. The house was built in 1901 for Norman Dickson Ferguson, third son of Thomas Ferguson, who had married in 1895 Jessie Mary Dickson of Edinburgh, daughter of Andrew John Dickson, Solicitor to the Supreme Court. Clonaslee is a fine Victorian villa, designed by the Dromore architect Henry Hobart, and built in Flemish bonded red brick with an entrance sheltered by a loggia style porch surmounted by a tiled roof. On the entrance front there is also a bay window which is topped by a tiled roof on a level with that of the porch, and the windows of the house, topped by flat arches, are recessed, sashed and silled. Clonaslee is a two storey plus attic house which has a tiled roof with deep eaves supported on console brackets. Henry Hobart, who favoured the use of redbrick for many of his buildings has

Clonaslee
COURTESY N.G.D. FERGUSON, CBE, DL

simulated in brick on the main front gable the beams which would have been found on the gables of a Tudor house.

Thomas Ferguson had five sons, the eldest dying in infancy, but three of his remaining sons entered the family linen business becoming directors, with Howard and Thomas in the warehouse and Norman in the factory. Ernie Gordon, a former works manager, writing about the 'Edenderry Works, Banbridge' in the *Banbridge & District Historical Society Journal*, 1993, states:

> In personality and outlook they were very different except for one very important factor and that was their complete dedication to the success of the business started by their father. They were all outstanding businessmen.

Norman Dickson Ferguson, of Clonaslee, is described by Gordon as an outstanding individual, tall and slim in appearance, who was respected in the linen community for his ability and determination. At one period he was Chairman of the Down County Council, Chairman of Belfast Ropeworks, a director of Banbridge Reservoir Company, and a Deputy Lieutenant for County Down. Norman Ferguson had two sons, Thomas and James, who in their turn became directors of Thomas Ferguson & Co., Ltd.

Clonaslee continues to be occupied by a member of the Ferguson family.

Jesse M.D. Ferguson and children outside Clonaslee
COURTESY N.G.D. FERGUSON, CBE, DL

IVEAGH HOUSE
BANBRIDGE

Iveagh House is situated a short distance out of Banbridge town on the Castlewellan Road. The house was designed by Henry Hobart and built about 1902, as a wedding present from the Smyth family, on the occasion of the marriage of Thomas Ferguson to Evelyn Smyth (Eva), a daughter of William Smyth of Brookfield. Iveagh is a two storey, three bay Victorian house built in red brick and having an imposing doorcase, set within an arch with keystone supported on two Tuscan pilasters and having an entablature designed to give the effect of a balustrade. There are bay windows extending to the first floor on either side of the front entrance with the windows recessed, sashed and silled and topped with a flat arch in brick. The roof is slated with deep bracketed eaves and two chimney stacks set centrally on the roof.

Thomas Ferguson, along with his brothers Howard and Norman, was a director of Thomas Ferguson & Co., Ltd., and took an active part in the management of the company. In *Bridges to Banbridge*, 1980, Dr W. Haughton Crowe

Iveagh House
COURTESY STANLEY M. FERGUSON

writes that Mr Tom was genial and approachable with a liking for sport. He was a fresh air lover and, rejecting the car as a means of transport over short distances, he always walked to his office making his way along the railway line to Scarva to the point where it ran nearest to the factory. Tom Ferguson loved hunting and no hunting Saturday passed without his familiar figure in leggings out in the fields.

Thomas's two daughters, Miss Janie and Miss Geraldine Ferguson continued to live in Iveagh after the death of their parents up until 1990 when Miss Janie died. The house is now a private residential home for the elderly, having been considerably extended.

Iveagh House
JFR

Aghaderg Glebe House
JFR

AGHADERG GLEBE HOUSE
LOUGHBRICKLAND

The Rev. Joseph McCormack had been Vicar of the Parish of Aghaderg for just three years when the Glebe House was built in 1801. The Church of Ireland, Board of First Fruits, gave one hundred pounds towards its erection and also purchased a glebe of twenty four acres. In 1857 Dean Jeffry Lefroy, Vicar of Aghaderg, carried out major renovations and enlargements to the Glebe House. The Rev. Jeffry Lefroy was the third son of the Rt. Hon. Thomas Langlois Lefroy, Lord Chief Justice of Ireland, and having spent eight years in the parish as a bachelor, he married in 1844, Helena Trench, eldest daughter of the Rev. Frederick Stewart Trench and Lady Helena Trench. They had nine children and when adults, two of them wrote in a book in 1908, for private circulation, their memories of the family and the following concerning the house at Loughbrickland:

> About a quarter of a mile east of the village on a rising ground overlooking the lake, and facing south, stood the Glebe House. Certainly founded on a rock

and fairly well built, but a very small and unpretending house with two small sitting rooms on either side of the door, the usual bedrooms above, and roomy offices and stabling at the back, it must have seemed a tiny home to our father and mother who had both been used all their lives to much roomier quarters.

However, during his incumbency Dean Lefroy had the Glebe house enlarged, with the addition at the west end of a good sized study and a bedroom and dressing room of corresponding size overhead. The study opened by folding doors into the drawing room.

Aghaderg was originally a three bay, two storey Georgian residence, with slated roof. The windows are recessed, sashed and silled and in the original house are of a tripartite form with the ground floor windows reaching almost to the ground. The house has a single storey projecting porch with moulded architrave, and with entrance at the side.

Aghaderg Glebe House and lands were sold in 1950 to James Dickson Ferguson, OBE, DL, who had served in the Second World War as Lieutenat Colonel in the army, and was a director of Thomas Ferguson & Co., Ltd., and Ballievey Bleaching Co., Ltd. He had been left Edenderry House by his uncle Howard Ferguson but did not live there, selling the house in 1947 after which it became Banbridge Academy. Jim Ferguson spent a considerable amount of money restoring Aghaderg Glebe House and lived there with his wife Jean, daughter of the late Malcolm Gordon, of Clonmore, Lambeg, until his death in 1979. The house remains in the ownership of the Ferguson family.

WARRAIN
BANBRIDGE

Warrain is situated on the Ballymoney Road, a short distance out of Banbridge, and on a hill north of the town. The house was built in 1935 by Mr Stanley Carr Ferguson, the architect being Reside of Newry. Warrain is a five bay, two storey stucco house, the main rooms facing the garden at the rear. There is a large conservatory, also overlooking the garden, which was laid out by Mrs Ferguson and planted by Daisy Hill Nurseries, Newry.

The name of the house is Australian being the Aboriginal for 'the sea'. Stanley Carr Ferguson went to stay with a member of the Liddell family, in Australia, in 1925, in order to recover from glandular fever. While there, he became a member of the Warrain Country Club on the outskirts of Melbourne, and so much enjoyed his time at the Club that he named his house, Warrain.

Warrain continues to be occupied by a member of the Ferguson family.

Warrain Country Club, Melbourne, 1925
COURTESY STANLEY M. FERGUSON

Warrain front and rear

JFR

THE COWDY FAMILY
OF BANBRIDGE

A John Cowdy (1770–1857) is recorded in the late eighteenth century as being in the linen trade in Dromore, which is near the original Cromwellian Grant of 1653 to a Cowdy, who was in Cromwell's army. John's son, Anthony Cowdy (1809–92) went to Portadown from Dromore where he built up a good linen finishing, making up, and merchandising business in the handkerchief trade. Later, in 1863, he acquired a small works on the Callan River at Greenhall near Loughgall, but in 1874, as a result of the slump following the American Civil War, he ran into severe financial difficulties and had to give up his home, Killycomain House, Portadown, and his interests in the Ravarnette Weaving Company. However, Anthony Cowdy, Sr., retained the Greenhall works and the Edward Street business in Portadown, where he did most of his merchanting activities.

At this point he handed over the business to his sons, William and Anthony, Jr., and this partnership continued until it was dissolved in 1879. The Portadown business then became William Cowdy & Sons, and in turn was continued by his son, William Laird Cowdy, until, unfortunately William Laird's only son was killed in the First World War. In 1929 the complete Portadown business was sold to Spence Bryson, who finally closed it down in 1957. After 1879 Anthony, (1844–1908), managed the processing works at Greenhall, County Armagh, and did a good business in the very heavy end of the linen trade, for use in soldiers' clothing and boot linings. Greenhall was a commission house and was processing merchants' cloth but the shortage of water from the Callan River restricted the expansion of the business, which was then beginning to do very well. Anthony (1844–1908), had six sons, five of whom went into the linen trade, and with the prospect of a further increase in the business, he acquired the lease of Millmount in Banbridge where there was ample water from the River Bann.

In 1796 William Hayes (1770–1827) acquired the lease of Millmount and its land in the townland of Edenderry from John Reilly, Esq. A survey of the site in 1796 by George Stuart shows a mansion house and several other houses and there was also a corn mill. Prior to this the McClellands of Banbridge had held a lease on Millmount from 1762, but William Hayes set up a bleach works and the Ordnance Survey, 1833–38, records industrial buildings which were erected in 1800 and 1806. William Hayes married, in 1796, Margaret Crawford of the Crawford family of Ballievey House and eventually had a family of ten children. The *Ordnance Survey Memoirs*, Mid-Down, 1833–8, list William Hayes & Sons

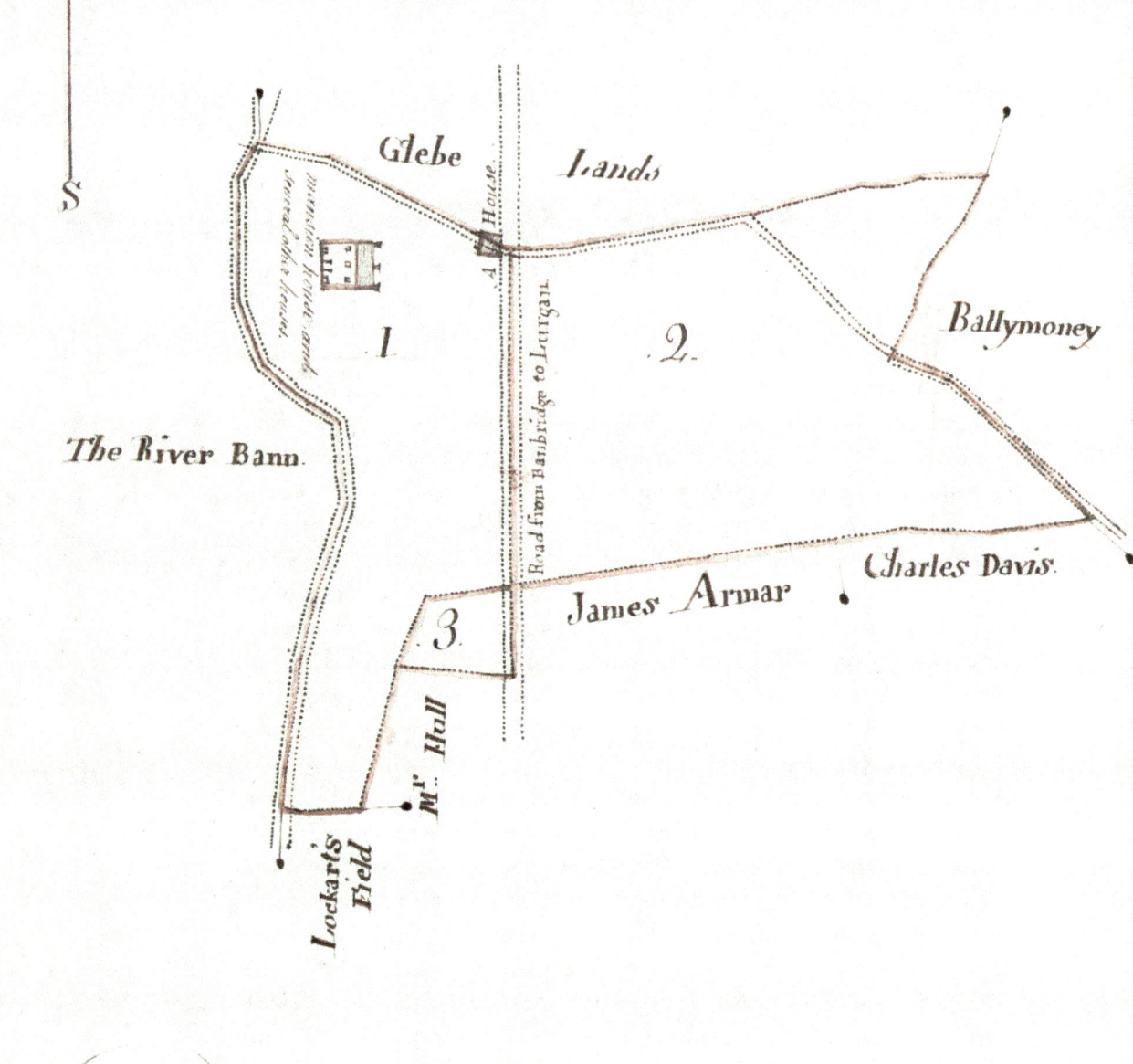

Millmount Farm, in Edenderry, being part of the estate of John Reilly Esq. Surveyd in June 1796 by

Geo: Stuart

Scale 20 perches to an inch.

Nº	A	R
1	20	2
2	28	"
3	1	2

Kane's Field.

Nº 3 Kane's field, one acre two roods twentytwo perches .... A.R.P 1.2.22
Nº 1 Under, or Westward of the broad road, twenty acres two roods nine perches 20.2.9
Nº 2 Above, or Eastward of the broad road, twentyeight acres 28.0.0
                                                                        50.0.31

Total of English measure. 50.0

THE COWDY FAMILY OF BANBRIDGE

as one of the principal bleachers in the parish of Seapatrick. Further buildings were added to the bleach works and after the death of William in 1827, Millmount was inherited by his eldest son Richard. However, he died intestate in 1864 and the bleach works were let to the Malcomson family who used it for cloth bleaching and finishing. E.R.R. Green, 1963, states that the works were then taken over by James McWilliam, a Banbridge manufacturer, but after his death it closed down until it was eventually re-opened when Anthony Cowdy acquired the lease to Millmount in 1892.

In 1895 Anthony Cowdy, (1844–1908), took the prestigious post of manager of the York Street Flax Spinning Company, Muckamore Works, one of the largest bleaching and dyeing units in the trade, in order to allow his sons experience in the business. Charlie, his eldest son, and Tony, his second son were sent to Millmount to start up the bleach works. Subsequently, they each, in turn, took up management positions in important linen companies in order to acquire experience, as did his other three sons, eventually returning to Banbridge. Anthony Cowdy died in 1908, and his eldest son, Charlie, became the main driving force, with his youngest brother Jack joining him at Millmount *c.* 1909. Over the ensuing years the business expanded very considerably with new buildings being added to the site. In 1924 Tony, his second son, applied for the post of Managing Director of the Greenmount & Boyne Linen Company, Drogheda, to which he was appointed and remained there for the rest of his life. The Greenhall works had been kept on when Millmount was acquired, and was managed by Edward, being assisted by Alfred after he had served in the 1914–18 war.

A very considerable customer base was built up by the company with a very strong position in the linen cambric trade. After the Second World War a large dye house was built at Millmount, Banbridge, and this again expanded the business making Anthony Cowdy & Sons, Ltd., one of the major commission bleachers and dyers in Ireland. The merchants enjoyed a significant recovery in business in the late 1940s and early 1950s, however this faded in the 1960s. The work for commission bleachers and dyers contracted to such an extent that several firms closed down. Anthony Cowdy & Sons, Ltd., decided to cease production in 1964, closing both the works at Millmount as well as at Greenhall.

Map of Millmount Farm in Edenderry
PRONI

BRANCH WORKS:—
    GREENHALL, LOUGHGALL, Co. ARMAGH.
Telephones:— { BANBRIDGE 3232 2 LINES.
                LOUGHGALL, MOY 214.
Telegrams:— { "COWDY, BANBRIDGE"
              "   "   LOUGHGALL."

ANTHONY COWDY & SONS, LTD.

Bleachers, Dyers & Finishers,
Millmount
Banbridge,
Co. Down

COWDY FAMILY TREE

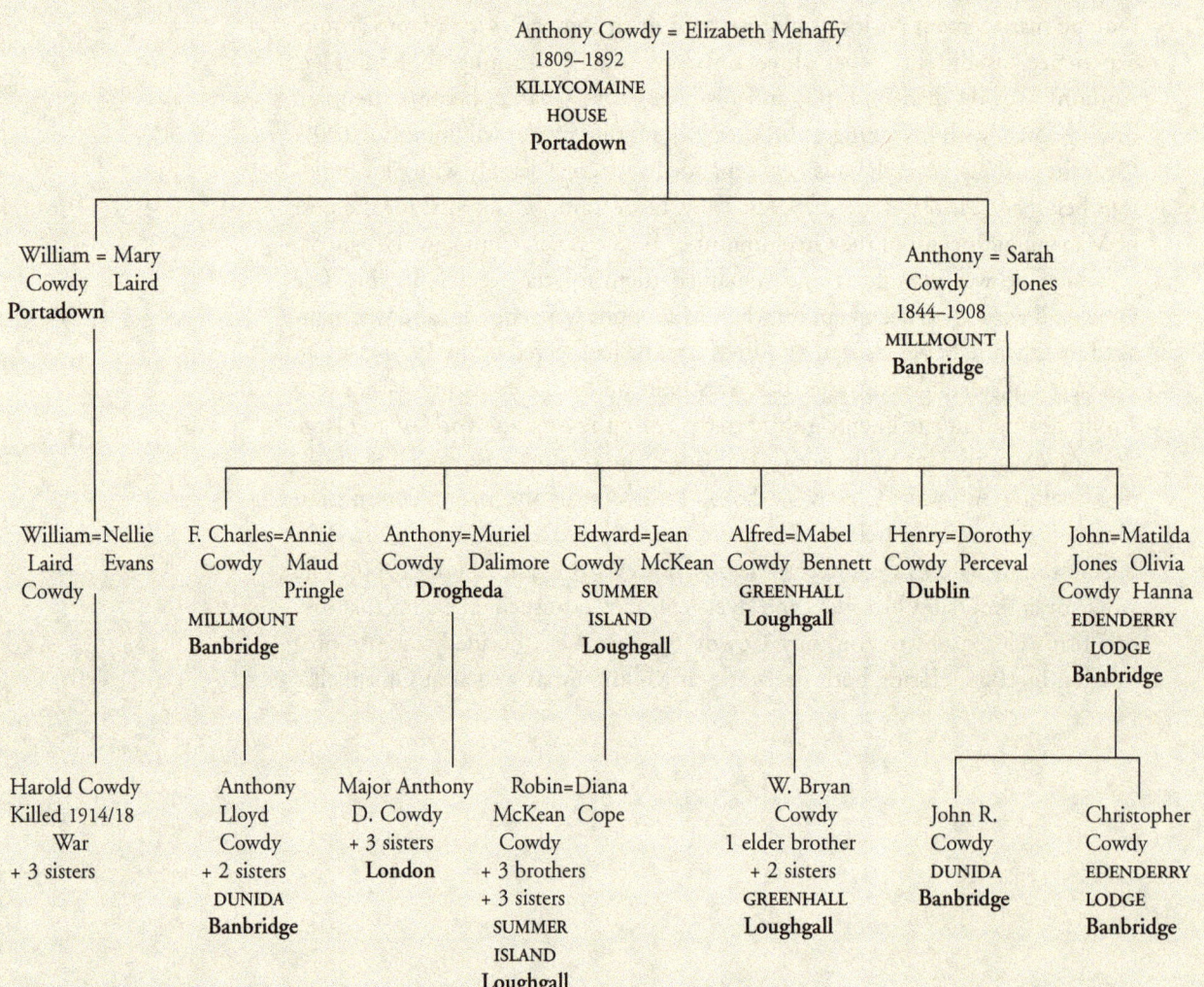

This is an abbreviated Family Tree showing the names of the members of the Cowdy family involved in Anthony Cowdy & Sons.

Millmount House
COURTESY COWDY FAMILY

MILLMOUNT HOUSE
BANBRIDGE

Millmount House is situated on the left hand side of the Lurgan Road out of Banbridge, and on the northern side of the River Bann. The *Ordnance Survey Memoirs* for the Parish of Seapatrick in 1834 state:

> About half a mile beyond Banbridge are the bleaching green and mills of Mr Richard Hays of Millmount and a few perches further, where there is a wooden bridge, is the thread manufactory of Mr Dunbar …

However, it was Richard Hayes' father, William Hayes, who, in 1796, took a lease for 900 years of Millmount House and lands in the townland of Edenderry from John Reilly Esq. Previously, the McClelland family had taken a lease of the property in 1762, when there was a corn mill on the site. However, it would appear that there was a house at Millmount in the late eighteenth century. William Hayes married, in 1796, Margaret Crawford of the Crawford family of Ballievey House, and had a family of ten children. He adapted the corn mill buildings for bleaching, and became very successful in this business, which, after his death in 1827 was carried on by his son Richard, who also lived in Millmount House. Richard Hayes died in 1864, after which the works were let for bleaching to the Malcomsons, and subsequently to James McWilliam, again for bleaching.

Richard Hayes' daughter Elizabeth married Robert Joy, JP, son of Robert Joy,

Millmount House stairwell
COURTESY COWDY FAMILY

F. Charles Cowdy
COURTESY COWDY FAMILY

QC, Dublin, and Bassett, 1886, records them living in the house at Millmount in 1886. Anthony Cowdy took a lease of the bleaching works at Millmount from the Hayes in 1892 and moved part of his business to Banbridge from Greenhall in Loughgall. Finally, at the close of the nineteenth century Anthony Cowdy bought the mansion house, works, and land at Millmount, occupying the house in 1902. After Anthony died in 1908, Charles, Edward and Jack carried on the company, Anthony Cowdy & Sons, Ltd., with great success, and Millmount House was occupied by members of the Cowdy family until the mid-1960s when Lloyd Cowdy moved to South Africa.

Millmount House, built in 1796, is a three bay, two storey Georgian house, which has at the rear a much older return section, and a more modern wing to the side of the main building which was once fronted by a conservatory. The ground floor is rusticated with a platband separating it from the top floor which has decorative quoins. There is a hipped roof with moulded eaves and cornice. A description of the detailing around the windows and the interesting doorway are given in *Linen Houses of Banbridge*, 1995.

The most appealing aspect of Millmount has to be the architectural detailing around the windows and the Venetian doorway. The bottom storey windows are slightly recessed, reaching to the ground. The tympanum above them have scrollwork, the whole entablature being supported on Corinthian pilasters. The windows of the upper storey have quite elaborately moulded architraves with keystone, all supported on console brackets. All the windows are sashed, the top having glazing bars while the bottom are glazed with plate glass. The door is recessed and flanked by sidelights framed by two engaged Doric columns set slightly forward and supporting a moulded architrave. A small fanlight surrounded by a shell hood sits atop the architrave.

Although Millmount is now used for sheltered accommodation, the house still retains some of the original character.

F. Charles Cowdy and his wife, formerly Annie M. Pringle, lived in Millmount House for a considerable number of years. He was the eldest son of Anthony Cowdy, Greenhall, County Armagh, and later Millmount House, Banbridge. After the death of his father, F. Charles Cowdy was the senior director of Anthony Cowdy & Sons, and died in March 1953, aged 82.

EDENDERRY LODGE
BANBRIDGE

Edenderry Lodge was situated on the southern side of the River Bann on the Huntly Road and close to Banbridge town, but was, unfortunately, burnt down about the year 2000. This fine Victorian villa was designed by the Dromore architect Henry Hobart, and built around 1870 for Robert Matier who was a linen manufacturer. Robert Matier (1816–73) was the eldest son of Robert Matier, a farmer of Tullyear, County Down, whose second son Henry Matier (1822–91) was apprenticed in the linen industry to Brice Smyth of Brookfield, Banbridge. He went on to found Henry Matier & Co., a well known Belfast linen company specialising in the manufacture of cambric handkerchiefs, which were exported to markets throughout the world. Robert married Ann Hawthorne in 1848 and they had one son John, who died in New Orleans, and six daughters, one of whom was Anna, who went on to become headmistress of Victoria College, Belfast, 1912–30.

Edenderry Lodge
COURTESY COWDY FAMILY

LINEN HOUSES OF THE BANN VALLEY

The following quotation is taken from *Victoria College, Belfast: Centenary 1859–1959*.

VICTORIA COLLEGE BECOMES A PUBLIC SCHOOL UNDER MISS MATIER

Miss Anna Matier, daughter of the late Mr and Mrs Robert Matier of Edenderry Lodge, Banbridge, succeeded Dr Margaret Byers as Headmistress. Miss Matier had been a pupil at Victoria; she had held a staff appointment as teacher of History and English, and had also been Vice-Principal in succession to Miss E.M. Cunningham during Dr Byers's later years.

Ann Matier, widow of Robert, died at Edenderry Lodge in 1901 and the house was then bought by F. Charles Cowdy who lived there until 1924 when he moved to Millmount House. J.J. Cowdy (Jack) then moved from Dunida to Edenderry Lodge where he maintained a large stable of horses for hunting. The Cowdy family sold Edenderry Lodge in the mid-1960s.

Edenderry Lodge was a two storey, three bay, gabled house built of Flemish bonded red brick. At the entrance there was a small wooden porch with tiled roof and the front door had a segmental arched fanlight above. The ground floor windows sat out from the façade and all were round headed sashed and silled, being topped by a flat arch in brick. The roof had deep eaves, with bargeboards on the gables, and three sets of double chimneys.

From the mid-1920s Edenderry Lodge was the home of Mr J.J. Cowdy, his wife, and family. He was a director of the company of Anthony Cowdy & Sons, Ltd., and a member of the Council of the Linen Industry Research Association. Above all, hunting was, for a considerable time, his main interest, being a member of the County Down Staghounds and the Iveagh Harriers, of which, for a period, he was the Master.

Edenderry Lodge stairwell
COURTESY COWDY FAMILY

Jack Cowdy, and his wife Hilda, at Edenderry Lodge before a Boxing Day Hunt.
COURTESY COWDY FAMILY

DUNIDA HOUSE
BANBRIDGE

Dunida was built around 1890, to a design by Henry Hobart, for Charles H. McCall who was the manager of F.W. Hayes mill at Seapatrick. The mill had been established in 1834 by Frederick William Hayes to produce linen cloth, but by 1840 he had started yarn spinning and thread making in the premises. During those early years, a good manufacturing base was established for his products, which were given the name 'Royal Irish Linen Threads'. Frederick William Hayes died in 1853 and was succeeded by his eldest son William, who successfully extended the premises. In order to meet the needs of an expanding work force, William Hayes commenced a programme of house building with rows of workers' dwellings being built along with a short terrace of management houses. A school house was also built by the company opposite the entrance to the mills, for the education of the children of the employees.

William Hayes died in 1876, and was succeeded in running the firm by his eldest son, Frederick William Hayes (2), although he was still a minor. The management team of F.W. Hayes & Co. was strengthened by the recruitment of

Dunida House
JFR

Charles H. McCall as general mill manager, who was to live in Dunida, and was the son of the linen historian, Hugh McCall of Lisburn. About 1920 the house was sold to the Cowdy family and Jack Cowdy lived there until he moved to Edenderry Lodge in 1924, when the property was let. In 1935 Lloyd Cowdy moved to Dunida on the occasion of his marriage, and the house was later occupied by John R. Cowdy and his family, until it was sold in the mid-1960s.

Dunida House is situated on the north side of the Lurgan Road, Banbridge, a short distance from the town and just beyond Banbridge Academy. This is a two storey, gabled house with a stucco finish hiding the brickwork, and having a string course separating the first and second storey. There is quite an elaborate porch sheltering one window, which like the others on the ground floor is sashed and silled. The windows of the upper storey are tripartite with architrave and large keystone. Dunida has a steep roof, with the gables having bargeboards and finials, but most distinctively there are three tall chimneys rising above the height of the roof.

SUMMER ISLAND
LOUGHGALL

Summer Island is situated north west of Loughgall and mid-way between Loughgall and Moy, adjacent to the River Callan where Anthony Cowdy set up his bleach works at Greenhall. Edward Cowdy bought Summer Island in 1908 from the Verner family. In 1888 Bassett listed the occupant of Summer Island as Joseph Atkinson, Jr., his father, who was Deputy Lieutenant for County Armagh, living at nearby Crowhill. However, it appears that the house was leased to the Atkinson family by the Verners who had bought the property from Walter Clarke at some date prior to 1837. According to Brett, 1999, a Henry Clarke is noted as 'of Summer Island' in 1769 and relatives of the Clarke family appear to have been in occupation up to 1816. Again, Brett, 1999, states that this attractive Georgian house is very difficult to date, since one does not know whether the house now standing is the original one or a rebuilding. From various sources a date between 1780 and 1820 seems possible and this is confirmed by Belinda Jupp in her *Heritage Gardens Inventory*, 1992. She states:

Summer Island
JFR

LINEN HOUSES OF THE BANN VALLEY

Demesne for house *c.* 1780. Mature parkland and shelter belt trees. Maintained ornamental garden at house. Walled garden. Gate lodge (pair).

Summer Island is an attractive Georgian two storey, stucco finish, five bay house with basement. Sir Charles Brett, writing on *Buildings of County Armagh*, 1999, gives the following description:

Summer Island doorway
JFR

> There is a very fine fanlight above the wide doorcase, which incorporates two engaged columns and two pilasters. The windows retain their Georgian glazing bars. The roof is hipped, with heavy dentils at the eaves, and a pair of fine big chimney stacks on the ridge, one carrying seven pots, the other eight.

Summer Island is particularly noted for the fine pair of gate lodges, situated at the entrance, which have been described by Dean, 1994, as, 'The prettiest pair of surviving Georgian Gothic porters' lodges in the Province'. They were built by the Clarke family as an introduction to their elegant classical villa and are situated to the back of a segmental lay-by approach. Dean, 1994, gives a date *c.* 1820 but Brett, 1999, states that both lodges are clearly shown on William Kigan's map of June, 1794. The lodges are now empty but are maintained by the Cowdy family.

Mr Edward Cowdy, DL, (1873–1934), who lived at Summer Island, was a director of the firm Anthony Cowdy & Sons, Banbridge, having charge of the works at Greenhall, Loughgall, County Armagh. For many years Mr Cowdy was a prominent figure in the public life of County Armagh, serving on the County Council, of which he became Chairman, and also on the County Education

Summer Island gatelodge
JFR

Committee. His public services were recognised in 1919, when he was appointed a Deputy Lieutenant for Armagh, and, in 1920, he was further appointed High Sheriff of the County. It was probably as an agriculturist that he was best known in Northern Ireland, being a leading authority on British Friesian cattle.

Summer Island remains occupied by a member of the Cowdy family.

Fireplace in the dining room and stairway
© *CROWN COPYRIGHT HMSO*

Edward Cowdy as high Sheriff, County Armagh, 1923
COURTESY COWDY FAMILY

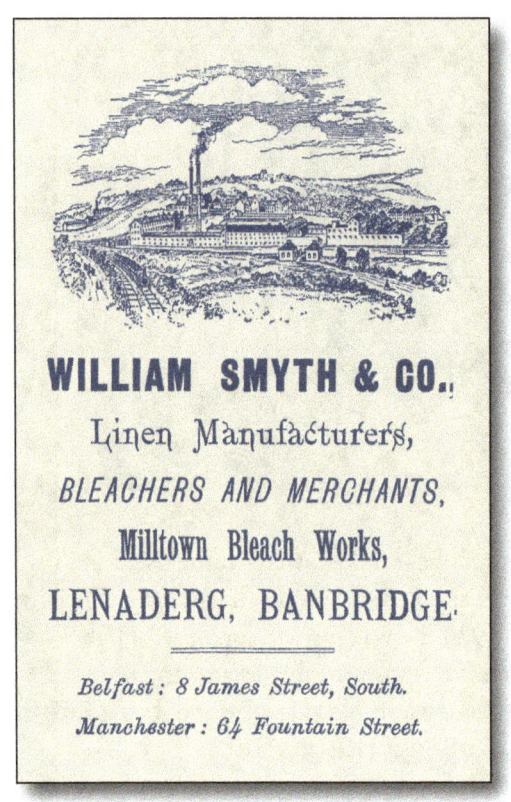

THE SMYTH FAMILY
OF BANBRIDGE

The family of Smyth was one of the oldest connected with the linen trade and was established in Banbridge for over two centuries. In 1663 a Brice Smyth settled in Derriaghy but the first of the family to settle in Banbridge was also a Brice Smyth who, in 1728, had a farm of fourteen acres in Ballyvalley. The Christian name Brice has occurred constantly through succeeding generations of Smyths, connected with the linen industry. In a census of 1766, the sons of Brice Smyth of Ballyvalley, Brice (2), James and Andrew, were living again near Banbridge in the townland of Lisnafiffy. Brice (2) had a son Brice (3), born in 1764, who married in 1785 Agnes Sterling and had at least three sons, Robert, Brice (4) and John. According to Lawlor, Brice (3) was engaged in the linen trade and prospered, eventually setting up and trading as Brice Smyth & Sons of Brookfield when his sons, Brice (4) and John came of age. Brice (3) lived until 1829, but in 1820 his younger son John (1798–1890) bought from the Crawfords their corn mill and surrounding land at Lenaderg where he erected extensive bleaching and finishing works. This became known as the Milltown Bleach Works, Lenaderg, which in time grew to be the largest on the River Bann. Essentially, from the death of Brice (3) in 1829 there were two Smyth families engaged in the linen industry, Brice (4) at Brookfield and John at Milltown.

THE SMYTH FAMILY OF BANBRIDGE

Brice Smyth (4) was born in 1796 but was unfortunately blinded at the age of twelve through an attack of smallpox. Nevertheless, he entered the family linen business and with great tenacity developed his other senses, being able to judge the quality of cloth or yarn by touch, and becoming one of the most renowned teachers in the trade. Brice (4) married Lucinda Running in Banbridge on 11th December 1829, and they had five children, only one of whom, William (1835–1913), entered the family business. After the death of his father in 1829, Brice (4) built Brice Smyth & Sons into one of the most respected linen firms in the country, specialising in the manufacture of heavy shirting linen. Unfortunately Brice (4) died in 1851 and did not live to enjoy the boom years in the Irish linen industry of the 1860s, due to the lack of cotton during the American Civil War.

Brice (5) died in 1836, and William Smyth was only fifteen when his father died but in a few years he had a complete grasp of the business which he carried on successfully for many years. However, in the 1870s the hand loom business was going into decline, and in 1883 William Smyth built a fully equipped power loom factory at Brookfield, manufacturing fine and coarse linens. The name of the firm was changed to Smyth's Weaving Co., Ltd. and William took into partnership his eldest son, William Anderson Smyth. William married twice, firstly to Catherine Anderson, having two sons, William Anderson, known as Jumbo, and Brice (6). Catherine died in 1871, and William married secondly Jane Robinson Wilson, having a further five children. William died in 1913 just prior to the outbreak of the First World War, in which two of his sons were killed.

Smyth's Weaving Co., Ltd., carried on under the management of William Anderson Smyth, D. Wilson Smyth and in time two of Wilson's sons William and Edmund Fitzgerald, (better known as Teddy). Eventually, after the Second World War, Smyth's Weaving joined with Stevensons of Dungannon, and the Braidwater Spinning Company, Ballymena to form Moygashel Ltd. In 1964 Courtaulds, Ltd., bought Moygashel and subsequently closed Smyth's Weaving in 1980.

Essentially the family evolved into three interwoven branches which were connected to Brookfield, Milltown, and Belmont, their homes, which were close to Banbridge. Returning to the second strand of the Smyth family set up by John (1798–1890), beside the bleach works at Milltown he built Milltown House *c.* 1825, and married Anna McClelland of Belmont House on 10th November 1825. They went on to have twelve children, three of their sons, William, John, Jr., and James Davis, eventually forming the company William Smyth & Co., which became a very successful business in the latter half of the nineteenth century. John Smyth, Sr., lived until 1890 when the family owned two hundred and twenty acres, some of which was in bleach greens, along with the Bannville Beetling Mills and an iron foundry on the opposite side of the River Bann. Bassett, in 1886, gives the following description of Messrs William Smyth & Co.,

> Messrs. Smyth are linen manufacturers, bleachers, finishers and merchants ... The main works at Milltown are about a mile and a half from Banbridge, and two and a half miles, Irish, from Gilford. The buildings are scattered over a considerable space. Steam and water are combined for driving power, the former being used as an auxiliary.

However, in the early twentieth century the family lost two very distinguished sons in the First World War, followed by a further two sons, who had also served in the First World War, being murdered in the early 1920s in the south of Ireland. The Milltown works ceased bleaching cloth in 1930, with yarn bleaching later coming to an end, and the works finally closed in 1947 under the Irish Bleachers' Association Redundancy Schemes.

For a considerable period in the nineteenth and early twentieth centuries the Smyths were one of the very important families in the linen trade in the Banbridge area, with many members of the family being involved.

SMYTH FAMILY TREE

Limited to male members involved in Linen Industry in Banbridge

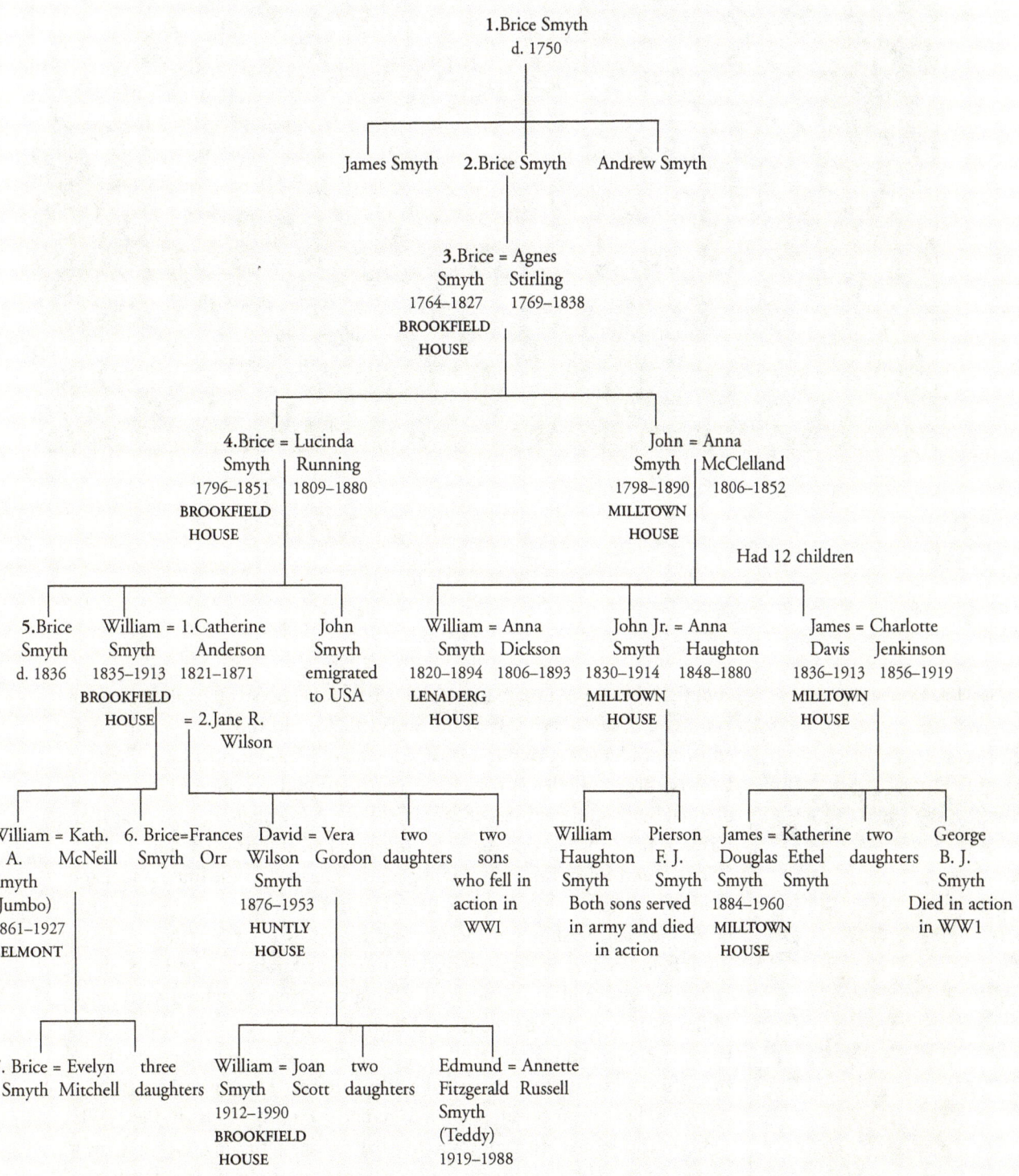

BROOKFIELD HOUSE
BANBRIDGE

Brookfield House and doorway
JFR

Brookfield House is situated one and a half miles west of Banbridge town centre on the northern side of the Scarva Road, and the house is surrounded by considerable grounds adjacent to the old Brookfield Linen Weaving Factory. Brice Smyth (2) may have been the builder, around 1760, of the original house and premises of Brookfield in the townland of Drumnagalley. His son, Brice (3) married Agnes Stirling and had at least three sons, Robert, Brice (4) and John. Brice (3) was apparently engaged in the linen trade, and prospered, so that when his sons Brice (4) and John came of age, they were taken into partnership and the business traded as Brice Smyth & Sons of Brookfield. Eventually, Robert settled in or near Strabane, and John, about 1820, bought land at Lenaderg, building extensive bleaching works and Milltown House. There is considerable similarity between Milltown House, Huntly House and Brookfield House and it has been suggested that Brookfield was possibly remodelled by the architect Thomas Jackson, who is known to have been commissioned to remodel Huntly House in the 1800s.

Brookfield House is a two storey, five bay house, with the upper and lower storeys separated by a platband, and the whole exterior is harled. The roof is hipped with overhanging eaves supported on paired console brackets and the

windows are simply silled and recessed. A particular feature at Brookfield is the single storey Ionic portico with fluted columns and a fine Adam's doorway with beautifully glazed sidelights and fanlight, showing a similarity to Milltown. The house is approached by a long driveway, and has a modest pair of gate lodges, facing each other across the avenue entrance.

Brice Smyth (4) was born in 1796 but at twelve years old was blinded by smallpox. Nevertheless, he succeeded his father in the business, living at Brookfield House, and building Brice Smyth & Sons into a very eminent linen firm which specialised in the manufacture of heavy shirting linen. He died in 1851 and was succeeded in Brookfield House by his second son William, under whom the firm expanded and modernised with William's son, William Anderson Smyth, working in partnership with his father. In 1884 a new power loom factory was built beside the family home at Brookfield, and the name of the firm was changed to Smyth's Weaving Co., Ltd. William Smyth (1835–1913) was one of the largest employers in the neighbourhood of Banbridge, and took an active interest in public affairs throughout his career, representing Banbridge district on Down County Council, along with taking a leading part in the work of the Banbridge Agricultural and Farming Society. He was very much involved in Scarva Street Presbyterian Church, occupying the position of senior elder, and superintendent of the Sabbath School for fifty years. William Smyth married twice, his first wife Catherine Anderson died in 1871, and he remarried Jane Robinson Wilson, having in all five sons, two of whom were killed in the First World War.

Brookfield House was occupied by the Smyth family until 1993 when it was sold, and the contents auctioned, bringing to an end over two hundred years of continuous ownership of the site.

Mr E.F. Smyth outside Brookfield House *c.* 1912. The car is an early Renault. Edmund Fitzgeral Smyth was born in 1868 at Brookfield House, the third son of William and Jane. He served in the First World war becoming Major E.F. Smyth, MC, but was killed in 1917 at Mercoing, West Cambrai.

William Smyth (1835–1913)
Smyths of the Bann

MILLTOWN HOUSE
LENADERG

Milltown House
JFR

Milltown House was built *c.* 1826 for John Smyth, son of Brice Smyth (1764–1829) of Brookfield House, but was remodelled by the architect, Thomas Jackson, in the late 1840s. While his brother Brice (4) remained at Brookfield working in the family firm, Brice Smyth & Sons, John purchased from the Crawfords their corn mill and surrounding land at Lenaderg about 1820. Here he set up his bleaching plant, which was to become Milltown Bleach & Weaving Works, and which expanded to become one of the largest on the River Bann. John Smyth, Sr., married Anna McClelland, a sister of Robert McClelland of Belmont, and together they went on to have twelve children, of whom William, John, Jr., and James Davis, followed by another generation were to become directors and managers of the bleach and weaving works.

Ceiling rose
JFR

Milltown House is situated on the southern side of the Banbridge to Gilford Road, about a mile and a half from Banbridge, adjacent to Lenaderg, and built not far from the bleaching works on the River Bann. This is an ashlar

MILLTOWN HOUSE

John Smyth with his wife Anna. John (Sr) 1798–1890, was founder of the Milltown Works
Smyths of the Bann

faced Georgian house, which is five bay and two storey, with a platband separating both storeys. The design of the house is very similar to Brookfield House in having a hipped roof with moulded eaves and cornice supported on paired console brackets. Again, as in Brookfield, the windows are recessed, sashed and silled, with those on the upper storey retaining their glazing bars, while the lower storey windows are glazed with plate glass. At the front of Milltown House there is a single storey portico with fluted Ionic columns, similar to that of Belmont House, where again the architect was Thomas Jackson.

John Smyth died in 1890, aged ninety two, and was succeeded by his sons William and John, Jr., who had formed the company William Smyth & Co., which consisted of the bleach works, the Bannville beetling mills and an iron foundry on the other side of the River Bann at Lisnafiffy. William married Anna Dickson, of the Gilford Dicksons, and lived at Lenaderg House, while John, Jr., who had married Anna Haughton, lived with his father at Milltown House. Douglas Smyth, a grandson of John, Sr., was, with his wife Katherine, the last of the Smyths to live in Milltown House which was sold about 1954.

Stained glass window on the staircase of Milltown House
JFR

Linen stamp

Bellfield House
JFR

BELLFIELD
LENADERG

Bellfield is situated on rising ground on the northern side of the Banbridge to Gilford road just beyond Lenaderg and not far from Milltown House which lies closer to the River Bann. John Smyth, Sr., brother of Brice Smyth of Brookfield, who had built Milltown House for himself *c.* 1825, also built Bellfield, slightly later, for his cousins the Weirs. Henry Weir owned a linen business in Belfast with Henry Smyth. Lawlor, 1941–43, states:

> In 1849, Henry Smyth, apparently a son of Robert, elder son of Brice Smyth (3) started a linen business in Belfast with his cousin Henry Weir, as Smyth, Weir & Co. The Weirs lived at Lenaderg, Banbridge. Smyth, Weir & Co. had their office first in 11 Donegall Place, moving afterwards to 1 Donegall Square West, Belfast, where now stands the Scottish Provident Building. Weir died in 1856, when Sir John Preston took Smyth into partnership in a new firm as Preston, Smyth & Co., Linen Merchants.

The name of the house was originally Bellevue, as can be seen on the map of 1859, but Bassett in 1886 lists the house as *Bellefield*, when it was occupied by Thomas Dickson, one of the owners of the Hazelbank Weaving Co., Ltd. This company, formed in 1880, manufactured very fine linens and the factory stood on the southern bank of the River Bann at Lawrencetown. Thomas Dickson,

Bellfield and the grounds
JFR

who had previously leased the house, finally bought Bellfield from William Alexander in 1913, and in 1935 the house passed to his son Norman, who lived there until his death in 1975.

Bellfield has been described as a mid-nineteenth century, five bay, two storey house built in the Georgian style, with the ground floor being rusticated, and separated from the upper storey by a platband. The ground floor windows are taller than those of the top floor, while the window above the porch is wider than the others. Bellfield is unusual in having the façade broken by four giant pilasters of the Tuscan order. There is a small square porch, which is also rusticated, and has two Tuscan pilasters, the whole porch rising slightly above the platband, and being topped by a flat roof with moulded cornice.

Bellfield was vacant for a few years but the house and grounds have now been restored.

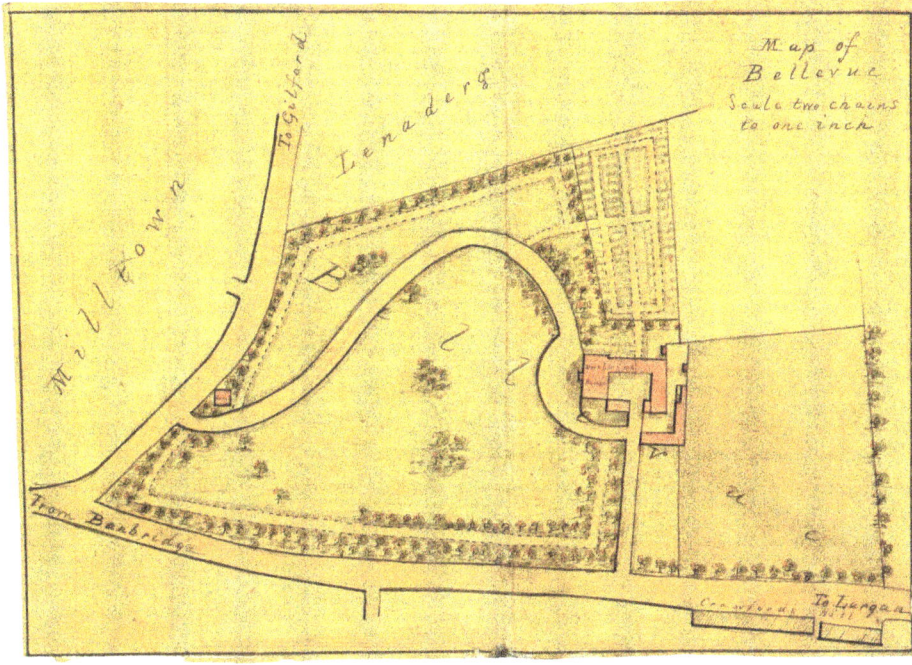

Map of 1859 showing Bellfield as Bellevue
PRONI

LENADERG HOUSE
LENADERG

Lenaderg House
JFR

Lenaderg House is situated on the northern side of the Banbridge to Gilford road, and mid-way between Lenaderg and Lawrencetown. The house has been recorded as late eighteenth century, but a portion at the rear was originally built to house English army officers around the 1690s. Lenaderg is a two storey, five bay house, which has moulded architraves surrounding the sashed and silled windows. The roof has a slight concave curve with bracketed eaves, and has tall, roughcast chimneys rising from it. Lenaderg House was refaced in the late nineteenth century and it may have been at the same time that a lower two storey wing was added at the side of the building along with the two storey porch on the entrance front. The front door is surrounded by a moulded architrave, and above it on the first floor are two small round headed windows.

Lewis, in 1837, records the principal seats in the neighbourhood of Banbridge, including 'Lenaderg Cottage of T. Weir, Esq.', and this refers to the renamed Lenaderg House. Thomas Weir, of Lenaderg, is named as a subscriber to the *Topographical Dictionary of Ireland*, 1837, published by Samuel Lewis. By 1855 Lenaderg House was the residence of William Smyth, eldest son of John Smyth, Sr., of Milltown House, who had originally established the Milltown Bleach Works. William Smyth's wife, Anna Dickson, was a sister to both James and

Benjamin Dickson, who were associated with the linen firm Dunbar, Dickson & Co. An obituary, in the *Belfast News Letter* of 8th March 1894, states that Mr William Smyth was open hearted, and kindly in disposition with a very genial manner. It also records that almost every Friday, Mr Smyth visited Belfast, where he had troops of friends who will deeply regret his death. Many linen merchants met in Belfast on a Friday to do business, and, indeed, this continued up to the start of the Second World War.

Messrs William Smyth & Co. are mentioned in Bassett's *Guide and Directory* of 1886,

> In the drive along the Bann from Banbridge to Gilford, among the many sites, there is none more beautiful than that occupied by the Milltown Bleach Works of Messrs. William Smyth & Co. Messrs Smyth are linen manufacturers, bleachers, finishers and merchants.

At this time the active members of the firm were William Smyth and John Smyth, Jr., although their father, who had set up the business was still alive, but very elderly and living in Milltown House. Bassett, 1886, also mentions that over two hundred and fifty people were employed in the various sections of the works and for the most part they lived in houses built by Messrs Smyth.

After the death of William Smyth in 1894, Lenaderg House was the residence of the manager of the bleach works, Mr J.H. Davies, who was succeeded in 1909 by his son, Crossfield Davies. In 1940, when the plant finally closed the house came into the possession of the Irish Bleachers Association Ltd., and was eventually sold to a private buyer.

Lenaderg House doorway
JFR

John Henry Davies, Manager of Milltown Bleachworks
Smyths of the Bann

HUNTLY HOUSE
BANBRIDGE

Huntly House
JFR

Huntly House is situated a short distance from Banbridge, close to the southern side of the River Bann, and adjacent to the ford of the Bann where William III crossed the river on his way to the Boyne in 1690. According to Lawlor, 1941–43, the house has been added to on several occasions, the oldest part, of one storey, being of a type common in the Queen Anne period or earlier. At a later date, a two storey front was added at right angles to the original house, with the architect thought to be Thomas Jackson. Huntly House is a five bay, two storey Georgian residence, which has an extra wing added to the side. The roof is hipped with moulded cornice and eaves, and there is a single storey tetrastyle Ionic portico. The windows are recessed, sashed and silled with moulded architraves, and the main front of the house is quoined.

The Dunbar family is recorded in Banbridge in 1766 and must at that time have been in the linen business, since the *Belfast News Letter*, 14th April 1758, carries an advertisement placed by a number of linen drapers complaining of the damage caused by hawkers at the linen markets, and amongst these was Hugh Dunbar. He leased twenty two acres in the townland of Drumnagalley from Charles Whyte of Loughbrickland, and his son Robert, who was a linen draper, was granted a lease on the same land with rights to 'water, water courses and pastures'. The Dunbars lived in the house then known as Huntly Glen, and the most well known owner is Hugh Dunbar (1789–1847), a grandson of the original Hugh, and founder of the large Dunbar McMaster & Co., Ltd., spinning mill at Gilford.

Early in the 1800s Hugh Dunbar developed the family business, which was the manufacture of linen thread, and this is borne out by the first Ordnance Survey maps of the 1830s showing a thread manufactory located at Huntly in the townland of Drumnagalley. However, the production of linen yarn was revolutionised by the wet spinning process, and in 1834 Hugh Dunbar decided to erect a wet spinning and twisting mill, driven by steam power, at Gilford.

Capital was required for expansion of the business and, in 1837, John Walsh McMaster became a partner with Hugh Dunbar. Two years later they were joined by James Dickson and the manufacture of linen thread and brown linen was carried on at Huntley Glen while the mill at Gilford was built, finally opening in 1838.

Hugh Dunbar was very much involved in community matters in Banbridge and in particular in the affairs of First Presbyterian Church, Banbridge. He looked after the people in his employment, and had a list of four hundred paupers to whom he gave out money at his own house, weekly. Hugh Dunbar died in 1847 unmarried, leaving his four surviving sisters his estate, including all the land, buildings and machinery at Gilford and Huntly Glen. Hugh's sisters, the Miss Dunbars, lived on in Huntly, continuing his generosity to the community, until the death of Jane in 1874. She left a very considerable amount of money, not only to the Presbyterian Church, but also for the building and running expenses of a non-denominational school in Banbridge, known as the Dunbar Memorial School.

Finally, another well known owner of Huntly, with very significant linen connections, was Mr D. Wilson Smyth, DL, great-grandson of Brice Smyth, (3), of Brookfield.

D. Wilson Smyth with his children Vera, William and Moira, in the late 1920s
Smyths of the Bann

Huntly House doorway
JFR

DUNBAR FAMILY TREE

Hugh Dunbar
d. 1784

Robert Dunbar = Mary McWilliam
d. 1805   d. 1814

Agnes Dunbar	Mary Dunbar	Margaret Dunbar	Elizabeth Dunbar = Henry Herron	Jane Dunbar	Hugh Dunbar	Isabella Dunbar
b. 1780	d. 1798	1781–1833	1783–1852 d. 1868	1786–1874	1789–1847	1791–1871

Finally, another well known owner of Huntly, with very significant linen connections, was Mr D. Wilson Smyth D.L., great grandson of Brice Smyth (3) of Brookfield.

5
GILFORD

WOODLANDS PARK, GILFORD
formerly part of the grounds of Bannvale House
Reproduced with the kind permission of Dr R.A. Logan

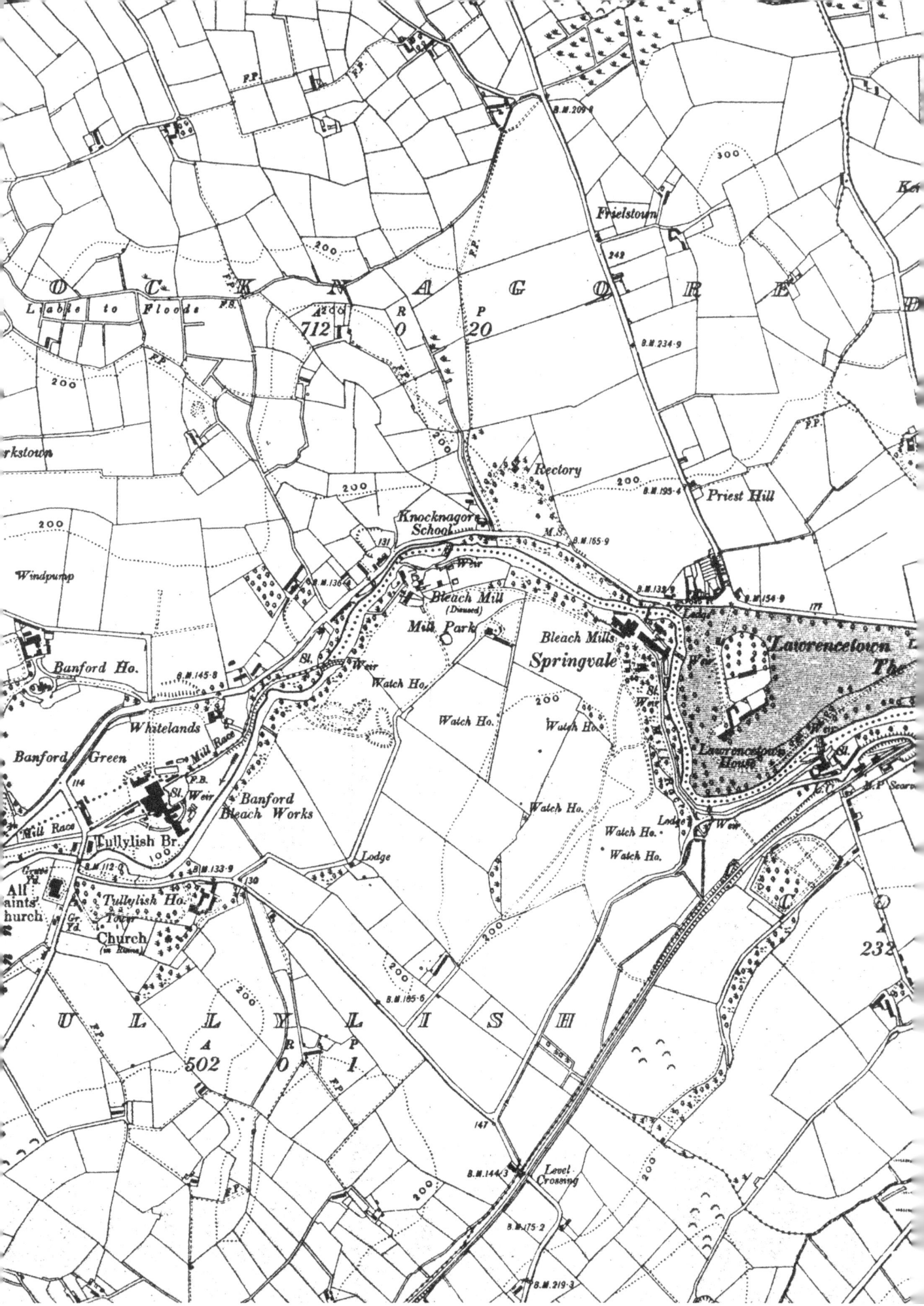

HAZELBANK
LAWRENCETOWN

Hazelbank, now demolished
COURTESY CARSWELL FAMILY

From at least the middle of the eighteenth century, the Law family was in the linen business, and owned both Hazelbank and Glenbanna House or Coose Vale as it was then called. R.S.J. Clarke has recorded in *The Heart of Downe*, 1989, a gravestone inscription to John Law of Ballydown in the county of Down, linen draper who died in 1758. Various members of the Law family are named in a survey for 1771 for the townland of Ballyvally where they held leases on land adjoining the River Bann, most likely for the bleaching of linen. In 1820, Samuel Law of Hazelbank was mentioned in a memorial to the Linen Board for the appointment of Sealmasters. Later, about 1834, the first spinning mill on the River Bann was built at Hazelbank, in Coose near Lawrencetown, by bleacher Samuel Law. This is confirmed by the *Ordnance Survey Memoirs*, 1834, which describes Law's bleach green as having two large water wheels, one of which turned machinery for spinning linen yarn. Lewis, writing in 1837, mentions a mill for spinning linen yarn at Coose, and adjoining it, chemical works for the supply of the bleachers.

Hazelbank, at Lawrencetown, about three miles from Banbridge, was the main seat of the Law family and Samuel Law is recorded as living there in 1816, in a list of churchwardens for Seapatrick Parish. Prior to this, in 1815, he had married Jane Hayes, eldest daughter of William Hayes and Margaret Crawford of Millmount, Banbridge. Hazelbank was demolished as recently as 1997, but photographs remain to show a nineteenth century six bay, two storey gabled house possibly built at right angles to an older house, shown at the rear. The ground floor windows were recessed, silled and had Tudor revival hood mouldings, while the windows of the first floor were round headed and recessed with the platband forming their sills. There was a recessed front door with an entablature supported on console brackets.

Samuel Law died in 1867, and, due to a dispute regarding his will, a judge ordered the sale of the whole property, the factory appearing to have closed about ten years later. The Hazelbank Weaving Company was set up in 1880 for the weaving of very fine linens, and was owned by Mr Thomas Dickson and Mr William Walker, a linen draper of Banbridge. They had bought the Law premises and had increased the number of looms from seventy five to two hundred. Bassett, 1886, records a Mr G.M. Rogers, JP, living in Hazelbank in 1886.

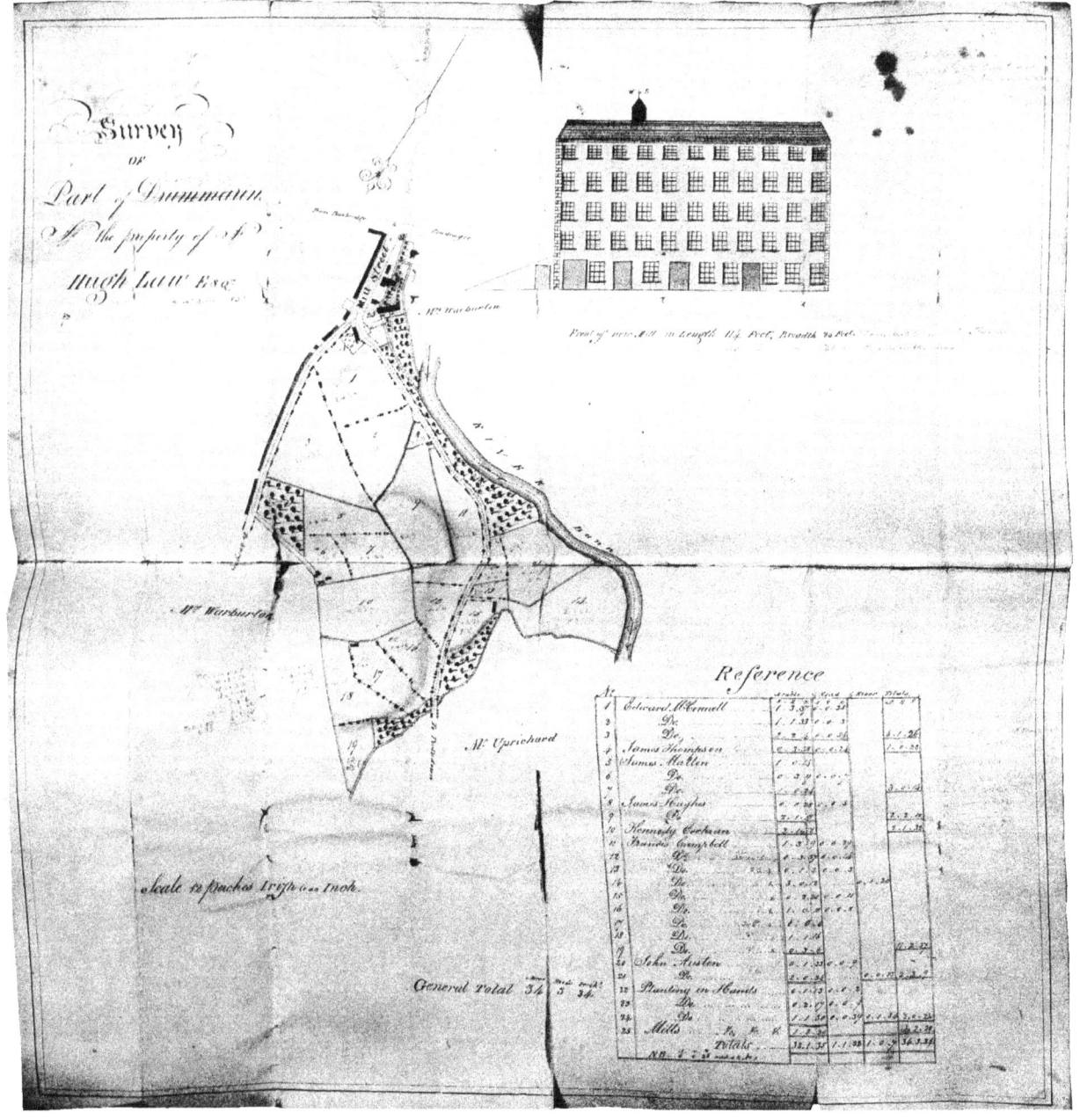

Survey of Hugh Law's property in Drumaran, 1831, showing the front of the new yarn spinning mill
PRONI

GLENBANNA HOUSE
LAWRENCETOWN

Glenbanna House is on the southern side of the River Bann, and is approached by crossing a bridge at Lawrencetown on the Banbridge to Gilford road, about three miles from Banbridge, and approximately three miles from Gilford. The original house on the site was built by the Law family in the late eighteenth century and was called Coose Vale, the present house being known as Glenbanna. Pigot's *Directory* for 1824 lists Joseph Law at Coose, but he died in 1831, aged 82 years, leaving his property to his nephew, Samuel Law of Hazelbank.

Glenbanna is a two storey, cement faced house with quoins, which has three bays between two three sided bows on the ground floor. The windows are sashed and silled, with three dormer windows to the front surmounted by finials, on the first floor. There is a double gabled roof, with deep eaves and highly decorated bargeboard and the porch is topped by a similarly decorated balustrade. Bassett in 1886 stated that the avenue to Glenbanna lay through two rows of giant beeches, the branches forming a beautiful bower, fifty feet wide, and the trees still remain. At that time, the occupant of the house was Mr William Walker, one of the owners of the Hazelbank Weaving Company. Coose Vale is listed by Dean, 1994, as having had a gate lodge, built pre-1834, but it has been demolished.

Glenbanna House
© CROWN COPYRIGHT HMSO

THE UPRICHARD FAMILY
OF SPRINGVALE BLEACH WORKS

The Uprichard family came to Ireland from Wales early in the eighteenth century, settling at Fairview, near Lurgan. Henry Uprichard, who was born in 1752, married Margaret Dawson, who was a daughter of Margaret Christy and Thomas Dawson. The Christy family have been credited with the introduction of linen bleaching on the River Bann at Moyallon in 1675, and John Christy originally owned Springvale. Indeed, it is thought that it was the marriage connection to the Christys which prompted Henry and Margaret's sons to acquire the Springvale bleach works and found the company, J.T. & H. Uprichard, soon after 1830. Prior to this, between 1816 and 1825, there are references to James and Thomas Uprichard at Bann Vale, which had been around 1800 the 'extensive and high finished bleach green of Richard Blood'. While Thomas lived at the old family home, Fairview, it appears that James lived at Bann Vale House, which he may have built.

The great Gilford mill of Dunbar McMaster was built in the 1830s and the tail race from the mill cut through Bann Vale, thus ending the bleach green. This may have been the reason for the Uprichards taking over the Springvale Bleach

Works along with the fact that they owned part of the land on which the mill was built, thus releasing money for the purchase. Springvale, until it was stripped in 1962, was a very fine example of an old fashioned bleach works, remaining virtually unchanged since it was expanded by William Uprichard, who spent £10,000, in 1884. The original buildings on the site dated from 1808.

Of the three brothers who bought Springvale only James married, and when he and Thomas died the business was run by the remaining brother, Henry. Subsequent to Henry's death it was inherited by William, second son of James of Bann Vale House, who also lived in his father's house. Henry James, the eldest son, lived at the original family home, Fairview, Tannaghmore. William married twice – first to Sarah Jackson, they had no issue, and secondly to Sarah Maria Malone, who had six children.

1	James	b 1845	d 1854
2	Elizabeth	b 1846	
3	**Henry Albert**	**b 1848**	
4	Susanna	b 1849	
5	**Anna Maria**	**b 1851**	
6	Ellen Malone	b 1854	

The Uprichards had a talent for making good marriages and of the six children, the two who are of interest are Henry Albert and Anna Maria. Apart from William's children, his sister, also Anna Maria, married James G. Bell of Tullylish House, who was also a Quaker and had linen connections. William's daughter, Anna Maria married Frederick Woods, and two of their daughters married into the Sinton linen family of Banford House. William Uprichard, of Bannvale House, previously known as Bann Vale House, died in 1884 leaving the very much improved Springvale Bleach Works to his son Henry Albert.

Henry Albert Uprichard married Emily Green in the mid-1870s and they lived at Lawrencetown House until 1884 when they moved to Elmfield Castle, which had been bought for them by Emily's father, Forster Green, a very wealthy tea and coffee merchant from Belfast. Sadly, Emily died in 1887 two weeks after giving birth to Emile Llewellyn, leaving Henry Albert with five young children. However, Henry Albert married for a second time, to an English lady called Beatrice Taylor, and they had a daughter – Beatrice Eileen b.1899. Henry Albert died in 1901, aged only fifty four. Two years later, in 1903, Henry's father-in-law, Forster Green, died leaving his five Uprichard grandchildren the majority of his wealth, which amounted to £139,000, being equivalent to eight million pounds in the early twenty first century.

The Springvale Bleach Works were inherited by Henry Albert's sons, William (better known as Willie), Forster and Emile. However, Emile decided to take his inheritance and move to England, Willie and Forster having to buy him out. Their other brother, Henry Albert, did not enter the linen business but became Managing Director of the Belfast Company, Forster Green & Co. Later, during

Willie Uprichard and Howard Ferguson, Iveagh Harriers, unknown but possibly c. 1920s

the First World War, as a Major in the 13th Royal Irish Rifles, Henry Albert was killed at Thiepval on 1st July 1916. As the eldest son, Willie Uprichard inherited Elmfield Castle, and, thanks in part to their grandfather Forster Green, the Uprichards' lives at Elmfield entered a golden age in the early twentieth century. Willie was an enthusiastic huntsman, amateur jockey, and race horse trainer, bringing the sport to a new level in the Uprichard family. A replica of Punchestown racecourse was laid out at Elmfield Castle and in 1923 his horse, 'The Monk' won the Punchestown Gold Cup, which is still in the Uprichard family. For more than eighty years the family was associated with the Iveagh Harriers, and also hunted regularly with the County Down Staghounds.

Willie Uprichard married Nancy Kane, daughter of the Rector of Tullylish, and had four children, three sons and one daughter. Forster Uprichard died in 1945, and Willie in 1949, leaving Elmfield Castle to his eldest son, Richard Rutledge Kane, known as Rut, and Lawrencetown House to Henry Albert. At this point Albert, his mother Nancy and butler Bobby Dawson moved to Mill Park House, having previously lived at Elmfield Castle. After the Second World War, Rut and Albert attempted to run the bleach works, Rut having served his time at Kirkpatrick Brothers, Ballyclare, and Albert at Anthony Cowdy & Sons, Banbridge. However, after a few years it was clear that the linen industry in Ulster was in decline and the Springvale Bleach Works had to close in 1955.

Mill Park was another very old bleach works which was part of the Uprichard

UPRICHARD FAMILY TREE

Henry Uprichard = Margaret Dawson
1752–1794
FAIRVIEW, Lurgan
daughter of Thomas Dawson and Margaret Christy

- James = Susanna
  1777–1840
  BANNVALE HOUSE
- Ruth
  b.1780
- Thomas
  1783–1850
  FAIRVIEW
- Mary
- Margaret
- Mary Margaret
  1790–1878
- Henry
  b.1793

Children of James = Susanna:
- Anna Maria
  b.1809
- Henry = Mary Anne
  1811–1879
  FAIRVIEW
- William = 1st Sarah Jackson (no issue)
  1813–1884   2nd Sarah Maria Malone
  BANNVALE HOUSE
- Anna Maria = James G. Bell
  TULLYLISH HOUSE
- Susanna

Children of Henry = Mary Anne:
- James
  FAIRVIEW
- Gertrude

Children of William = Sarah Maria Malone:
- James
  1845–1854
- Elizabeth = ?Jackson
  b.1846
- Henry Albert = 1st Emily Green
  1848–1901   2nd Beatrice Taylor
  LAWRENCETOWN HOUSE / ELMFIELD CASTLE
- Susanna
  b.1849
- Anna Maria = Frederick W. Woods
  b.1851
- Ellen Malone
  1854–1889
  BANNVALE HOUSE

Children of Henry Albert:
- Mary Green = FCC Bland
- William Forster = Nancy Kane
  d.1949
  ELMFIELD CASTLE
- Henry Albert
  d.1916
  BANNVALE HOUSE
- Forster Green
  d.1945
  LAWRENCETOWN HOUSE
- Emile = Betty Llewellyn White
  Lived in England
- Beatrice = KC Kirkpatrick
  Eileen

Children of William Forster = Nancy Kane:
- Richard Rutledge = Grace Kane
  ELMFIELD CASTLE
- Henry
  died young
- Henry Albert
  MILL PARK
- Maureen = Duncan Hill

J. T. & H. Uprichard
PARTNERS:- R.R.K. UPRICHARD H.A. UPRICHARD

TELEGRAMS
UPRICHARD LENADERG

TELEPHONE
LENADERG 207

SPRINGVALE BLEACH WORKS   LAURENCETOWN   CO. DOWN

Miss Moore (Springvale Cottage, Gilford) makes a presentation to the Irish Linen Queen, Miss Clarke, outside Springvale Bleachworks. Looking on is Albert Uprichard of JT and H Uprichard, Bleachers and Finishers. 1938

property, but has been in ruins for more than a century. This 'Bleachyard on the River Ban [sic]', was advertised in the *Belfast News Letter*, 8th January, 1782, as belonging to the late Thomas Christy. At that time it was capable of finishing 8,000 pieces of linen a year, and there was a newly erected house along with 50 acres of land. The *Ordnance Survey Memoirs* describe John Christy as operating a bleach works at Mill Park in 1834, and records show that he bleached about 15,000 pieces a year in 1839. John Christy continued to bleach at Mill Park after Springvale had been sold to the Uprichards, but in 1852, there was a conveyance of Mill Park to Henry Uprichard of Fairview, who may have lived at the house. At the entrance to Mill Park there is a pair of old gates, which are still referred to as Christy's Gates, and this was also the entrance to the old bleach works at Springvale.

Christy gates
JFR

FAIRVIEW HOUSE
TANNAGHMORE, LURGAN

Fairview House was the original home of the Uprichard family, when they came to Ireland from Wales, in the late seventeenth century. The present house was built by Henry Uprichard, possibly around 1776, on the occasion of his marriage to Margaret Dawson. Fairview is recorded in the *Ordnance Survey Memoirs* of 1837 as being the residence of Mr Thomas Uprichard, and he was the second son of Henry and Margaret Uprichard. Thomas Uprichard was one of the three brothers who ran the Springvale Bleach Works at Lawrencetown.

Fairview House is a seven bay, two storey Georgian farmhouse, which remains much as the original except for a two bay extension at the east end, possibly added in mid-nineteenth century by Henry James Uprichard. The walls of the house are roughcast and painted white, with black quoins, and the original doorway with radial fanlight remains. Fairview House, along with Mill House, and with a fine Victorian garden, was acquired by the Craigavon Development Commission, the grounds being opened to the public in June 1969 as a park. However, due to vandalism, both houses were refurbished in 1979 by Craigavon Council and Fairview House is now occupied by a private tenant, although the park remains open to the public.

Fairview House
© *CROWN COPYRIGHT HMSO*

BANNVALE HOUSE
GILFORD

Bann Vale is recorded, around 1800, as the 'extensive and high-finished bleach-green' of Richard Blood. The *Ordnance Survey Memoirs*, 1834, make no mention of any bleach works, but the Valuation Books under Ballymacanallen refer to 'old mills with old machinery' belonging to James Pritchard, i.e. Uprichard. However, it is quite clear that when Dunbar McMaster's mill was set up in the 1830s the tail race from the works cut through Bann Vale ending its history as a bleach green. There are references to James and Thomas Uprichard at Bann Vale, near Gilford, between 1816 and 1825, and it is thought that James Uprichard built Bannvale House, in the early years of the nineteenth century. The house name always had the two words Bann and Vale put together as Bannvale. William Uprichard inherited Bannvale on the death of his father in 1840 and the house remained in the ownership of the Uprichard family into the twentieth century. However, a few years after the death of Henry Albert Uprichard in 1916 the Uprichard family sold Bannvale House. This modest but important country house is now an Administration Building for the Southern Health and Social Care Trust.

Bannvale is a two storey, five bay Georgian symmetrical house which is classically proportioned. There is a modern two storey annex and a single storey lean-to at the south west side of the property. The duo pitched roof has natural Welsh slates and roll top black ridge tiles and there is a raised gable to the front centre

Bannvale House
JFR

Uprichard family at Bannvale House c. 1905

Henry Albert Uprichard outside Bannvale House, c. 1912

of the building. On the front of the house are very distinctive windows which are two, twelve and twenty pane with double mullioned vertical sash painted timber frames and having stone sills. There are labels over the upper floor windows and curved hood moulds over the ground floor windows, with recessed heads to large windows. The entrance is set in the front central projection which has a raised stone string course at first floor level on stone brackets on three sides, and stone string course on first floor ceiling level at front. The front door has three bottom panels with two clear glass panes above and to each side are four pane sidelights which are painted.

Dean, 1994, lists two gate lodges at Bannvale, South Gate *c.* 1850 and North Gate *c.* 1880, which were distinctive being built in black basalt with yellow fireclay brick dressings and quoins, however, only one lodge remains and is in a state of disrepair.

In the early twentieth century, Major Henry Albert Uprichard lived at Bannvale House, but served in the army in the First World War, and unfortunately was killed in action in the attack on Thiepval on 1st July 1916. He is commemorated by the Major Uprichard Memorial Orange Hall, Tullylish. Henry Albert Uprichard did not enter the linen business but instead became Managing Director of Forster Green & Co., his late grandfather's company. As well as being a well known polo player, he was also a rider at point-to-point and steeplechase meetings, and hunted regularly with the County Down Staghounds and the Iveagh Harriers. Prior to the First World War, he was Commander of the 2nd Battalion of the West Down Regiment of the Ulster Volunteer Force.

Lawrencetown House
JFR

LAWRENCETOWN HOUSE
GILFORD

Lawrencetown House, and the village of Lawrencetown, which is in the parish of Tullylish, take their name from the Lawrence family. The Springvale Bleach Works was on the opposite side of the River Bann from Lawrencetown, where many of the workers lived, and a wooden foot bridge connected the village with the works.

Colonel Thomas Dawson Lawrence was born about 1730, and was originally known as Thomas Dawson but changed his name to Dawson Lawrence when he inherited the Lawrencetown estate from his cousin Henry Lawrence, in 1781. Thomas Dawson was a great-grandson of the Rt. Hon. Henry Lawrence, Lord President of the Council, 1655.

Dr R.A. Logan of Gilford, in his book *A Window on the Past*, 2000, states that Colonel Lawrence built Lawrencetown House and that it was later described as being,

> very commodious and washed by the River Bann – the offices slated and finished in a superb manner. There are six acres of fine orchard, the gardens extensive and highly ornamental, in one of which there is a fountain that hath a sulphurous water. The estate is well wooded and does not contain one unprofitable acre, the most of it being rich meadow.

Mr Hugh Lyons Montgomery lived in the house *c.* 1823, and other owners

Emily Green on the left with her future husband, Henry Albert Uprichard in the doorway c. 1875.

included Mr A.J.R. Stewart of Ards House, County Donegal, a brother of the 1st Marquess of Londonderry, and Joseph Wakefield, owner of Moyallon bleach green. Henry Albert Uprichard bought Lawrencetown House about 1875 on his marriage to Emily Green, and lived there till 1884, when they moved to Elmfield Castle. Other members of the Uprichard family continued to live in the house, and in 1908, Captain Forster Uprichard had it rebuilt as it is today. Lawrencetown House was sold after his death in 1945, and after several owners, the house is now used as a Bible College.

Lawrencetown House is a three bay, two storey house, which also has a lower two storey wing of six bays to the left of the front. The house is cement faced and has a hipped and slated roof, with moulded eaves and cornice. There is a single storey projecting porch with two round headed windows and the door at the side is surrounded by an architrave with keystone. All the windows are sashed and recessed, with the bay windows on the ground floor having above them, on the upper floor, three windows of smaller width. There are two bay windows on the garden front looking down towards the River Bann.

Emily Green, daughter of Forster Green, who was a very wealthy Belfast tea and coffee merchant, is shown on the left hand side of the photograph, which was taken in the mid-1870s, shortly before her marriage to Henry Albert Uprichard (1848–1901), who, in the photograph, is standing in doorway of Bannvale House. After their marriage they lived in Lawrencetown House until 1884, when they moved to Elmfield Castle.

Captain Forster Green Uprichard of Lawrencetown House on the right

TULLYLISH HOUSE
GILFORD

The *Ordnance Survey Memoirs* of 1834 record Tullylish House in the townland of that name and state that it is the residence of H. Hamilton, agent to Alexander Robert Stewart Esq. (of Ards House, County Donegal), and a magistrate, attending in the Justice Room in Gilford. Tullylish is primarily a parish, covering a large area which extends from Lawrencetown in the east to the border of County Armagh in the west. Lewis, 1837, states 'The River Bann passes through it in a winding course of five miles from east to west, passing by the town of Gilford, which is nearly in the centre of the parish.' Tullylish House, which is on a hill on the southern side of the River Bann, about one mile from Gilford, overlooks an old stone bridge which crosses the river, and is not far from Tullylish parish church.

Tullylish House appears to have been built about 1775, and in 1785 was owned by William Meeke, who was a Justice of the Peace for the area and may have built the house. However, it seems that an earlier house, possibly dating from the Cromwellian period, already existed on the site. A photograph of the house in 1870 shows it is a five bay, two storey building with sashed and silled windows, with decorated entablatures over the ground floor windows on the main front, which is quoined. The roof, with its elaborately moulded cornice, is hidden behind a parapet with only the chimney stacks to be seen. The 1870

Tullylish House
COURTESY CARSWELL FAMILY

James Greer Bell
Portrait from *The Quakri at Lurgan and Grange*

photograph shows the door set in a single storey porch, but this has now been removed and replaced by a handsome recessed doorway. In 1919, the owner David McAuley, Esq., put the house up for auction, and the accommodation was described as three reception rooms, six bedrooms, dressing rooms, store and box rooms, pantries, servants' apartments and fitted up throughout with hot and cold water. Tullylish House was then bought by Nathaniel Carswell and it remains in the ownership of the Carswell family.

James Greer Bell (1806–80) became the owner of Tullylish House about 1841, when he and his wife Anna, née Uprichard, moved there from York Street in Belfast. Anna was the sister of William Uprichard of Bannvale House, Gilford, but died in 1851, and James married again in 1854 to Eliza Greer of Belfast. He must have had extensive farming interests since he owned ninety eight acres in the locality and built stabling at Tullylish House. Dean, 1994, lists a gate lodge built *c.* 1870, but this has been demolished.

Bill Jackson, 2005, has described James Greer Bell as a prominent Quaker but a worldly man who exercised his own mind where the Scriptures were concerned. Indeed, he was important enough to be profiled by James Nicholson Richardson, 1911, in his *Reminiscences of Friends in Ulster*:

Old Tullylish House *c.* 1870

My early recollection of James Greer Bell was something of the nature of trying to get out of his way, for fear of his walking over me. Six feet four in height, with a long beard (then an unusual appendage), he was quick in his movements, and stalked like some tall ostrich among lesser birds … He retired, at 39 years of age, from business in Liverpool, with a comparatively small sum, resolving as he used to tell me, only to spend half his income each year. That income, by dint of accumulations, must have become pretty large during his lifetime, for he lived handsomely and was generous to causes which appealed to him. The great kindness and quiet hospitality of himself and his wife (well known round their neighbourhood as Eliza Greer Bell) will long be remembered.

Eliza Greer Bell, second wife of James Greer Bell
Portrait from *The Quakri at Lurgan and Grange*

James worked originally with his Malcomson cousins, Joseph, David and Andrew, in Messrs Malcomson, Bell and Co. of Liverpool, which may have been a subsidiary company of one of a similar name at 9 Donegall Quay in Belfast. Bill Jackson, 2005, states:

> The company handled much of the transiting freight of Abraham Bell & Co. of New York, and certainly of many Ulster linen firms. James' retirement in 1845 may have come about the point when Abraham and his son James Christy Bell appear to have decided to get out of shipping.

Despite his retirement from Liverpool, James Greer Bell appears to have had business interests in the transport and shipment of linen from Gilford and also for his relatives in business in Lurgan. He died, aged 74, a very wealthy man, in 1880, leaving not only the house and farm at Tullylish House to his wife, but also a warehouse in Little Donegall Street, which was let on lease to Robert Watson. He also owned lands and mills at Milltown in the townland of Ballymurphy. However, his will reveals clearly that he believed in the newly built railways for transport as he owned six thousand pounds of stock in the Great Northern Railway Company of Ireland along with shares in the Belfast and Northern Counties Railway Company, and many other railway companies. As Bill Jackson, 2005, records:

> His will bequeathed thousands of pounds worth of stocks, particularly in Ireland's burgeoning railway companies, [and] the value of his stock and cash legacies alone would come to three or four million pounds of purchasing power today.

Public auction of Tullylish House, 25 January 1919

Tullylish House today

JFR

BANFORD HOUSE
TULLYLISH

Banford House
JFR

Banford House is situated about one mile from Gilford, and was built *c.* 1780 by Thomas Nicholson, (1730–94). John Nicholson, father of Thomas, had set up what was probably the earliest bleach yard on the River Bann, with money being granted to him by the Linen Board between 1727 and 1729. According to Bassett, 1886, in 1795 the bleach works was owned by Robert Jaffrey Nicholson, son of Thomas. There were also buildings in which brown linens were woven on the site. However, in 1815 both the business and the house were sold to Benjamin Haughton, and the business was carried on under the name of Benjamin Haughton & Co. Benjamin Haughton died in 1862, and Daniel Jaffé joined Thomas Haughton to form the Banford Bleach Works Co., since the weaving end had ceased in 1860. Thomas Haughton, eldest son of Benjamin, succeeded his father in Banford House and lived there until his death in 1888.

James N. Richardson in, *Reminiscences of Friends in Ulster*, 1911, states:

> Banford House was and is still a fine old-fashioned square Irish house, looking down on a bleach green and beautifully wooded landscape in front, and with a particularly fine old-fashioned garden behind. It is now occupied by Frederick Sinton, one of a large and important family of "Friends", but of whose members I have not many recollections in my earlier days.

BANFORD HOUSE, TULLYLISH

In Benjamin Haughton's time Banford was a rendezvous and place of hospitality for many, so rendered, not only by the geniality of its owner, but by the peculiar circumstances of his large family – or families, I should say – for by his first wife he had several children, and married secondly, Rachel Fennell, a widow, (born Malcomson) who brought to Banford her five children: added to these, there was a second family of younger Haughtons. In all, I think, some fourteen or fifteen young people, who helped to make Banford lively when I was a child.

Banford is a five bay, three storey house with semi basement, which was described in the 1786 edition of *The Post-Chaise Companion* as an 'elegant new house'. The walls are roughcast with quoins and there is a hipped slated roof with moulded eaves and cornice. The windows are recessed, silled and surrounded by a moulded stucco architrave, with a diminution of window height with each succeeding floor level. The entrance is recessed in a segmental arched

Doorway, Banford House
JFR

Haughton family photograph 1855–60
Benjamin Haughton, proprietor of the Banford Bleaching Linen Mills sits on the far left

opening with decorative sidelights within an engaged Ionic-plastered portico with enriched frieze, and above the frieze is a segmental fanlight of spider-web glazing. On the first floor, above the entrance, is a tripartite window which follows a similar arrangement. Internally there is a central stair hall with the main stair rising to the first floor, and a service stair, which is screened from the landing, continues to the second storey. Major renovations were carried out in the mid-Victorian period, which involved the extension of the house to the rear and the addition of a large conservatory.

Banford House is a Grade 1 listed Georgian building, which is set on a hill and has views across its own land and the nearby Tullylish Cricket Ground. The house, which has two separate tree lined driveways, is set in ten acres, and has a formal garden of lawns, flower beds, shrubberies, mature trees, and a tennis court. The grounds also contain an old watch tower, which was erected by Robert Jaffrey Nicholson for purposes connected with yeomanry activity. In the disturbed state of Ireland before the Rebellion of 1798, yeoman corps were raised to assist the government. John Nicholson of Stramore and his brother Robert Jaffrey Nicholson of Banford were both involved with the Bann Infantry.

In 1900 Banford House was bought by Frederick Buckby Sinton, and for more than sixty years was a very important Sinton residence.

Yeomanry tower in the grounds of Banford House
JFR

Belfast News Letter 18 October 1814

MOUNT PLEASANT
TULLYLISH

Mount Pleasant is situated on the northern side of the Banbridge Road about a mile from Gilford and four miles from Banbridge. This is a five bay, two storey house over a semi basement with walls rendered in stucco. The house has V-channelled quoins and moulded cornice. There is a central entrance which is approached by steps and recessed within a segmental arched recess with moulded architrave and topped by a fanlight with leaded spider-web glazing. On either side of the entrance the windows are of tripartite composition and are deeply recessed, being surrounded by moulded architraves. All the other windows are rectangular, deeply recessed, again surrounded by moulded architraves, and are sashed, retaining their original glazing bars. One of the most prominent features of Mount Pleasant is the battlemented parapet on top of the main front, the side wing and the archway to the side of the house.

Although it has been suggested that Mount Pleasant was built by George Darley in the late eighteenth century, the present owner has records giving the date of the original building as 1760, indicating that Thomas Christy of Moyallon may have built the house on land originally held by Sir Richard

Tullylish Bridge and the River Bann
JFR

Mount Pleasant
JFR

Johnston of Gilford Castle. In the 1880s the flour mills at Mount Pleasant, adjoining Banford, and the associated lands including the house, were acquired by Thomas Haughton on behalf of Banford Bleach Works. The old flour mill, which was adapted to be the Major Uprichard Memorial Orange Hall, has a stone marked '1844', which may be the date of the building of the mill. However, the flour mill itself was built on a site formerly occupied by a very old bleach works. According to the *Ordnance Survey Memoirs*, 1834, the Mount Pleasant bleach works were built in 1786. They belonged to George Darley until his death in 1825, when the property passed to Issac Stoney of Frankford in King's County, now known as County Offaly. Nevertheless, the bleach works may have originally been set up in the mid-eighteenth century by Thomas Christy of Moyallon.

Doorway, Mount Pleasant
JFR

DUNBARTON HOUSE
GILFORD

Dunbarton House is a mid-nineteenth century, three bay, two storey house which was built in considerable grounds on a slight hill overlooking the great Dunbar McMaster mill in the centre of Gilford for Hugh Dunbar. He had previously lived at Huntly House with his four sisters and indeed died there while giving out alms to the poor of Banbridge. Dean, 1994, has attributed Dunbarton House and the gate lodge to the architect Thomas Jackson with a building date of 1845. There is no doubt that the house shows a close resemblance to Huntly House, Milltown House and Belmont which were all Jackson houses. A good description of Dunbarton House is given in *Linen Houses of Banbridge*, 1995:

Dunbarton House
JFR

LINEN HOUSES OF THE BANN VALLEY

Dunbarton gate lodge
JFR

The ground floor is rusticated with a platband separating the two storeys. The most pleasing aspect of Dunbarton House is the windows which lend an air of space and lightness to the house. The bottom storey windows reach almost to the ground. Like the other windows, they retain their glazing bars, are recessed, sashed and silled, and are surrounded by moulded architraves with dentilled cornices. The window of the central bay, above the portico, is wider than the rest and of a tripartite form, while a tripartite bay window adorns the side of the house. On both these windows, the entablature is supported on console brackets. A balustrade sits atop the bay window. Like Huntly House, Milltown House and Belmont, Dunbarton has a single portico of engaged Ionic columns, with a moulded architrave and dentilled cornice, topped by a balustrade the same as that above the bay window. The roof is hipped with deep, bracketed eaves, the underneath of which are decorated with rosettes. A dormer window rises from out of the roof above the bay window while the chimney stacks are cleverly hidden from view by a surrounding balustrade.

During the First World War Dunbarton House was converted into a military hospital under the auspices of the Ulster Volunteer Force as a Convalescent Home, in connection with their large hospital in Belfast. The hospital was staffed by fully trained nurses and probationers, all of whom were members of the Ulster Volunteer Force Nursing Corps. Additionally, in the autumn of 1916, Bannvale House, the residence of the late Major Albert Uprichard, was opened as an annex to Dunbarton House, with thirty beds. Major Uprichard died, when leading his men of the 13th Royal Irish Rifles, in the battle of the Somme on 1st July 1916. A framed address of thanks for the use of Dunbarton during the

Gilford branch of the UVF hospital, County Down

Nursing staff at the Gilford branch of the UVF hospital, County Down

Great War, 1914–18, was sent by the War Office, and signed by Winston Churchill.

Dunbarton House has an Air Raid Shelter from the Second World War, which is constructed of concrete, and is buried in a knoll to the south west of the house. A very narrow passageway leads to a chamber about four metres by six metres. Externally only a sheeted door may be seen. The shelter was used by the military during the Second World War as an adjunct to the convalescent home in the main house. This rare survival of the conflict is of interest to the military historian, and is an important part of the history of Dunbarton House.

In 1834 Hugh Dunbar of Huntly entered into a partnership with W.A. Stewart of Edenderry to build a spinning mill at Gilford. Stewart died in 1839, the year the mill opened, but meantime linen thread continued to be made at Huntly until 1843, when Robert Thompson took his place forming Dunbar, Thompson & Co. However, Thompson was soon bought out by Dunbar and replaced by J.W. McMaster of Armagh. In 1839 James Dickson was also taken into the partnership and the business was divided into two distinct firms in 1843, firstly, Dunbar McMaster & Co. for thread spinning, and secondly, Dunbar, Dickson & Co. for manufacturing and bleaching. The *Ordnance Survey Memoirs* of 1837 record the five storey spinning mill in course of erection, and by 1846 the Gilford mill was described as one of the largest in Ireland.

Address of thanks for the use of Dunbarton House during the Great War of 1914–18 signed by Winston Churchill

Hugh Dunbar began, almost immediately, a large house building project in order to accommodate the large number of workers encouraged to come to Gilford in search of employment mainly from Counties Monaghan, Fermanagh and Armagh. One hundred and eighty houses were built in close proximity to the mill with a large number of workers coming from the Keady district of south Armagh. Ultimately, many of these 'two up, two down' type houses accommodated two families. Hugh Dunbar was concerned for the welfare of his workers and in 1843 gave land for the building of a Methodist Church, followed in 1844 by a further grant of land for the Presbyterian Church, contributing generously to the building of these churches. He gave, out of his estate, a rent free site to the Roman Catholics for the building of St. John's Church, dedicated in 1850 – a church placed in a pleasing position on Castle Hill. Two of the houses at the bottom of Hill Street were set aside for a fever hospital and these accommodated large numbers suffering from typhoid fever during the famine. Dr R.A. Logan writing in *A Window on the Past*, 2000, states,

> Finally before he died Dunbar built a school that opened in 1846 consisting of three separate infant, male and female schools. The cost to the firm of providing the three room schoolhouse, teacher's salaries, fire light, annual painting and lime-washing was £104 per year. The supervising surgeon for the factory was also physician and apothecary and had care of the hospital as well.

Hugh Dunbar died intestate in 1847, his sisters inheriting all his estate and mills, and the firm continuing to trade under the former names. Several new partners were added, namely Benjamin Dickson (brother of James), William Spotten and W.R. Masaroon and in 1858 John Walsh McMaster bought out the Dunbar sisters, essentially, personally owning the whole complex of buildings and land, including Dunbarton House. During the great linen boom resulting from the American Civil War (1861–65) the trade of the firm was very substantial, with sales amounting to up to one million pounds. In 1866 the partnership was dissolved but the Dicksons were dissatisfied with the terms, and a protracted legal battle ensued which was eventually settled in favour of John Walsh McMaster. Finally, the Dickson brothers went into partnership with their brother-in-law Thomas Ferguson of Banbridge forming Dickson, Ferguson & Co. for the power loom weaving of linen. This became the well known linen company Thomas Ferguson & Co., Ltd., when the Dicksons retired from business in 1883.

John Walsh McMaster was also philanthropic towards his workers, and recognised the need for a parish church in Gilford, giving land and money in 1869 for the building of St Paul's Church of Ireland. He died in 1872, leaving Dunbarton House and all his land to his eldest son, Hugh Dunbar McMaster, and a memorial window was erected in St Paul's. In spite of difficult conditions Hugh, with some of his brothers, carried on the flax spinning and thread manufacture in Gilford, eventually in 1886 forming a private company. In 1901, Dunbar McMaster & Co. joined the Barbours in the Linen Thread Co., Ltd., and the factory carried on until the late 1980s when it was forced to close.

However, Dunbarton House, which is very significant in terms of the history of the linen industry, remains in private ownership, and is extremely well maintained.

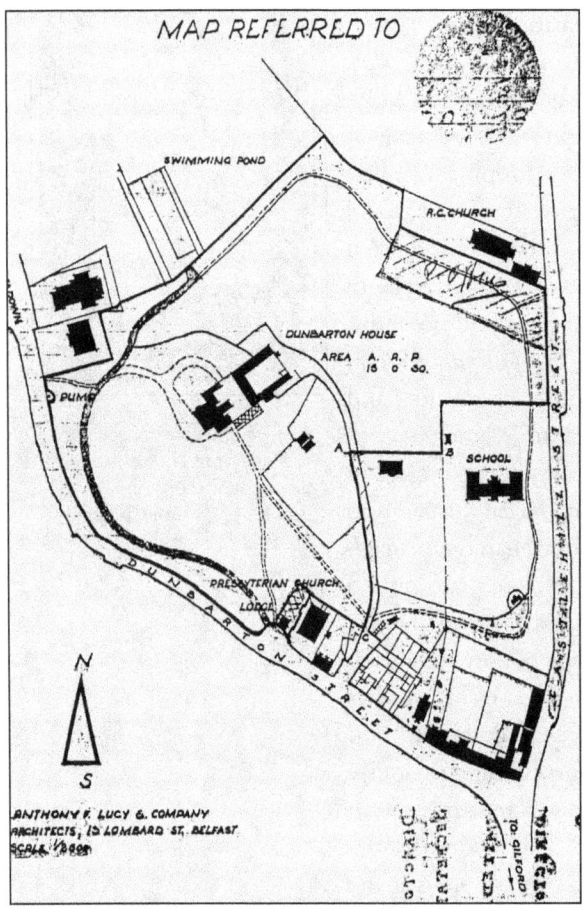

Map of Dunbarton House and grounds

MCMASTER FAMILY TREE

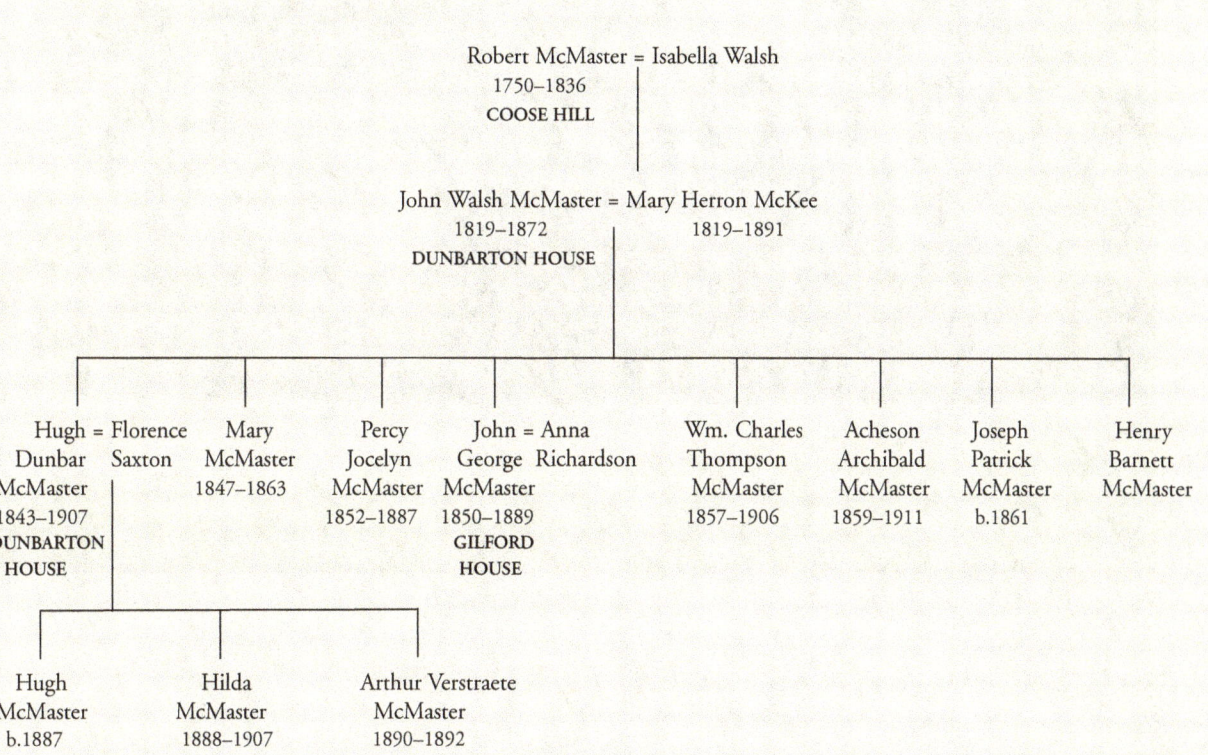

Robert McMaster = Isabella Walsh
1750–1836
COOSE HILL

John Walsh McMaster = Mary Herron McKee
1819–1872   1819–1891
DUNBARTON HOUSE

- Hugh = Florence Dunbar Saxton McMaster 1843–1907 **DUNBARTON HOUSE**
- Mary McMaster 1847–1863
- Percy Jocelyn McMaster 1852–1887
- John George McMaster = Anna Richardson 1850–1889 **GILFORD HOUSE**
- Wm. Charles Thompson McMaster 1857–1906
- Acheson Archibald McMaster 1859–1911
- Joseph Patrick McMaster b.1861
- Henry Barnett McMaster

Children of Hugh and Florence:
- Hugh McMaster b.1887
- Hilda McMaster 1888–1907
- Arthur Verstraete McMaster 1890–1892

THE McMASTER FAMILY, 1898

From left:

Unknown; unknown; Lucy Saunders (née Saxton, step sister of F. McMaster; Lily Temple (née Brooke); H.D. McMaster; Florence McMaster (née Saxton) Arthur Vaerstrate McMaster; Hugh McMaster;

In front:

Henry Saunders, son of L. Saunders; Kathleen Swinton Lee (née McMaster); Hilda McMaster

PRONI

GILFORD CASTLE
GILFORD

Gilford Castle
JFR

Armorial glass
R.A. LOGAN

The old Gilford Castle was for many years the property of the Johnston family, probably having been built by William Johnston in the late seventeenth century. Harris in the *Antient and present state of County Down*, published in 1744, states:

> Gilford, a village on the River Bann, about three miles S.W. of Waringstown, belongs to Richard Johnston, Esq., who has here a house and garden. The meanders of the river about this place (over which there is a good stone bridge) and the rising grounds surrounding it, adorned with woods and the bottoms variegated with bleach yards, afford altogether an agreeable prospect.

An old map of Portadown district, which includes Gilford, dated 1703, shows a large house marked as Mr Johnston's, which would appear to be the old Castle, beside a few houses. The Johnston family continued to live at Gilford Castle until the death of Sir William Johnston in 1841, but after this date it was not occupied and gradually fell into decay, being later completely demolished. The old Gilford Castle stood on the south side of the present Castle Street, close to the road, the front facing southwards.

About 1855 the estate of the Johnston family was bought by Benjamin Dickson, who with his brother James, were partners in the Dunbar McMaster linen thread company which was doing a large amount of business. Benjamin Dickson employed the Scottish architect William Spence to design the new Gilford Castle which is on a site much farther back from the road. The building is of Scots baronial style with a slender turret on the entrance front rising through three storeys, topped by a candle-snuffer roof. The bay windows of the lower storey are surmounted by a quatrefoil balustrade, while those of the upper storey are hood moulded. One of the most striking features of Gilford Castle is the portico, which is topped in the same way as the bay windows with two stone urns resting on the two corners. The roof is slated and multigabled. The Castle, which is built of Portland stone and Scrabo sandstone, is set in magnificent grounds, containing various types of oak and pine. There are two entrances to the property but only one with a lodge, the Banbridge Gate, which was built about 1860, the architect perhaps William Spence.

Auction poster
PRONI

After the death of Benjamin Dickson in 1894 the property passed to his trustees, and was eventually bought by Mr James Wright whose family still own Gilford Castle.

Castle entrance
R.A. LOGAN

ELMFIELD CASTLE
GILFORD

Elmfield Castle
JFR

Elmfield Castle is situated to the north west of Gilford, about half a mile from the town on the northern side of the Portadown Road. The lands known as Elmfield were in the latter half of the eighteenth century the property of the Christy family. In 1806 James Christy of Stramore granted them by a sub-lease for ever to William Dawson, who resided in the old house at Elmfield. However, in 1832 James Uprichard of Bannvale bought the head rent payable to the Christys. There was a further change of ownership in 1861 when the lands were purchased by James Dickson, a wealthy partner in Dunbar, Dickson & Co., Gilford. The Dickson family were already in the linen business as James was the elder son of Andrew Dickson, linen bleacher of Glenavy, County Antrim.

James Dickson, who married a daughter of Benjamin Haughton of Banford, built Elmfield Castle on the same lines as his brother Benjamin built the

Elmfield Castle *c.* 1920

new Gilford Castle and using the same architect, William Spence of Glasgow. Elmfield Castle was built *c.* 1864 in the Scots baronial style around the earlier Georgian house and, like Gilford Castle, it is constructed from Portland stone

Elmfield Castle front showing the turret
JFR

and Scrabo sandstone. The building is very grand, having numerous crow-stepped gables, small corbelled turrets with beautiful candle snuffer roofs and finials. There is another similarity to Gilford Castle in that a fine slender turret rises from the entrance front to above the roofline. Decorative quoins adorn the main façade with hood mouldings surrounding the windows of the upper storeys. The bay windows of the bottom storey are surmounted by a quatrefoil balustrade and there are armorial bearings above the front entrance. There are two gate lodges to Elmfield Castle, the one at the main entrance having been constructed *c.* 1860, the architect probably William Spence, and the other rear lodge which is pre-1833.

Elmfield Castle doorcase
JFR

According to the 1833 valuation the original house at Elmfield, belonging at that time to William Dawson, was considerably smaller in size than Woodbank, which was immediately opposite on the other side of the road from Gilford to Portadown. Nevertheless, there are listed a number of additional buildings such as coach houses and offices. At Elmfield a garden has existed since the eighteenth century complementing the original house, however, most of the planting took place in the 1860s at the same time as the building of the present Scottish baronial house. The grounds were planted mainly with rhododendrons, azaleas and specimen trees with rose gardens around the house, and the walled garden laid out as a kitchen garden. In the mid-twentieth century the grounds became rather run down but after the Shaw family bought the estate in 1958 they began a restoration programme. Francois Goffinet, a Belgian landscape designer who had worked on large gardens in parklands in the United States and Europe, was commissioned to develop an overall plan in 1989. There is now a framework in place for an ongoing programme of tree and shrub planting in the grounds of Elmfield Castle for the next twenty years.

H. Albert Uprichard, far right, with a hunting party leaving Elmfield, 1948

In 1866 the Dunbar McMaster partnership was dissolved and John Walsh McMaster agreed to pay out James and Benjamin Dickson in accordance with the terms of the partnership – as he interpreted them. This gave rise to a law suit in that the Dicksons claimed that the payment to them should include the value of the name and goodwill of the business. The matter was argued in the court of law, and in 1866, the Lord

Chancellor of Ireland decided in favour of McMaster. In the following year the Court of Appeal reversed this, but McMaster carried it to the House of Lords, which gave the final decision in his favour. However, in 1866 James and Benjamin Dickson went into business with their brother-in-law Thomas Ferguson setting up the partnership, 'Dickson, Ferguson & Co.', for power loom weaving of linen. In the 1870s there was a downturn in the linen trade, resulting in a loss of wealth, and James Dickson had to sell Elmfield Castle. This was bought, in 1884, by Mr Forster Green, a wealthy tea and coffee merchant in Belfast, for his daughter Emily, wife of Henry Albert Uprichard.

Henry Albert Uprichard and his wife Emily had previously lived at Lawrencetown House but from this point in time Elmfield Castle became the principal Uprichard residence, where the family were the embodiment of 'landed gentry' owning approximately six hundred acres in the surrounding area. The Uprichards were, like so many of the linen families of this area, members of the Society of Friends, and worshipped at the Meeting House at Moyallon. The very considerable business conducted at the Springvale Bleach Works gave employment to around one hundred and thirty workers, in the late nineteenth century and early twentieth century. Horses, dogs, and hunting were an integral part of life at Elmfield and over the years the extensive stables at Elmfield were home to many fine horses. William Forster Uprichard was an accomplished amateur jockey and went on to be Irish Amateur Champion, a feat replicated by his son, Richard Rutledge Kane Uprichard, known as 'Rut', in 1938. William Forster Uprichard died in 1949, leaving Elmfield Castle to his eldest son 'Rut', who unfortunately died in 1952, at a comparatively early age leaving no heir, and Elmfield Castle was later sold to the Shaw family.

Elmfield *c.* 1948
From left: Kane Uprichard, Jimsie Nicholson, Albert Uprichard, Alec Adamson, North Armagh Hounds, Grace Uprichard, Penelope Uprichard, Rut Uprichard, Diana Sinton, Tim Sinton

STRAMORE HOUSE
GILFORD

Stramore House is situated on the Stramore Road, approximately one mile from Gilford. This is a three storey, seven bay cement faced house, with quoins, and having a hipped slated roof. The windows have Georgian glazed sashes to the upper floors and plain sashes to the ground floor, while as the façade is ascended the windows of each storey decrease in height. All the windows are surrounded by moulded architraves and shallow sills, those on the ground floor having blank entablatures with string coursing running along the top of them. There is a single storey projecting porch topped by a dentilled cornice, with round headed windows on the sides and having a recessed doorway flanked by two very narrow round headed sidelights. On the south west side of the house the ground floor has a three light bay window which allows views over the parkland.

Stramore House
JFR

Stramore House
PRONI

Hugh Watson
JFR

Marianne Watson
JFR

The first Stramore House was built about 1694 by William Crozier, who was granted a lease forever of the lands to the north west of Gilford, in 1692 by Sir John Magill. William Crozier, a soldier, and son of John Crozier, a cavalry officer who came to Ireland in 1631 from Scotland, had three sons, John, Samuel and William, Jr. They all settled around Gilford, John marrying Mary Frazer from Scotland and having six sons, who were all over six feet tall. His eldest son William, a cavalry officer, succeeded him in Stramore but in 1764 sold part of the estate to Thomas Christy, a wealthy member of the Quakers in the neighbouring townland of Moyallon. Thomas Christy bought Upper Stramore in 1764, for his stepson Joseph Richardson, and conveyed the estate to him when he came of age in 1771. Joseph Richardson lived at Stramore but built the present Stramore House in 1794. Unfortunately he died young in 1801, leaving the estate to his step-niece, Isabella Wakefield who was married to John Nicholson and whose brother lived at Banford House.

John Nicholson lived at Stramore House with his wife Isabella and they had a large family, the eldest of whom was Alexander Jaffrey Nicholson. He became a doctor in Dublin and was the father of General John Nicholson, the great soldier of Indian fame, whose statue is in Lisburn. There is a watch tower at the gates of Stramore House whose construction appears to be linked with the local yeomanry company raised by the Nicholsons, with a similar one at Banford. This is a two storey, square tower, built *c.* 1801 of rubble stone. John Nicholson died in 1825, leaving Stramore to all of his children, however, one son, Rawdon Hautenville Nicholson lived at Stramore House, looking after the property until his death in 1863. The house and lands were sold in 1865 to Benjamin Dickson and Thomas Ferguson who immediately sold the house and 206 acres to Hugh Watson of Beechpark, Lurgan. He had set up with his brother-in-law, in 1860, Watson, Armstrong & Co., linen manufacturers, at the Edenderry Factory, Watson Street, Portadown.

Hugh Watson also bought an additional seventy acres of land, and about 1870 employed the architect, Thomas Jackson, to make improvements to Stramore House. Unfortunately, he died in 1871, but his wife stayed on in the house until 1879, when the property was sold by auction in Belfast. In 1920, Harry P. Watson of Beechpark, Lurgan, bought back Stramore House and the property was eventually left to C.S. Waller Watson (1889–1973). His son, Ivan V.W. Watson (1920–2002) inherited Stramore House

Yeomanry Tower
RA LOGAN

LAKEVIEW
LURGAN

Lakeview is situated in its own grounds on the eastern side of the Gilford Road, Lurgan, about two miles from the town, and is approached by a long sweeping avenue which is tree lined. The house is five bay, two storey, cement faced with windows which are sashed, recessed and silled, having moulded architraves over the ground floor windows, which are of greater height than those of the first floor. The architraves and quoins are picked out in contrasting colour to that of the rest of the house. The roof is hipped and has moulded eaves and cornice. There is a two storey porch on the entrance front, with three narrow sash windows with architrave, and above on the first floor, a further three narrow round headed windows. On the ground floor, on each side of the building, are rooms with round bay windows. Lakeview has recently been restored to its original state, with intricate plaster work in the main reception rooms.

Lakeview, Lurgan, was occupied in the mid-1800s, and indeed, the present house may have been built *c.* 1870, to a design by Thomas Jackson, on the site of the original house, by Francis Watson (1809–79), eldest son of Robert Watson, Ballyblagh, County Armagh, a linen merchant. The company operated under the title Robert Watson & Sons, The Flush, Lurgan, but after the death

Robert Watson 1776–1848
JFR

Lakeview
JFR

Ceiling rose
JOHN MORTON

of Robert Watson in 1848 the partnership was dissolved with the business carried on by the eldest son, Francis, under the style and title of Robert Watson & Sons. Bassett, 1888, records Francis, Joseph and Thomas Watson, along with some sisters, all living at Lakeview in the 1880s. Thomas Watson, son of Francis, carried on the business and lived at Lakeview until his death in 1923. The company still manufactured handkerchiefs in the 1950s under the title Robert Watson (Lurgan), Ltd. Members of the Watson family occupied Lakeview until the mid-1950s.

During the early years of the nineteenth century Lurgan was the centre of an area producing a variety of linen, however, it was the finer cloths, cambric, lawns and diapers which dominated the production. The linen establishment founded in 1808 by Robert Watson at 'The Flush', in Lurgan, may have been one of the earliest hand loom factories in Ireland. According to McCorry, 1993, Watson's of the Flush was sited at the end of Ballyblagh Street, at a point where the extended main street of Lurgan branches in three directions, to Belfast, Waringstown and Gilford.

The Watson family were known for the keen interest which they took in the welfare of their employees, and they gave support to the Orange Order. In 1861 the parish church of Lurgan was rebuilt, and the principal window in the chancel by Meyer of Munich, consisting of three lights featuring the four Evangelists, was presented by Francis Watson. Furthermore, when a peel of eight bells was installed in the church tower in 1878, the largest individual subscription of £200 was received from William Watson of New York.

Lakeview hallway
JOHN MORTON

Shankill Parish Church
East window
JFR

Beechpark house and doorway
JFR

BEECHPARK
LURGAN

Beechpark, in the townland of Ballymacateer, is situated on the southern side of the Dromore Road leaving Lurgan and is about two miles from the town. An early nineteenth century two storey house, Beechpark is a five bay dwelling of blackstone, with slated roof. The windows, which retain their glazing bars, are silled and have a brick dressing which also surrounds the doorcase. The doorway has beautifully glazed sidelights and a fanlight of spider-web glazing.

Hugh Watson (1815–71), a younger son of Robert Watson, married Marianne Armstrong, a daughter of William Armstrong of Lurgan, in 1843 and lived at Beechpark before buying Stramore, Gilford, in 1865. Hugh worked in his father's business, Robert Watson & Sons, Linen Merchants, Flush Factory, Lurgan, along with his elder brother Francis, who lived at Lakeview. After their father's death in 1848, Francis carried on the family business but Hugh set up a new factory in Portadown with the Armstrongs. Watson, Armstrong

& Co. was a very large linen weaving enterprise established in 1860 in Watson Street, Portadown, which by 1909, was listed as having 600 looms. Hugh's eldest son Robert followed him into the linen business becoming a partner in Watson, Armstrong & Co.

Hugh Watson, Jr. (1847–1907), fourth son of Hugh Watson of Stramore, was educated in Trinity College, Dublin and was afterwards called to the Bar. However, in 1889, he enrolled as a solicitor and worked in the practice, which became known as Watson & Neill, doing a large and lucrative agency business, including the agencies of Lord Lurgan. He had married Mary Gregory Jones of Dublin in 1874, having a family of twelve children, and lived firstly at Stramore, and then at Beechpark, Lurgan until his death in 1907.

James Watson with Thomas Armstrong outside his home Eden Hall, Portadown

Thomas Armstrong died 29 April 1871

CRAIGAVON MUSEUM

THE SINTON FAMILY
OF TANDRAGEE

In 1881, Slater's *Directory of Ireland* listed Thomas Sinton as a linen manufacturer with premises at Thomas Street, Portadown, and in Laurelvale and Tandragee, County Armagh. Thomas Sinton (1826–87) was born at Tamnamore House, County Armagh, and was the son of David Sinton who was a linen draper. According to Bassett, 1888, Thomas Sinton set up his manufacturing business at Laurelvale in 1852, where he manufactured linens and sheetings, using yarns which were spun at Tandragee and Killyleagh, County Down. The factory was built on four acres of a site encompassing one hundred and fifty acres.

The spinning factory at Tandragee was purchased in 1868, being previously known as Laurelvale. It was a mile and a half from Tandragee, and three and a half miles from Portadown railway station, which was the shipping point for the manufactured linens. Thomas lived in a large house adjacent to the factory, but it was demolished some time ago. After the death of Thomas Sinton in 1887, the business was carried on by his sons, Messrs Maynard, Arthur, Thomas and Frederick Sinton. Maynard married Miss Myra Atkinson, of Tandragee, and they had two children, Maynard, Jr., and Brigid. As a young man Maynard, Jr., joined the Royal Scottish Fusiliers and became a Second Lieutenant in 1936, but unfortunately, he was killed in action in the Second World War during the 1940 Norwegian campaign. His father never recovered from his son's death and died in December 1942.

The factory at Laurelvale closed in the 1950s, and the family carried on the business at Tandragee until the early 1990s, under the title, Thomas Sinton & Co., Ltd., Tandragee.

Thomas Sinton of Laurelvale
JFR

SINTON FAMILY TREE

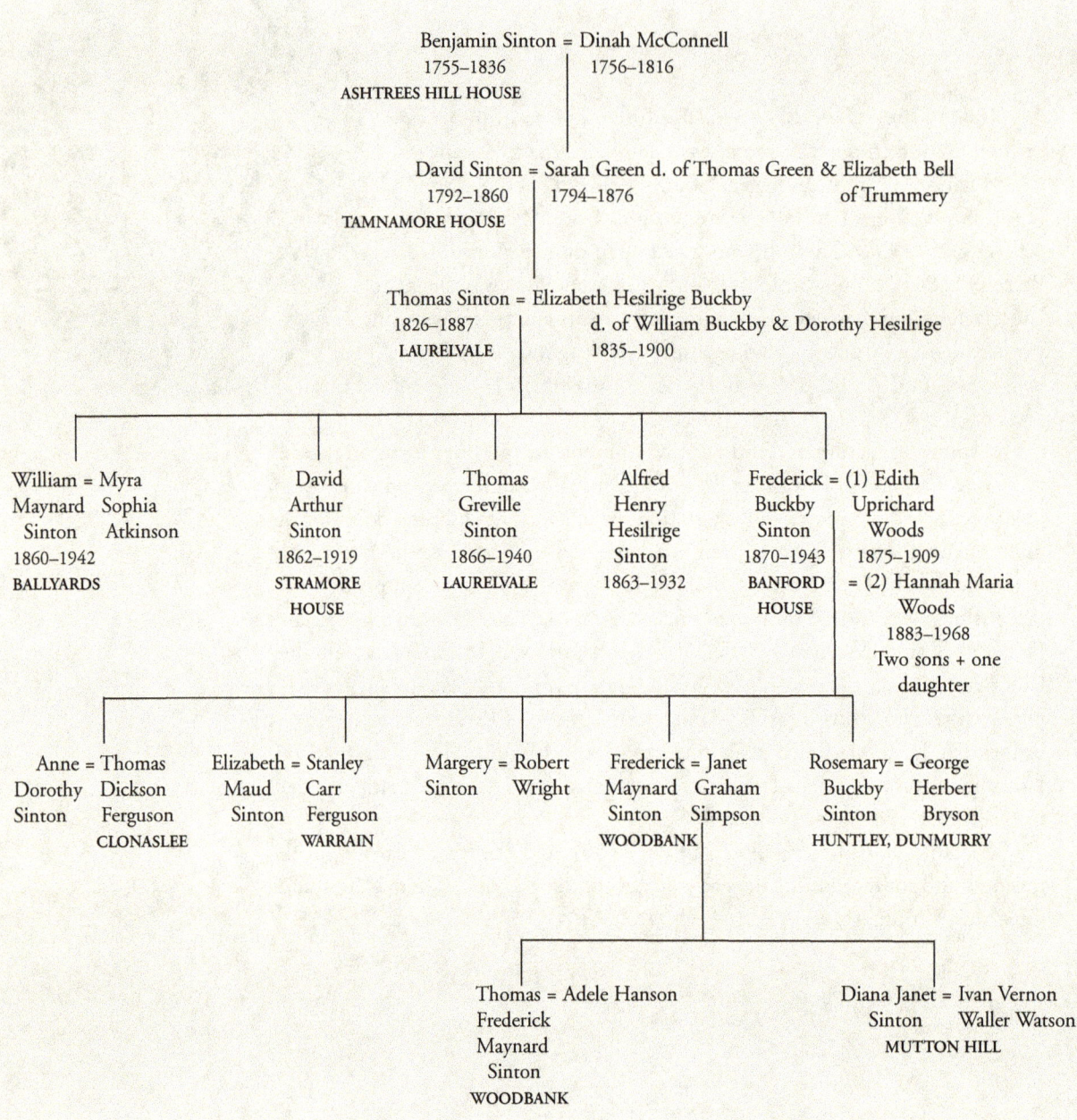

BALLYARDS CASTLE
MILFORD

The Simpson family acquired land at Ballyards in the year 1713 and appear to have prospered in the locale, around the late eighteenth century, having a record of military achievements in the Royal Irish Fusiliers and also as magistrates in the local area. The family used the waterpower of the Callan River and derived their substantial fortune from linen which was laid out to bleach in the fields around Ballyards. Linen Hill House was originally the home of Thomas Simpson and his wife Margaret, who died in 1796. In the year 1820 he built Beech Hill House, but by the 1860s Colonel Thomas Simpson wanted a more up to date home and had Ballyards House built.

Ballyards Castle
JFR

The present house was built in 1868 to designs by Charles Sherry and Robert Hughes, whose short lived Belfast partnership was responsible for completing

Ballyards Castle, 1921
PRONI

Maynard Sinton
PRONI

the Albert Memorial Clock after the death of W.J. Barre in 1867, and for the designs for the Belfast Theatre Royal. The house is a fine example of High Victorian mixing of styles. The plan is irregular with an entrance porch set in a re-entrant angle beneath a lean-to roof. The ground floor windows are pairs of severe rectangular openings with two sashes of single-sheet plated glass in each (very expensive in 1868, but very much the fashion for the best rooms). The single upper windows have vertically divided sashes. Above this, the house becomes typically eventful with shouldered gables (Tudor), heavily bracketed balconies (Venetian), files of linked chimney stacks (Tudor again), of which one low wing is supported on sets of corbels flanking an arch (Scottish). At one corner a circular tower rises to a conical capped belvedere with a complete vantage gallery again supported on heavy Italian brackets. The stonework, regularly coursed but with rustic facings, is reminiscent of the work of W.H. Lynn (Culloden Hotel) and of Young and Mackenzie (Queen's University, Belfast, Vice Chancellor's Lodge).

Mr Rowe, the Sinton family chauffeur in the Daimler
PRONI

Hugh Dixon wrote the above description, which is recorded in the Monuments and Buildings of Northern Ireland, showing how Sherry and Hughes combined a wide variety of architectural styles in Ballyards House. The coat of arms found on the skylight in the main entrance hall belongs to the Simpson family.

The house, which is situated near Milford, was sold in 1908 to Mr Maynard Sinton, JP, who made considerable improvements to the property, renaming it Ballyards Castle. Ballyards Castle is situated in forty acres of parkland and has two gate lodges, which were built in 1870, the Keady Road Entrance being designed by the architect Charles Sherry. Dean, 1994, states that

The music room
PRONI

Brigid on horseback
PRONI

the Milford Entrance, which was the original main access by the Callan River, has square ashlar Georgian piers contemporary with the old family home.

Maynard Sinton died in December 1942, but Mrs Sinton and their daughter Brigid lived on at Ballyards Castle during the later 1940s and the 1950s. After Mrs Sinton's death in 1962, Ballyards Castle was sold to Vernon College as a private school for boys, but the school eventually closed. Ballyards Castle was eventually sold to the Hospitals Authority to be used as a special care unit. However, the building now belongs to the Stauros Foundation, who run it as a residential unit for people suffering from addiction.

Ballyards today
JFR

Banford House front
JFR

BANFORD HOUSE
TULLYLISH

Banford House is thought to have been built *c.* 1780 by Thomas Nicholson, being described in the 1786 edition of *The Post-Chaise Companion* as an 'elegant new house'. Thomas Nicholson's father John came from a County Armagh Quaker family and he owned the bleach green at Banford. Towards the end of the eighteenth century members of the Nicholson family were also living in Stramore House, later to belong to the Watsons. After the death of his father, Thomas (1730–94) succeeded to the two bleach mills, Hall's Mill and Springvale, and built Banford House but subsequently his son Robert, in 1815, sold both the house and the business to Benjamin Haughton (1781–1866). The house has already been described in connection with the Haughton family but, in 1900, Banford was bought by Frederick Buckby Sinton, fifth son of Thomas Sinton of Laurelvale.

Frederick Sinton ran a fine bleaching business at Banford green and in the early years of the twentieth century the surrounding fields were covered by the brown linen being bleached.

He married firstly Edith Uprichard Woods in 1899 and had a family of four girls and one boy, Frederick Maynard Sinton, born in 1904. Unfortunately his wife died of tuberculosis in 1909, but he married again, in 1912, his wife's sister, Hanna Maria Woods, who had helped look after her sister's children. He had a second family of two sons and one daughter. These eight children required considerable accommodation in Banford and Fred Sinton built on a complete wing at the back of the house. There was a glass porch and iron steps leading to the ground floor, including a cloakroom, two pantries and a back staircase, which led to a small bedroom, bathroom and pantry on the first floor. A further two small bedrooms and a bathroom were on the second floor.

Rosemary B. Bryson, née Sinton, (1907–2005), recorded in 1985, her memories of Banford in 'Harking Back', which was deposited in the British Library National Sound Archive, and gives the following description of the two main reception rooms in the house.

> At the front of the house there was a very large dining room, out of which one could go down steps into the rather elegant conservatory, always full of exotic flowers all the year round. The dining room had a high ceiling, and in winter the windows had, as well as the long net curtains, golden brown chenille curtains with lovely 'bobbles' all the way up; these were removed at spring cleaning time. There were also Venetian blinds with wooden slats, which we children were never allowed to touch as they went wrong very easily. The furniture was large and atrocious Victorian stuff, but lovely and homely to me as a child. On each side of the fireplace was a very large leather chair, and, as a fire was always lit, my parents sat there in the winter unless there were visitors.
>
> The drawing room was smaller, and had pleasanter furniture including plenty of chintz covered chairs and sofas. Out of the drawing room there was what was called the veranda, a really very large sun room with glass on three sides, a parquet floor with Turkish mats, and rattan sofas and chairs. Here, as we grew older, we just rolled up the mats and danced to an old gramophone. To get from the veranda to the back part of the house one came through what was called the smoking room; but I never remember it being used as anything but a passage, for although it had a fireplace, it was too narrow.

West side
JFR

Frederick Sinton died in 1943, aged 73, but his wife lived on at Banford House, until her death, aged 84, in 1968. In recent years Banford House has had a number of owners but is not now connected to the linen industry.

East side
JFR

WOODBANK
GILFORD

Woodbank
JFR

Doorcase
JFR

Woodbank is situated on the southern side of the Gilford to Portadown road, about half a mile from Gilford and almost opposite Elmfield Castle. This is a five bay, two storey, bow ended house over basement, the building being cement faced and quoined. The central entrance is set in a single storey Tuscan porch, which has round headed side windows, and all the windows are Georgian glazed, sashed, silled, having plainly moulded architraves. There is a shallow hipped and slated roof, with a moulded cornice and substantial chimney stacks rising above it. In the twentieth century an extension was made to the rear of the house by the Sinton family along with modernisation of the kitchen quarters. The Ulster Architectural Heritage Society, Craigavon, 1970, date the house to late eighteenth/early nineteenth century, with a complete range of outbuildings. They also state:

> The setting and planting do a great deal to enhance the value of the building group.

Dean, 1994, has recorded a gate lodge at Woodbank first erected *c.* 1840, and later improved *c.* 1880, but now demolished, along with octagonal stone entrance piers with friezed caps which may have been built at an earlier date.

Ballymacanallen is the townland to the north of Gilford, and in 1693 Sir John

Side view of Woodbank
JFR

Magill made a grant of lands in the area to Thomas Kennedy, on a renewable lease. These lands immediately adjoined Gilford and are often known as 'Kennedy's Farm', but include within the area, the houses Bannvale, Elmfield and Woodbank, with a very extensive portion of land.

The Kennedys were a family who had come from Ayrshire, Scotland, where Colonel Gilbert Kennedy was a brother of John, 6th Earl of Cassilis. Rev. Gilbert Kennedy, son of Colonel Kennedy, came to Ireland in 1668, to the parish of Dundonald and Holywood. His son, Thomas Kennedy certainly built the original house known as Woodbank in 1693, and appears to have farmed the land, including linen bleaching, with the McCreight family who were linen merchants, as one land boundary is the River Bann. According to Dean W.R.M. Orr, Rector of Gilford, Bannvale was in the possession of Andrew McCreight, linen merchant, in the eighteenth century, and it seems probable that the Kennedys and the McCreights were related as Thomas Kennedy was buried in the McCreight tomb at Tullylish.

Several generations of the Kennedy family lived at Woodbank until 1791, when Thomas Kennedy of Dundonald assigned the lease of one quarter of the land, with all houses and plantings, at Ballymacanallen, to Abraham Atkinson, of Stramore, who was a linen draper.

Abraham Atkinson would appear to be the person who built the present Woodbank, although some of the original building remains. However, apart from the house, the 1833 valuation lists very extensive outbuildings, including a lapping room, two stables and lofts, a steward's house

Staircase
JFR

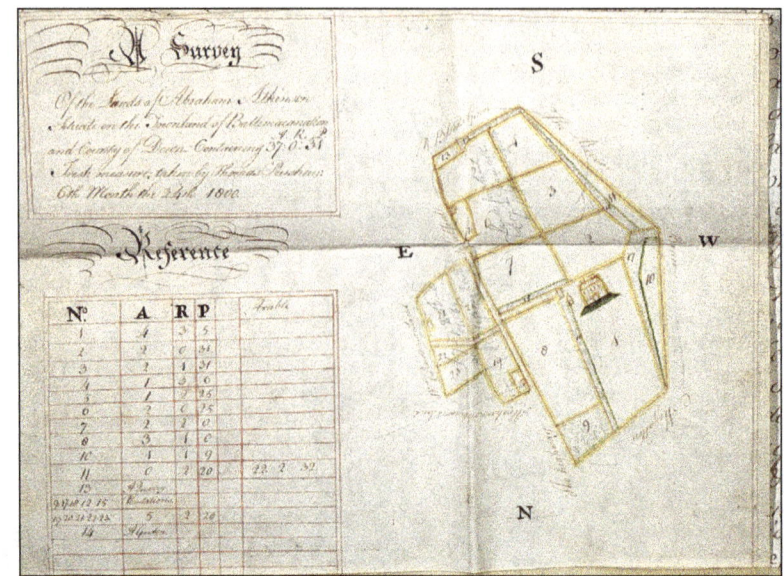

Survey of Ballymacanallen, 1800
PRONI

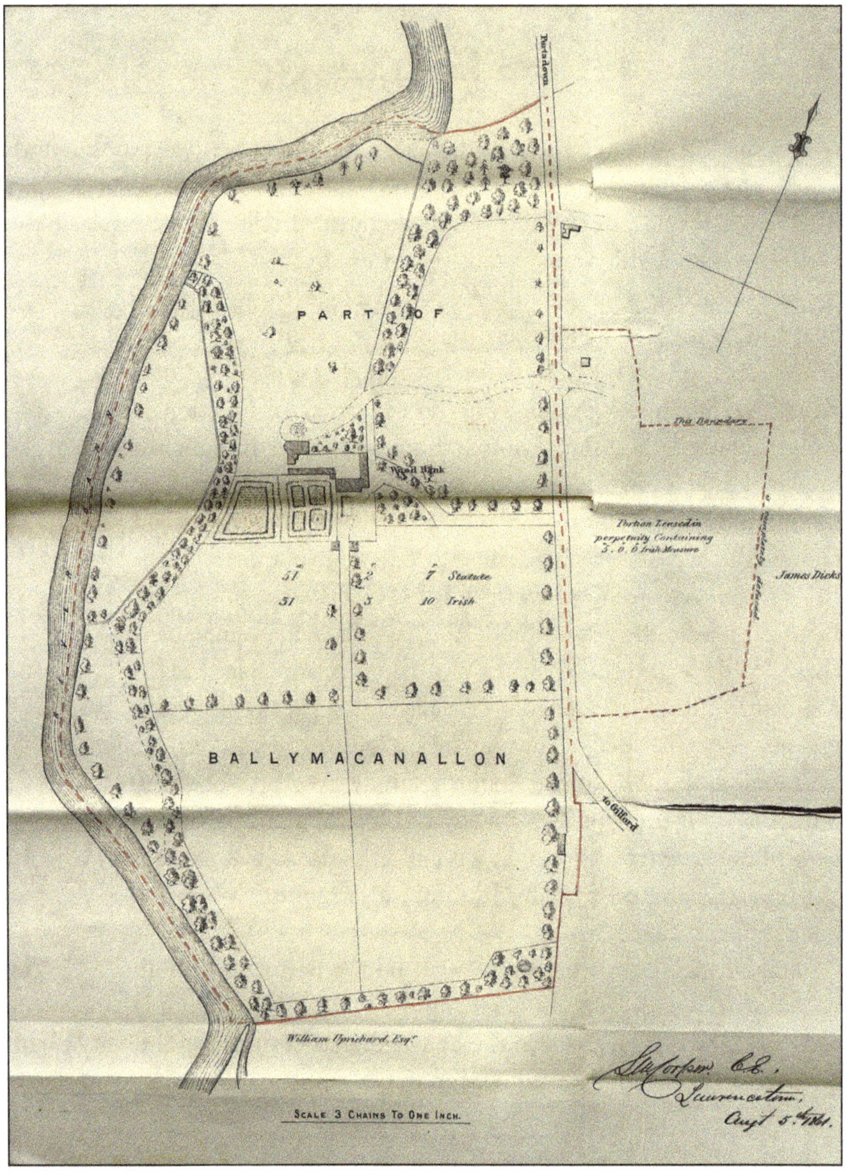

Map of Woodbank and grounds, 1861
PRONI

and a gate house. Abraham Atkinson died in 1809, and bequeathed the lands of Ballymacanallen, with all houses, plantings and improvements made thereon, to James Christy of Stramore, and after his death, to his daughter Mary Christy. However, Mary Christy married Abraham Bell in 1812 and they eventually emigrated to America, where her husband became head of a substantial company of Quaker shipping and commission merchants in New York City. James Christy was a partner in the Moyallon Vitriol Company, and according to Bill Jackson, writing in *Ringing True*, Abraham Bell possibly worked in the Christy undertaking from 1812 to 1816. James Christy died in 1820 and the lands and houses, including Woodbank, became the property of Mary Bell née Christy, until her death in 1832, when her husband inherited the holding.

Following the death of Abraham Atkinson, William Dawson, of Woodbank, is named as an executor in the will of Margaret Sinton née Christy written on 15th December 1810. William Dawson, a relative of the Christys, was in business with John and Joseph Christy, in the Christy and Dawson bleach works at Millpark and Springvale. In 1830 the business became insolvent, being sold to the Uprichard family, but at this point William Dawson was living in the old house at Elmfield. Meanwhile in 1835 Hugh Law was living in Woodbank, but in 1861 the whole property was auctioned, being bought by James Dickson of Elmfield for £2,500. Another occupant of the house in 1889 was John George McMaster, a brother of Hugh Dunbar McMaster of Dunbarton House and the Gilford Mill.

In the early 1930s Woodbank was purchased as a wedding present for Frederick Maynard Sinton and his bride Janet Graham Simpson. Unfortunately, Fred Sinton was killed in a car crash in 1936 but his widow lived on at Woodbank with their two children, Tim and Diana. Meanwhile in the twenty first century the Sinton family continue to occupy the property, which since 1693, has been associated in various ways with those involved in the linen industry.

Photograph taken at Retirement Dinner in 1989 for Peter W. Larmor, Chairman, Ulster Weaving Co., Ltd.

From left: T.F.M. Sinton, Chairman, Thomas Sinton & Co., Ltd., who lived at Woodbank; Peter W. Larmor, Chairman, Ulster Weaving Co., Ltd.; Joe A. Johnston, Chairman, Johnston, Allen & Co., Ltd.; John B. Bryson, former Chairman, Spence Bryson & Co., Ltd.

6
MOYALLON

HINCKS PRINT PLATE VI
Spinning, reeling and boiling the yarn

WILLIAM HINCKS 1783

THE RICHARDSON FAMILY
OF MOYALLON

John Grubb Richardson
COURTESY RICHARDSON FAMILY

The Richardson family appear to have been among some of the earliest settlers, who were encouraged to come over to Ireland from the west of England and Wales, to live in Lisnagarvey, the modern Lisburn. There are records showing that in 1610 there were Richardsons occupying some of the fifty two houses centring on Lisnagarvey, an estate which had been granted to Sir Fulke Conway. Similarly, another early settler was the Rev. John Richardson, rector of Loughgall, County Armagh, whose brother Zachary also settled in Loughgall and had a son Jonathan Richardson (1) who became a member of the Society of Friends in company with the Nicholsons of County Armagh, the Greers of County Tyrone, and the Grubbs of County Tipperary. The Society of Friends actively discouraged marriages outside their religion and the Richardson family observed this rule for many generations, the first Jonathan's grandson Jonathan (2) (1681–1737), marrying Elizabeth Nicholson. His son John (1719–59) served his time to the linen trade with his relatives the Hoggs of Lisburn, settling there permanently after marrying Ruth, daughter of William Hogg, who had a bleach green at Glenmore, Lambeg. Their son, Jonathan (3) b.1756, bought the Hunters' bleach green at Glenmore and was the first to succeed in winter bleaching, which meant he was able to run his bleach works all the year round.

Undoubtedly, the Richardsons are one of the oldest of the linen families, who, generation after generation, pursued the making and marketing of linen. The bleaching business at Glenmore expanded substantially and about 1830 the firm purchased the adjoining bleach green from the Handcocks, amalgamating it with their existing works. Jonathan (3) married Sarah Nicholson, having three sons, James Nicholson (1), John and Joseph, who were to lay the basis for the large Richardson business. In 1810, James Nicholson Richardson (1782–1847) married Anna Grubb of Anner Mills near Clonmel, County Tipperary, a lady who brought him a large amount of money. Under his active guidance the Richardson linen business prospered and in 1825 he took into partnership John Owden, founding the company of J.N. Richardson, Sons & Owden, Ltd. James Nicholson Richardson lived until 1847, leaving seven sons, some of them becoming men of distinction in the linen trade.

Jonathan (5) (1811–69) of Glenmore, Lambeg
John Grubb (1813–90) of Brookhill, Lisburn; Moyallon and the Wood House, Bessbrook
James Nicholson (2) (1815–99) of Lissue

Joshua Pim (1816–82) of Cheltenham
Thomas (b. 1818) of New York
Joseph (1821–1906) of Springfield, Magheragall, Lisburn
William (1824–62) of Brooklands, Belfast

J.N. Richardson, Sons & Owden, whilst being very successful, was, in 1845, a bleaching and warehousing firm, which was anxious to enter into the manufacture of linen. John Grubb Richardson, the second son, was in many ways the most remarkable of the seven brothers, and he showed great foresight when in 1845, he purchased from Lord Charlemont the Mount Caulfield estate in County Armagh, where his cousins the Nicholsons had been in the linen trade since 1802. Records show that in 1817 the Nicholsons had no looms in their premises but they gave out yarn to be hand woven in people's homes. However, by 1839, they owned a spinning mill of 1,024 spindles, a scutch mill, a hackling house, and sundry other buildings.

John Grubb Richardson conceived the idea of a model village at Bessbrook, shaping it to his Quaker and temperance ideals by providing houses for his workers, a school, churches, a shop but no place where drink might be purchased. The village of Bessbrook gradually grew with the building of houses, the addition of large spinning mills and eventually weaving factories, all working in conjunction with the Glenmore Bleach Works and the Belfast warehouse of Richardson Sons & Owden.

In 1863 John Grubb Richardson, through the sale of an inherited estate in County Tyrone, became the sole owner of the entire business, works and village of Bessbrook, and in 1878, the firm was incorporated as a limited liability company, under the title of the Bessbrook Spinning Company Limited. Although John Grubb Richardson died in 1890 the Richardson business flourished in Bessbrook for a considerable period but eventually, after the Second World War, there was a decline in the linen industry when many mills and factories in Northern Ireland closed. The eventual closure of the Bessbrook Spinning Company in 1967 had a profound effect on the community of Bessbrook and the surrounding areas.

MOYALLON HOUSE
GILFORD

Moyallon House
JFR

Moyallon House is situated on the Stramore Road, but is immediately adjacent to the Gilford to Portadown road, about two miles from Gilford. This is a two storey, three bay classically styled rendered house, which is quoined. The main block with parapeted roof was built in 1794, and the hip-roofed extensions and veranda were added in the late nineteenth century by John Grubb Richardson. On each side of the doorway are tripartite windows, the middle lights of which are flanked by two narrower sidelights, and the architraves surrounding these windows reach to the ground. On the upper storey elaborately moulded architraves reaching to the sills surround the windows. The doorway is flanked by sidelights, while the frieze above the door is supported by Composite columns with Composite pilasters framing the sidelights. There is a segmental fanlight of spider-web glazing above the frieze. Moyallon House has a fine group of two storey roughcast outbuildings with hipped roofs and rendered walls with stone dressings about a courtyard. According to Dean, 1994, in contrast to the graceful neo-classical villa there are two sturdy late Victorian picturesque gate lodges both constructed *c.* 1880, the architects probably being Thomas Jackson and Son.

Doorcase
JFR

A year before the Bessbrook purchase John Grubb Richardson married Helena Grubb, of Cahir Abbey, County Tipperary, but five years later, in 1849, she died, leaving him with a son, James Nicholson (3), who eventually became chairman of the company, and a daughter Helena. However, in 1853 he married Jane Marion Wakefield of Moyallon House, Gilford, which is seventeen miles from Bessbrook. Initially they lived at Brookhill, near Lisburn, but in the 1880s they moved to Moyallon House and had one son, T. Wakefield Richardson and seven daughters, the sixth of whom, Ethel, married her cousin, R.H. Stephens Richardson, DL, who in time became the Chairman of Richardson Sons & Owden, Ltd. and the Bessbrook Spinning Co., Ltd. Thomas Wakefield Richardson and his wife Hilda lived firstly at the Grange and after his mother's death in 1909 at Moyallon House. Thomas died in 1921 without children, and was succeeded in Moyallon House by his nephew Alexander Richardson. In the twenty first century the house is still owned by the Richardson family.

The townland of Moyallon was a very early centre of the linen industry on the River Bann. Alexander Christy, who was born in Scotland in 1642, settled here in 1675, and the family is thought to have introduced the linen trade into this

Helena Grubb
COURTESY RICHARSON FAMILY

Mrs Jane Marion Richardson with her famous white pony Sweet Pea and butler for 50 years, Robert McCormick, 1898
PRONI

Moyallon House to rear
JFR

part of the country. Before the end of the seventeenth century there were members of the Society of Friends living in the area, and as the linen industry developed, a group of closely related Quaker families became engaged in it along the River Bann between Moyallon and Lawrencetown. Thomas Christy (1711–80) was the grandson of Alexander, and lived in the old Moyallon House on the opposite side of the road to the present Quaker Meeting House. He was a linen merchant, owning several bleach works apart from that in Moyallon – the Springvale and Millpark works near Lawrencetown.

In the latter part of the eighteenth century Moyallon bleach green belonged to Joseph Wakefield, who had married Hannah, daughter of Thomas Christy, having both a son and a grandson called Thomas Christy Wakefield. He had come originally from Westmorland to learn the linen business with Joseph Richardson of Stramore, and he lived at Lawrencetown. Thomas Christy, who died in 1780, left the Moyallon property to his grandson, Thomas Christy Wakefield (1772–1861). He was responsible for building the new Moyallon House in 1794, which, after the old house had been destroyed by fire, became the principal residence of the Wakefields.

Thomas Christy Wakefield had a son, Thomas Christy Wakefield (junior), who died in 1878, and left the property, including Moyallon House, to one of his daughters Jane Marion Richardson née Wakefield (1831–1909).

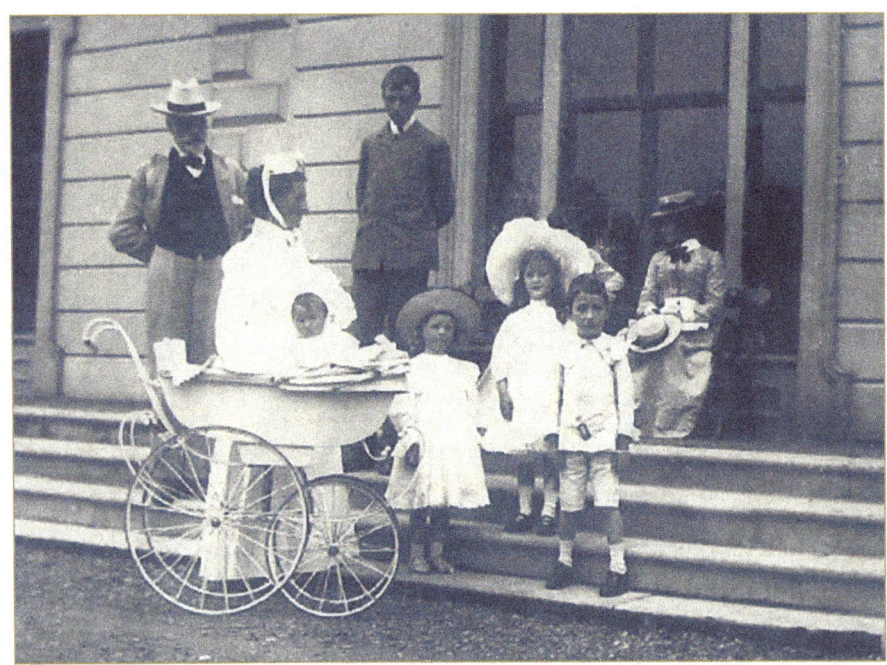

The Richardson children at Moyallon House, 1890
COURTESY RICHARDSON FAMILY

OLD DRUMLYN HOUSE
PORTADOWN

Old Drumlyn is situated on the main Gilford to Portadown road almost mid-way between the two towns. It is thought to have been an old stage coach inn and is shown on the 1835 Ordnance Survey map. According to the Ulster Architectural Heritage Society book on Craigavon, 1970, the building could be late eighteenth century, but seems to have been re-fenestrated with Venetian sashes in the 1820s. Old Drumlyn House is informal but attractive in appearance, being two storey, rendered, and having a slate roof. The outbuildings appear to be later additions to the property.

R.H. Stephens Richardson (1869–1957) and his wife Ethel Joanne Richardson lived for some years after their marriage in 1897, at Old Drumlyn. R.H. Stephens Richardson's great-grandfather, John, was a brother of the first James N. Richardson, and his father was Alexander Airth Richardson of Aberdelghy, Lambeg, who was head of the firm of Richardson & Nevin, Lambeg Weaving Factory. However, his wife Ethel was born at Moyallon, being the daughter of John Grubb Richardson and his second wife Jane Marion Wakefield.

Old Drumlyn House
© CROWN COPYRIGHT HMSO

Stephens Richardson and his wife had two sons, John Stephen Wakefield Richardson (1899–1985) and Alexander Reginald Wakefield Richardson (1902–84), both sons being born while the couple lived at Old Drumlyn. They built a new house, Drumlyn not far from their original residence and moved there in 1908.

A member of the Richardson family in a 1900 De Dion Bouton motor car
CRAIGAVON MUSEUM

DRUMLYN HOUSE
MOYALLON

While Moyallon House is the last house in County Down, on the road from Gilford to Portadown, Drumlyn House is the first in County Armagh; the county boundary following a stream in a wooded glen between the two properties. This new Drumlyn House was built for R.H. Stephens Richardson in 1909 to designs in the 'Dutch' style by the architect W.J.W. Roome, and cost £5,000. In the early 1900s Drumlyn was the epitomy of Edwardian style having a staff of twelve, which ensured that standards were maintained for the comfort of the Richardson family.

Drumlyn is distinguished by its prominent Dutch gabling, and it sits appropriately on the brow of a rolling hill, the garden front having views to the south over the River Bann and to Slieve Gullion in the distance. Drumlyn is a two storey house, with Dutch gabling rising to the same height as the roof, and being a very elongated house, requiring six separate chimney stacks. The windows are slightly recessed, being sashed and silled, with moulding above some of the windows. The recessed front door with overhead shielding, is approached by three shallow steps, and is at the extreme right front of the building. An entrance courtyard to the north of the building was formed when road widening occurred in the 1960s, and is enhanced by urns

Drumlyn House
R.A. LOGAN

R.H. Stephens Richardson

Drumlyn House frontage
R.A. LOGAN

which originally came from Drumbanagher House near Poyntzpass. To the south, the gardens are laid out in a series of terraces enclosed by formal yew hedging, and having open views over the countryside. To the west lies a charming rose garden, laid out by Alex Richardson, with shrubberies and paths beyond.

R.H. Stephens Richardson and his wife Ethel had two sons, ensuring the continuation of the Richardson line. The elder son, John Stephen Wakefield Richardson, known as Jack, eventually lived at Bessbrook, remaining unmarried. He was one of the managing directors of the company, and a member of the Board of Directors of J.N. Richardson, Sons & Owden, Ltd., Belfast. The younger son, Alexander Reginald Wakefield Richardson, known as Alex, lived with his wife at Drumlyn House after the death of his father in 1957, and farmed the land associated with the property. Alex Richardson had married Edith Cecilia Marianne Boultbee, the daughter of an English vicar, in the early 1930s, but their early married life was marred by the death of three of their four children, which are recorded as taking place at Moyallon House. Alex Richardson died at Drumlyn in 1984, but Marianne lived into her 100th year and was much admired, holding a deep and sincere faith. An oak tree was planted in the grounds of Drumlyn House on what would have been her 100th birthday.

Drumlyn House remains a Richardson family home, lived in by the great-grandson of the builder, his wife and children.

Drumlyn House stairway and first floor landing
© CROWN COPYRIGHT HMSO

The Woodhouse
PRONI

THE WOODHOUSE
BESSBROOK

In 1863 John Grubb Richardson inherited an estate in County Tyrone, which he sold, and subsequently bought the village of Bessbrook including the Camlough estate of Lord Charlemont. He also became the sole owner of the works and the entire linen business at Bessbrook, and with the passing years he watched the village grow, having a constant concern for the social and moral welfare of the inhabitants. Some years after 1863 John Grubb Richardson made one of his homes at The Woodhouse, Bessbrook, which was built in the grounds of an older residence, named Derrymore House, built before 1787 by Isaac Corry, MP for Newry and last Chancellor of the Irish Exchequer. The Woodhouse is situated close to the entrance of the village of Bessbrook and not far from the Quaker Meeting House, where the Richardson family worshipped. This is a many gabled two storey late Victorian house with eaved roofs and elaborate bargeboards, having tall recessed sashed windows and a platband separating the ground and first floor.

Dean, 1994, lists a gate lodge *c.* 1880 with the architect probably Thomas Jackson and Son, due to the long lasting Quaker relationship between family and architect. There is considerable similarity in the detail of the gate lodge as

The Woodhouse
JFR

described by Dean and The Woodhouse. Both appear to have matching cream fireclay brick in bands on the red brick chimney stacks and the gate lodge has the eaves carried on large wooden brackets as has the house. Dean records a nice pair of 'portcullis' carriage gates, hung on chunky quarry-faced stone pillars at the entrance.

John Grubb Richardson died at The Woodhouse in March, 1890, and was succeeded in the business by his eldest son James N. Richardson who lived at Mount Caulfield, Bessbrook. Mrs J.G. Richardson lived at Moyallon House until her death in 1909, when the Derrymore estate passed to her twin daughters, Mrs Ethel Williams and Miss Anne Richardson. Mrs Williams lived at The Woodhouse for over half a century, assisting with the work of the Society of Friends and taking an active part in their meetings in Bessbrook.

Ethel Richardson (Mrs Williams) in the conservatory
PRONI

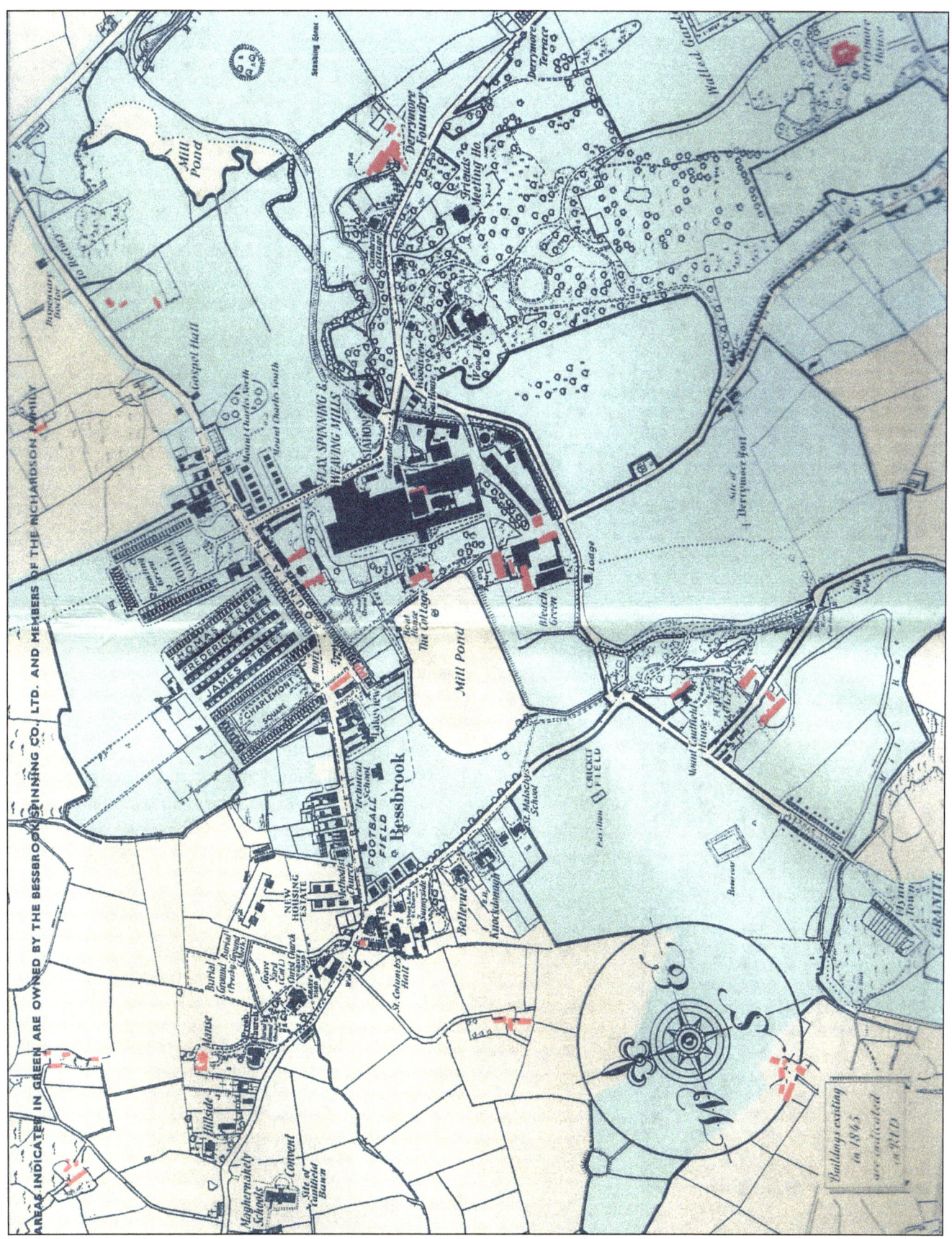

Map of Bessbrook showing the Richardson houses
The Woodhouse and Mount Caulfield

From a publication on Bessbrook

PRONI

MOUNT CAULFIELD HOUSE
BESSBROOK

James Nicholson Richardson, 1901
From 'Bessbrook'

Mount Caulfield House is situated on the south eastern side of the village of Bessbrook in well planted grounds and adjacent to Hill Street. This is a stucco house with diamond pattern slates on a complicated roof structure which shows evidence of the extension of the house. Bence-Jones, 1988, has given the following description:

> A house of two storeys with a dormered attic, a gabled projection at one end of its front and a curvilinear gable at the other; probably a C19 rebuilding of a C18 house. Seven bay front, plus the gabled projection: window surrounds with blocking. Charming wooden porch, in the Chinese taste. In 1814, the residence of William Duff.

The house has also been listed as being in existence in 1839 and extended in 1867. According to Brett, 1999, the listers say:

> Two storey mansion with attics. Originally symmetrical with Dutch gables and other generally 17th century detail. The southern bay has been extended with canted bays.

Unfortunately the charming wooden porch has disappeared to be replaced by an inappropriate modern one.

Mount Caulfield House
JFR

Brett, 1999, has suggested that, from the name, the original house belonged to the Caulfield family, but after several owners, it was occupied by Joseph Nicholson, who is recorded in 1836 as the occupier of what was then a single storey dwelling. At that time Nicholson, who had bought the property in 1802, was operating a power mill at Bessbrook, which spun a considerable quantity of flax per week. According to Horner, Secretary of the Irish Linen Board, Joseph Nicholson & Sons had a spinning mill, which was the largest in Ireland at that time, together with a scutch mill, and for a time a bleach green at Mount Caulfield. However, in 1839 the mill burnt down, and remained unoccupied until the property was sold to the Richardsons in 1845.

John Grubb Richardson gave Mount Caulfield to his eldest son James Nicholson Richardson on the occasion of his marriage, in 1867, to Sophia, daughter of William Malcomson of Portlaw, near Waterford. The house stands on a hill just above the mills and the grounds were planted and laid out for the couple by John Grubb Richardson. Unfortunately Sophia Richardson did not enjoy good health and she died at Torquay in the early summer of 1886. In 1893, James Nicholson Richardson married Sara, often referred to as Sissillia, elder daughter of Samuel Alexander Bell, of Bellevue, Lurgan. In succession to his father James Nicholson Richardson became Chairman of the Board of Directors of the Bessbrook Spinning Company, and he and Sissillia continued to live at Mount Caulfield. He took a leading part in the care of the entire village of Bessbrook and in 1913 the workpeople of Bessbrook, Craigmore and district presented him with a framed and illuminated address, and to Sissillia they gave a beautiful solid silver rose-bowl.

Mrs James Nicholson Richardson, 1901
From 'Bessbrook'

James Nicholson Richardson died in 1921, and his widow Mrs J.N. Richardson later left Mount Caulfield to live with her sister in her old home at Bellevue, Lurgan. The house was requisitioned during the Second World War, and was later subdivided into three flats. According to the Monuments and Buildings Record of Northern Ireland, Mount Caulfield has unfortunately been 'at serious risk' since 1996, with leaking roof and internal damage to ceilings.

7
LURGAN

OLD LURGAN MILL
Early 19th century watercolour by Jean Adair Warren

Donated to PRONI by H.P. Watson of Beechpark, 1965

THE BELL FAMILY
OF LURGAN

Hand bill reproduced from George Bassett, County Down, 100 Years Ago

During the nineteenth century County Armagh played a very important part in the manufacture of linen, particularly in weaving. Indeed, the Lurgan/Portadown area was known for the excellence of its fine linen, and held the supreme position in the production of fine handkerchief linens. In the first half of the nineteenth century Lurgan was the centre of a large hand loom weaving industry, eventually using yarn produced in the new spinning mills in the Banbridge area, such as that built at Hazelbank, about 1834, by Samuel Law, and in 1838 at Huntly by Hugh Dunbar. Crawford, 2005, states,

> Yet it has to be recognised that after the introduction of the wet-spinning process into Ireland in the late 1820s, the great bulk of the yarns spun in Irish mills were woven into cloth by handloom weavers throughout the countryside of the province of Ulster.

As stated by E.R.R. Green, 1949,

until the eighteenth century the making of linen cloth was still little more than a supplement to the main business of farming.

This altered in the early eighteenth century when many of the Lurgan Quaker families were involved in tanning and linen. However, by the middle of the eighteenth century there was a rise in commercial undertakings and McCorry, 1993, states,

> The enterprise and endeavour of Quaker and Church of Ireland principal tenants in exploiting linen manufacture and tanning had pushed Lurgan's evolution into a well established market and distribution centre.

The Bell family were Quakers from an early date, and the records of the Quaker meetings of Lurgan, where the Society of Friends first met in Ireland, survive from the mid-1670s and contain incidental references to the linen trade and to people engaged in the industry. In his extensive history of the Bell family and their occupations over a period of 350 years, Bill Jackson, 2005, states,

> Two branches of the Bells, one Belfast – the other Lurgan-based, were to become significant when linen in Ulster moved into its industrial phase.

It is clear that various Bell families, either at Trummery or Lurgan, were involved in the making of linen in the early eighteenth century, and one such was Richard Bell (1694/5–1764) of Trummery, who was a co-signatory to a letter from the linen weavers and manufacturers in Lurgan. In the nineteenth century a Thomas Bell was listed as a muslin manufacturer in Bradshaw's 1819/20 *Directory for Lurgan*.

Again, Bill Jackson, 2005, refers to Abraham Bell (1787–1859) of Lurgan, who, as he states, undoubtedly must have prospered as a merchant in the town as, on his death, his effects amounted to something short of £60,000. His eldest son Thomas and brother Samuel Bell, both of Main Street, Lurgan, appear in Slater's 1846 *Directory* as cambric manufacturers and linen yarn merchants and ten years later there is an entry for the firm 'Thomas Bell & Co., Bellview'. Unfortunately Thomas died in 1852, leaving his father to manage the firm until he himself died in 1859. Jackson, 2005, states,

Samuel Bell (1821–1901)
COURTESY RICHARD DERMOT BELL

> The evidence is an indenture of January 31, 1865. Its preamble notes that Samuel Alexander Bell (1821–1901) of Bellevue, William Bell (1833–79) of Solitude and George Bell (1813–88) had carried on business in partnership as linen and cambric manufacturers under the name of Thomas Bell and Company of Bellevue, 'from the date of the death of their father in or about the tenth of August 1859' up to the month of November 1864.

In effect they agreed to terminate the partnership and allow Samuel to buy out the others. There is no doubt that Thomas Bell & Co. was trading by the 1850s, specialising in cambric, a very fine linen, which was used in handkerchiefs, and in the 1860s benefiting from the impact of the American Civil War which stopped the import of cotton. In the Lurgan area the factory system was slower in coming to the linen industry due to the low cost of hand loom weaving, which made factory methods uneconomic. Bellevue was a centre of collection where quantities of handkerchiefs came in from cottage weavers and were washed, smoothed, hemmed and folded before being placed in presentation boxes. Bassett, in 1888, lists Thomas Bell & Co., Bellevue, under Handkerchief Manufacturers, but due to competition from power loom weaving the company closed in the 1920s.

However, in the late nineteenth century, the Bells in Lurgan were involved in power loom manufacture of linens, cambrics and handkerchiefs, since they became directors of the Lurgan Weaving Company, Ltd., which was set up in 1881. This company purchased a power loom factory adjacent to Brownlow Terrace from Messrs William and James Macoun which had been making cambric and cambric handkerchiefs since the 1860s. Bassett, 1888, names two Bells in the list of seven directors, namely Mr Samuel A. Bell, JP, Belle Vue, Lurgan, Chairman, and Mr Frederick W. Bell, Belle Vue, Lurgan. The Lurgan Weaving Company was highly successful and had a considerable overseas market for fine handkerchiefs, but was eventually taken over by the Blackstaff Flax Spinning & Weaving Co., Ltd.

FAMILY TREE OF SAMUEL A. BELL OF LURGAN

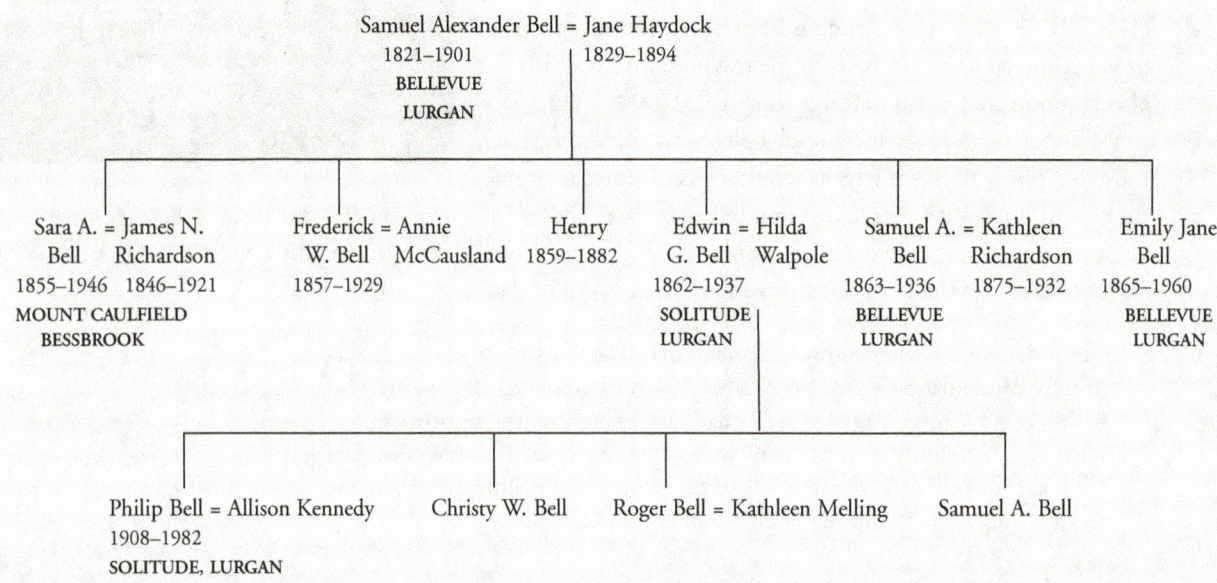

BELLEVUE
LURGAN

Bellevue was situated to the north east of Lurgan just off the Kilmore Road. The house is thought to have been commissioned about 1853 by Abraham Bell for his son Samuel Alexander Bell (1821–1901) prior to his marriage to Jane Haydock. It was adjacent to the factory, Thomas Bell & Co., where Samuel A. Bell was a director. Bellevue was designed by Thomas Jackson and the building shows similarities of design to earlier houses, such as Huntly House and Milltown House, Banbridge, which were built for linen merchants.

Bellevue was a five bay, two storey house, a platband separating both storeys. The windows of the upper floor had Georgian type glazing, and were recessed sashed and silled. The roof, with its moulded cornice, was hidden behind a parapet, but a dormer was added in 1939 with three windows, to provide additional accommodation. Like Jackson's other houses in the Banbridge area Bellevue had a single storey Ionic portico. It would seem possible that the two bay windows on the ground floor were later additions to the house. Bellevue was burnt down

Bellevue

COURTESY RICHARD DERMOT BELL

in the early 1970s, and two gate lodges, mentioned by Dean, 1994, have also been lost.

In the late nineteenth century Samuel Alexander Bell was the main director of both Thomas Bell & Co. and the Lurgan Weaving Company Ltd. He married Jane Haydock, and had six children, the eldest of whom, Sara, married James N. Richardson of Mount Caulfield, Bessbrook. Bellevue was inherited by Samuel and Jane's fourth son, who was called after his father, and was actively involved in both companies as were his elder brothers. He and his wife Kathleen Richardson had no children, but his sister Emily lived on at Bellevue to the venerable age of ninety-five, accompanied by her nephew Christy Walpole Bell (1910–71), who had changed his name by deed poll from his birth name of Edward Christopher Bell.

Emily Jane Bell (1865–1960) daughter of Samuel A. Bell. Although the yougest in the family she took an active part in the business.

COURTESY RICHARD DERMOT BELL

SOLITUDE
LURGAN

Solitude is situated to the north east of Lurgan, off the Kilmore Road, and not far from the former Bell residence, Bellevue, and the industrial works of Thomas Bell & Co. The 1834 Ordnance Survey map shows an unnamed house at the site with the lane running round the outside of Lord Lurgan's Estate, just in front of it. Solitude is named on the 1859 Ordnance Survey map and is shown as having an extensive garden and orchard at the rear where eventually there was a walled garden.

The original house was a two storey, three bay building with a slated roof, and sashed and silled windows. Solitude is recorded as being occupied in 1865 by William Bell (1833–79), youngest brother of Samuel Alexander Bell, but eventually

Solitude
COURTESY MRS ALLISON BELL

Solitude, 1976
© CROWN COPYRIGHT HMSO

he retired to live at The Croft, Holywood. Some years later Frederick W. Bell (1857–1929), eldest son of Samuel A. Bell, is stated by Bill Jackson, 2005, to have added a wing on the left of the house *c.* 1906. However, shortly after this, he retired from the business and went to live in Rosebank, Donaghadee. At this point Edwin George Bell (1862–1937) and his wife, the former Hilda Walpole, moved into Solitude, adding a matching wing to the right of the house. In 1940 their son George Philip Bell (1908–82) married M. Allison Kennedy and they lived at Solitude until the 1980s. This branch of the Bell family have left Lurgan and the house is now surrounded by an estate of substantial modern houses.

Edwin George Bell in his 2-cylinder Darracq
COURTESY RICHARD DERMOT BELL

DERRY LODGE
LURGAN

Derry Lodge is situated in its own considerable grounds to the north west of Lurgan, off Lough Road and adjacent to the Lord Lurgan Memorial Park. The Ulster Architectural Heritage Society volume on Craigavon, 1971, describes Derry Lodge as,

> Handsome single storey dwelling on outskirts of town, apparently c. 1820, set back from road behind a fine row of lime trees.

However, Brett, 1999, states that the house appears neither in the Valuation Book nor in the Ordnance Survey map or memoir of 1836. The title deeds show that Joseph Wilson, who was a linen merchant, took a 2,000 year building lease in 1852 from Lord Lurgan. Derry Lodge is a pleasant single storey house, the walls being roughcast stucco, with coupled pilasters at each corner. The windows are long reaching almost to the ground and there is a complex graduated slate roof.

There is the possibility that the architect of Derry Lodge was Thomas Jackson, since he was in mid-career at this date and the interior detailing of the house is of the highest quality. Again Brett, 1999, states,

Derry Lodge
© *CROWN COPYRIGHT HMSO*

The rooms, the doors, the windows and the shutters are all splendidly tall; the central roof-lit corridor has massive full entablatures around each side doorcase, and jewel like coloured glass in the central doorways at either end. Drawing room, dining room and breakfast room are handsomely proportioned and richly detailed.

Joseph Wilson died in 1868, and his wife Margaret with their three children possibly lived on in Derry Lodge for a period. However, by 1888 Bassett records it as the residence of Mr H.G. MacGeagh, the Managing Director of the Lurgan Weaving Co., Ltd., which had been set up in 1881. After the death of Joseph Wilson's widow in 1911, Derry Lodge was bought by William Waite, who lived there for a considerable period until 1952, when it was again sold. The house has recently undergone extensive restoration.

Derry Lodge interior
JFR

Derry Lodge
© CROWN COPYRIGHT HMSO

THE JOHNSTON FAMILY
OF LURGAN

James Johnston and Joseph Allen formed a partnership in 1868, Johnston, Allen & Co., for the manufacture of linen and cambric handkerchiefs by hand loom. They began in a terrace house in William Street, Lurgan, supplying yarn to about five hundred cottage weavers. The business obviously flourished since, ten years later, the number of weavers had increased to one thousand, the cloth they wove all being sold in the unbleached state. The increase in business made it necessary to acquire larger premises in William Street and this included accommodation for a stitching factory and finishing room, where eventually three hundred inside workers were employed in hemming and making up linen handkerchiefs. Early in 1888 the firm decided to erect a power loom factory, with capacity initially for five hundred looms, on a three acre site in Victoria

James Johnston, one of the founders of Johnston, Allen and Co., in 1896, with three of his sons (from left) Jim, Arthur and Joe.

COURTESY JOHNSTON FAMILY

Hand bill reproduced from George Bassett, *County Down, 100 Years Ago*

Street, Lurgan, and on the hundredth anniversary in 1968, this site remained the head offices of the company.

The original partnership came to an end in 1890 with the death of Joseph Allen, when his son William James took over, but he left in 1905 to set up his own business. Two of the sons of James Johnston, John and Thomas, were admitted to partnership in 1900, and the firm continued to grow rapidly, trading now in finished linen handkerchiefs with the USA and most European countries. James Johnston died in 1915 and in the year following his death the firm became a limited company. His eldest son, John, whilst remaining a senior partner in the business, became MP for North Armagh and was eventually knighted. During both World Wars the company was involved in making aeroplane linen and other materials for war purposes. In the period between the wars the company acquired an interest in the Milltown Bleaching Co., Ltd., and new markets were gained in China and South America. Later an interest in the Brookfield Spinning Co., Ltd., was purchased and a subsidiary, Gallagher & Johnston Allen Ltd., was bought to handle sales and distribution in Great Britain, through offices in London and a warehouse in Macclesfield.

Over the years the sons and grandsons of James Johnston joined the company and specialised in the management of different aspects of the business. Post-war years saw sweeping changes in the Northern Ireland textile industry, and while Johnston, Allen & Co., Ltd., did diversify, fine handkerchiefs were always a main line. The end of the company came when Marks & Spencer, who had annually placed £750,000 business with them, decided they were not going to run handkerchiefs any more. Johnston, Allen & Co., Ltd., ceased trading in 1981–82.

In the early days Johnston, Allen & Co. had links to two other companies involved with the linen industry. The original James Johnston had a large family and one of his daughters, Margaret, married W.F.B. Baird, a mathematics teacher from Campbell College, Belfast. James Johnston was a very generous man, and he set his son-in-law up in the linen business in Union Street, Lurgan, with the workers in this factory coming from Johnston Allen. The Johnston family retained an interest in the company, which became very successful in weaving very fine linen for handkerchiefs. W.F.B. Baird had two sons James and William, who were equally successful in running the business, and they have been followed by his two grandsons, Hugh and James, who have opened up the business in different directions commensurate with late twentieth and early twenty first century industrial requirements.

The second company link was with James Clendinning, Lurgan, which was first established in 1850 by James Clendinning. Bassett, 1888, lists them as manufacturers, bleachers and printers of linen, cambric, hemstitched and embroidered handkerchiefs. Arthur Johnston, youngest son of James Johnston, was a friend of James Clendinning and put money into the business in 1920, eventually buying the firm and running it. In those days the company specialised in block printing in their old Market Street premises in Lurgan, with the bulk of their production in printed Irish Linen handkerchiefs for the American market.

However, the company made steady growth, and after the Second World War combined with Moygashel of Dungannon to set up a new screen printing company in Lake Street, Lurgan. By 1970 James H. Clendinning & Co., Ltd., were the largest commission textile screen printers in the United Kingdom due to the drive of Arthur Johnston. He died in 1967, aged seventy-two, and his son Joseph Allen Johnston succeeded him as owner and Managing Director of Clendinnings. A new subsidiary company, Arthur Johnston & Co., Ltd., was opened in Portadown in September 1970, for the bonding and laminating of fabrics. While originally Clendinnings dealt with eighty per cent linen fabric, that figure decreased in the late twentieth century to no more than five per cent with many other fabrics being printed and bonded. In common with many other textile related companies, James H. Clendinning & Co., Ltd., closed in the early years of the twenty first century.

The final Board of Directors of Johnston Allen, 1989

Standing from left: David Johnston, Michael Johnston, Prof David Hadden

Sitting from left: J.J. Johnston, Joe A. Johnston (chairman), George Johnston (d. 2006)

COURTESY JOE A. JOHNSTON

Family group of Johnstons and Bairds outside Fallowfield
COURTESY JOHNSTON FAMILY

FALLOWFIELD
LURGAN

Sir John Johnston (1874–1952)
COURTESY JOHNSTON FAMILY

Fallowfield is situated to the north west of Lurgan on the Lough Road, and is now the property of the Southern Education and Library Board being known as the Silverwood Centre. This is a house designed in the Arts and Crafts style by architect James A. Hanna, 1910, and built by James Johnston of Johnston Allen for his eldest son John. Fallowfield is of two storeys with attic, roughcast on the exterior, with a steep red tiled roof, having deep eaves and small irregular windows. Considerable changes have been made to the house since it was acquired for institutional use.

Fallowfield was the home of John Johnston, who was the eldest son of James Johnston, one of the founders of Johnston, Allen & Co. He was admitted to partnership in 1900 with his brother Thomas, and some years later he and his brother alternated as Chairmen of Johnston, Allen & Co. Sir John Johnston, DL, (1874–1952) was knighted in 1945, after a number of years serving as MP for North Armagh. Sir John served on Armagh County Council, and as a member of Armagh Education Committee, he also was High Sheriff of the county in 1919 and later a Deputy Lieutenant. Sir John Johnston was a very prominent figure in the linen trade and at various

points in time was Chairman of Johnston, Allen & Co., Ltd., Lurgan, Chairman of W.F.B. Baird & Co., Ltd., Lurgan, a director of Milltown Bleaching Co., Donacloney, and Brookfield Spinning Co., Belfast.

After his retirement Sir John Johnston went to live in a substantial dwelling, Stone House, which he had built at Portavoe, Donaghadee, and his eldest son James E. Johnston, DL, succeeded him in Fallowfield.

Fallowfield from rear (top); front entrance (above)
© *CROWN COPYRIGHT HMSO*

Fallowfield entrance
JFR

The Demesne
JFR

THE DEMESNE
LURGAN

This house is situated in its own wooded grounds of twenty seven acres, adjoining Lurgan Golf Course, to the north east of Lurgan, and off the Antrim Road. On the Ordnance Survey map of 1935 it is called Demesne House, but is presently known as The Demesne. An Arts and Crafts style building in red brick, the house was possibly designed by the Dromore architect, Henry Hobart, who was greatly favoured by the linen merchants of the late nineteenth and early twentieth century. Demesne House was built in 1910 for Thomas B. Johnston, a partner in Johnston Allen, who felt that he required a large residence, since accommodation was required for visiting trade representatives, and no hotel was available in Lurgan. The house is essentially three bay, two storey with attic, and having a very large castellated front porch, with windows on either side of the recessed front door. Above the front entrance the roof is gabled and over all the building has deep eaves.

Thomas B. Johnston married Arabella Carter of Derryall, and their

Thomas B. Johnston
COURTESY JOHNSTON FAMILY

family included four boys who all entered the Johnston Allen business but also served in the Second World War. Their four sons were Thomas Carter b.1913, Joseph Julian James b.1915, Acheson who was killed in the Second World War, and John. Thomas B. Johnston was a director of Johnston, Allen & Co., Ltd., and of W.F.B. Baird & Co., Ltd., spending his whole working life in the linen business. He was succeeded in The Demesne by his son, T. Carter Johnston, who had entered the family company as a young man and initially spent time in Germany and also in China, learning the finer arts of embroidery. After serving in the Second World War, he returned to the family business, rising to be a director of both Johnston, Allen & Co., Ltd., and W.F.B. Baird & Co., Ltd. Such was Carter Johnston's interest in the textile industry that he continued working as a linen merchant with his brother Joe for many years after the family business ceased.

T. Carter Johnston, whilst very much involved in the business, also became High Sheriff of County Armagh, and continued to live at The Demesne until his death in October, 2005.

Thomas B. Johnston with his wife Arabella
COURTESY JOHNSTON FAMILY

Annadale
JFR

ANNADALE
LURGAN

Arthur Johnston (1895–1967)
COURTESY JOE A. JOHNSTON

Annadale is one of a pair of Victorian semi detached houses situated at 144 Lough Road, Lurgan, not far from Sir John Johnston's house Fallowfield. This house is in red brick and is five bay, two storey with dormer windows, and slated roof, built *c.* 1901 by the Johnston family on land which they had previously purchased. There is a single storey bay on the entrance front and beyond it is a very substantial flat roofed two storey extension, which was added by Arthur Johnston, possibly in the 1920s. The original sashed windows seen in the other semi detached house have been changed to windows with glazing bars. A single storey porch with slated roof has been added to the original house and shelters the front door.

Annadale was firstly the home of Thomas B. Johnston and his wife Arabella, in the early years of the twentieth century, prior to the building of Demesne House, Antrim Road, Lurgan in 1910. Annadale later became the home of Arthur Johnston and his wife Beatrice Matchett, who married in 1921, and had a family of one son, Joseph, and two daughters, Margaret and Eleanor. He was

ANNADALE, LURGAN

The Johnston windows, installed in Shankill Parish Church, Lurgan, 1989, with the lower portions depicting the linen industry
JFR

the youngest son of James Johnston and was for many years a director of Johnston, Allen & Co., Ltd. Arthur Johnston developed the skills of textile printing and was responsible for the large expansion of James H. Clendinning & Co., Ltd., a modern textile printing firm in Lake Street, Lurgan. Arthur Johnston died in 1967, aged seventy two, and his son Joseph Allen Johnston succeeded him as owner and Managing Director of Clendinnings. He also became in time the last Chairman of Johnston, Allen & Co., Ltd., having been on the Board for many years.

Annadale was occupied by Arthur Johnston until his death in 1967, however, it later became the home of Joseph A. Johnston, but after his retirement from business he went to live in Comber, and the house was sold.

The front door at Annadale
JFR

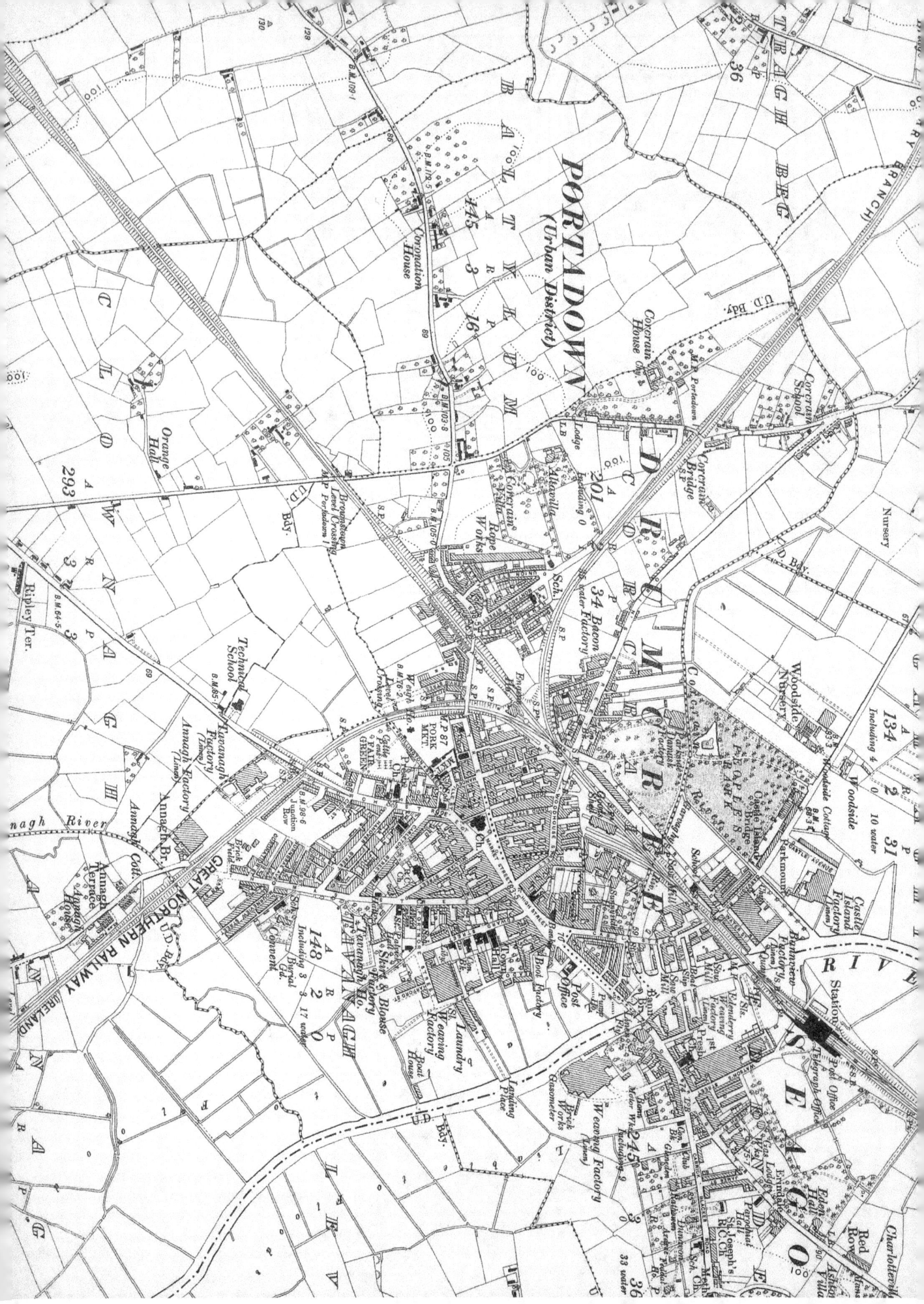

8
PORTADOWN

BANN BRIDGE, PORTADOWN
1861

BANNVIEW HOUSE
PORTADOWN

Bannview House
JFR

Bannview House was situated on the Garvaghy Road, Portadown, and as the mill manager's house, it was adjacent to the works of Achesons, Ltd., linen manufacturers. This was a five bay, two storey brick house, with the front door opening directly on to Garvaghy Road. The roof was slated and had three brick chimney stacks. The sash windows were round headed, silled, and topped by a flat arch in pale coloured brick. Beside the house was a stable for the horse, which was used for the transportation of linen cloth to the Portadown railway station.

Bannview House had a garden of considerable size to the side and rear, containing an orchard, and running down the side of the factory to the River Bann. The house remains unoccupied and boarded up.

In the late nineteenth century J. & J. Acheson & Co., were one of the major linen manufacturers in Portadown, at a plant known as Bannview, which was situated close to the River Bann in Portadown. The first plant on the site was set up by Dawson Tate Jr. in 1875, but Bassett records the works owned by J. & J. Acheson & Co. in 1888. A limited company, Achesons, Ltd., was formed in 1895, the directors being John Acheson, JP, chairman, and James J. Brown, who lived in Corcrain Villa. The company was later bought by the Brown family in the early twentieth century, being managed by James Nicholson Brown, who was also a director, and lived in Bannview House. James Nicholson Brown was a member of the Council of the Linen Industry Research Association, and for a term he was High Sheriff of County Armagh.

The Brown family had a long association with the linen industry and James N. Brown's great-grandfather was a linen merchant in Donaghmore. Achesons, Ltd. was the last linen weaving factory in Portadown to close down, which occurred in 1971.

CORCRAIN HOUSE
PORTADOWN

Corcrain House, demolished in the 1950s
JOHN GIRLING

Thomas Dawson
R.M. HADDEN

Corcrain House was situated to the west of Portadown, off Charles Street, but was demolished in the 1950s, to make way for a housing estate. The house and its grounds, along with a factory and premises, occupied an area of over fifteen acres, which were planted with beech, ash, birch and oak trees. Corcrain House was built *c.* 1840, and was three bay, two storey. The windows were recessed, sashed and silled, with plain entablatures over the first floor windows on the main front. The front door was on the side of the projecting single storey porch, which had Doric columns, and windows on the other two sides. The roof was hidden behind a parapet with only the chimney stacks able to be seen. There was a two storey extension to the left of the house of a lesser height than the main building.

Bassett, 1888, states that linen manufacturing by hand loom was commenced at the site in 1840 by Mr Joseph Druitt, who built stores, offices, thirty workers' houses and the porter's lodge. Mr Druitt was the lessee of Corcrain House which had already been built. Mr Thomas Dawson bought the whole site in 1872, erecting a hemstitching factory, and also adding steam machinery. He

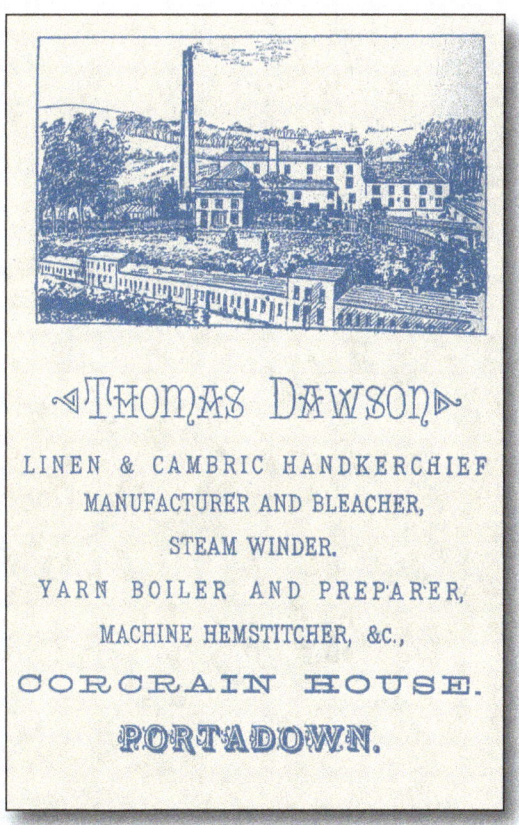

employed about four hundred hand loom weavers in the manufacture of linen and cambric handkerchiefs, with a further ninety employees associated with hemstitching.

Corcrain House was within the town boundary of Portadown, being bounded on the west by the Corcrain River and on the north by the Great Northern Railway.

Hand bill reproduced from George Bassett, *County Down, 100 Years Ago*

Hannah Robb (1854–1935) the second Mrs Dawson

R.M. HADDEN

Watercolour of Edenderry House, 1925
R.M. HADDEN

EDENDERRY HOUSE
PORTADOWN

Edenderry House was situated close to the River Bann in Portadown, in its own wooded grounds, and adjacent to the Bann Bridge. Hamilton Robb was a linen handkerchief manufacturer and lived in Edenderry House, built in 1865, close to his weaving factory, which was alongside the river and had a landing stage. Edenderry House was a two storey, three bay, brick built house with a hipped roof. The windows, which retained their glazing bars were silled and had a light brick surround. The door, set in a single storey porch, was treated in the same way as the windows.

John Robb lived in the country on a farm at Derrybrughas, about three miles north west of Portadown, and close to the River Bann. Records show that linen was produced there from 1830 in more than a dozen workers' houses on the farm, in all of which there were hand looms. Hamilton Robb, a grandson of John, set up a weaving factory in the 1860s in Portadown on a site bounded by Goban Street and the River Bann, and barges were used to move goods in and out of the works via the river. The business became highly successful, producing cambric cloth and sheeting. Hamilton Robb died in 1889 leaving his business to his sons Harford and Hamilton, Jr., but after the First World War the

Hamilton Robb (1827–89)
R.M. HADDEN

business got into financial difficulties. In 1924 a group of prominent citizens from Portadown bought Edenderry House, with the intention of starting, and carrying on a school to be called Portadown College. This has been very successful and large extensions were built around the original Edenderry House, but in 1962, due to a large increase in the number of pupils, a new building was erected for Portadown College on the Propect House site, Killycomain Road.

Mr William Mullen, who had worked in Hamilton Robb from 1895 for seven years, emigrated to New York where he became a very successful and wealthy businessman. However, in the 1920s William Mullen returned to Portadown to manage Hamilton Robb & Co., Ltd., and he eventually bought the business in 1934, reversing the fortunes of the firm. He became a leading businessman in Portadown, and died at the age of eighty-five in 1963, when the company was sold to Herdmans, Ltd., of Sion Mills, who eventually closed it down in 1968.

Elizabeth Montgomery (1827–77) married Hamilton Robb in 1852
R.M. HADDEN

Hamilton Robb jr. and family
R.M. HADDEN

THE SPENCE AND
BRYSON FAMILIES
OF PORTADOWN

Thomas Henry Spence and John Bell Bryson entered into a business partnership, Spence Bryson & Co., for the production of very fine linen in Portadown in 1884. In 1866 Thomas Spence had been apprenticed to the linen trade in the firm of Hamilton Robb of Portadown, who made linen handkerchiefs by hand looms and also did warp winding for Belfast firms. John Bryson was also apprenticed to the linen trade but somewhat later in 1873, in the firm of Robert Glass, Portadown, who were in the business of making cambric handkerchiefs. In the first years of the partnership in Meadow Lane, Portadown, the business consisted in buying linen yarn to have it woven by hand loom weavers in the townlands near Portadown. Spence Bryson sold linen to the Belfast warehouses such as Richardson Sons & Owden Ltd., York Street Flax Spinning Company, Henry Matier, and Brookfield Spinning and Weaving Company. From 1850 onwards power loom factories were set up in Belfast, and this increased in the 1860s with the demand for linen fuelled by the American Civil War, and the lack of cotton. Indeed, in the 1860s Watson Armstrong was the first Portadown firm to set up a factory with power looms. In 1891 Thomas Spence and John Bryson opened the Clonavon power loom weaving factory in Portadown for the production of cambrics, sheers and handkerchiefs.

Spence Bryson & Co., Ltd., was registered as a company in 1904 and, the first meeting of directors was held on 12th September 1904. An extract from the minutes reads:

> The first meeting of Directors was held this evening at Portmore Street, Portadown, the chair being occupied by Mr T.H. Spence. Directors present included Mr John Bell Bryson, Mr James Bryson, and Mr Samuel Lutton.

With a capital of £60,000 the company flourished and by 1908 it was in a position to sell directly within the United Kingdom and also to large American companies. In 1909 the company bought the linen weaving factory in Markethill, which had been established in 1888 by the late David H. Sinton. As the business continued to expand, premises were acquired in Great Victoria Street, Belfast, and in partnership with Johnston Allen of Lurgan, Spence Bryson purchased the Milltown Bleaching Company in 1924, making them both fully vertically integrated. Sales expanded with the opening of a New York office and further linen companies such as William Cowdy & Sons, Portadown, and Loopbridge Weaving Company were purchased in 1929. The Brookfield

Spinning Company in Belfast was bought from the liquidator in 1933, again in partnership with Johnston Allen and W.F.B. Baird of Lurgan. In response to a take over bid for Edenderry Spinning Company, Belfast, in 1946 by Isaac Wolfson, the directors of Spence Bryson, Johnston Allen and W.F.B. Baird put in a successful counter bid, placing a large Belfast spinning company, Edenderry, in their ownership.

The late 1940s and early 1950s saw the closure of some important South American markets and a gradual slowing down in sales of linen. This led Spence Bryson to diversify into expansion of laundry and dry cleaning companies, and in 1959 the manufacture of Corgi carpets at the Loopbridge factory in east Belfast. Northern Ireland Spinners, Killinchy, was gradually bought out by 1968 to safeguard carpet yarn supplies. A shirt factory was opened in Portadown in 1964, and gradually the linen side of the business decreased with the sale in 1973 of the Edenderry mill to Herdmans, Ltd., of Sion Mills, making the carpet end of the business more important.

Throughout the 1970s and 1980s trade in linen decreased very substantially as well as in the carpet business, and by the 1980s the directors were ageing and none had children interested in pursuing the business. In 1989 the company was sold to Richards, a Scottish company with similar linen and carpet interests.

River Bann & Bridge, Portadown.

GLENEDEN
PORTADOWN

Gleneden
JFR

Gleneden and Rathowen are two semi detached houses on the Carrickblacker Road, Portadown, which were lived in, and possibly built by, Thomas Henry Spence and John Bell Bryson *c.* 1895. Gleneden was the residence of Thomas Spence, who had married Jane Anne Lutton of Breagh, in 1893. The house is two storey with attics, and built of brick but being cement rendered. The rooms at the front have square headed sash windows on each floor surrounded by moulded architraves, and string courses run level with the sills of the windows. The entrance is set diagonally on the side of the house with a recessed doorway, having a decorative surround. Beyond the doorway, on the side of the house is a single storey bay window.

Thomas Spence and his wife lived in Gleneden until the end of the First World War, when he bought an estate near Lucan, County Dublin. At this point in time he was taking a less active role in factory affairs in Portadown. However, after the death of John Bell Bryson in 1923, Thomas Henry Spence came back

Thomas Henry Spence, one of the founders of Spence Bryson c. 1900

into active management of the firm, until he finally retired in 1929. He spent his latter years living in Belfast at 94 Malone Road, and died in 1937 in his mid-eighties.

Gleneden, Portadown, remains occupied at the start of the twenty first century.

Gleneden c. 1960
S.C. LUTTON

RATHOWEN
PORTADOWN

Rathowen
JFR

Rathowen, a substantial semi detached house, situated on the Carrickblacker Road, Portadown, was the mirror image of Gleneden, although it has now been slightly altered on the ground floor. This was the home of John Bell Bryson who had married Mary Halliday of County Armagh in 1892, and they remained in the house until 1910, when Spence Bryson acquired a Belfast warehouse. John Bell Bryson was primarily a manufacturer and merchant of handkerchiefs, and he undertook the management of the Belfast warehouse. The Bryson family therefore left Portadown and eventually took up residence in Deramore Park South, Belfast, off the city's Malone Road. Meanwhile Thomas Henry Spence, who was basically a cloth manufacturer remained living in Gleneden, Portadown. Samuel C. Lutton has recorded that the photograph of Rathowen, taken about 1905, shows a small boy standing on the steps in the garden, and this is George Herbert Bryson.

John Bell Bryson, one of the
founders of Spence Bryson, *c.* 1900

George Herbert Bryson and Thomas Everard Spence, sons of John Bell Bryson and Thomas Henry Spence, respectively, entered the business in the Belfast warehouse in 1919. They eventually became directors of Spence Bryson, and worked together as their fathers had, until they both retired in 1964.

Rathowen *c.* 1905
S.C. LUTTON

THE GREEVES FAMILY
OF PORTADOWN

From left: John Greeves holding Bertha J. Greeves; Gilbertina N. Greeves with Wilfred J. Greeves and Thomas J. Greeves holding Gilbert R.J. Greeves

COURTESY GREEVES FAMILY

The Portadown Weaving Company was started in December 1894 by Thomas Jackson Greeves and Owden Valentine Greeves, who were sons of John Greeves, Lismachan, Belfast. John and Thomas Malcolmson Greeves ran a large spinning mill in Belfast, known as J. & T.M. Greeves Ltd., but it was quite independent of the weaving business. The Portadown Weaving Company's Annagh Factory was situated at the lower end of Thomas Street in Portadown and close to the Annagh River, which flowed from the western side of Portadown into the River Bann on the east. The factory, which was built in brick, was also adjacent to the Great Northern Railway, providing ready access for shipment of goods to Belfast.

Owden and Jackson Greeves were later joined in the business by their nephew, William Edward Greeves, who was a son of Joseph Malcomson Greeves of Bernagh, Belfast, and a director of J. & T.M. Greeves. William E. Greeves ran the Portadown factory while Owden and Jackson were in the business end of sales. Portadown and Lurgan linen manufacturing was in the fine end of the trade, making fine cambric handkerchiefs and often having hemstitching works situated next to the weaving factories. Portadown Weaving Company bought their very fine yarn principally from J. & T.M. Greeves, Belfast, and made cambrics for the handkerchief trade in the home market.

THE GREEVES FAMILY OF PORTADOWN

In time the sons of Jackson Greeves, Gilbert and David, along with Owden's son, Edmund, joined Portadown Weaving Company eventually becoming directors. Later, in 1948, George Greeves, a son of William E. Greeves joined the company, and in 1953 became Technical Director as he held a degree in mechanical engineering. Edmund was the Sales Director and he gave constant warnings during the 1950s of the significant decrease in trade for linen handkerchiefs. The Portadown Weaving Co., Ltd., eventually closed in 1959 and the buildings were demolished, although the weaving shed remains used for a cattle market.

The Greeves of Portadown were related to the Greers, who, in the seventeenth century, settled at Redford near Grange, Dungannon, County Tyrone, and continued to live in that area in the eighteenth and nineteenth centuries.

SOME MEMBERS OF THE GREEVES FAMILY OF PORTADOWN

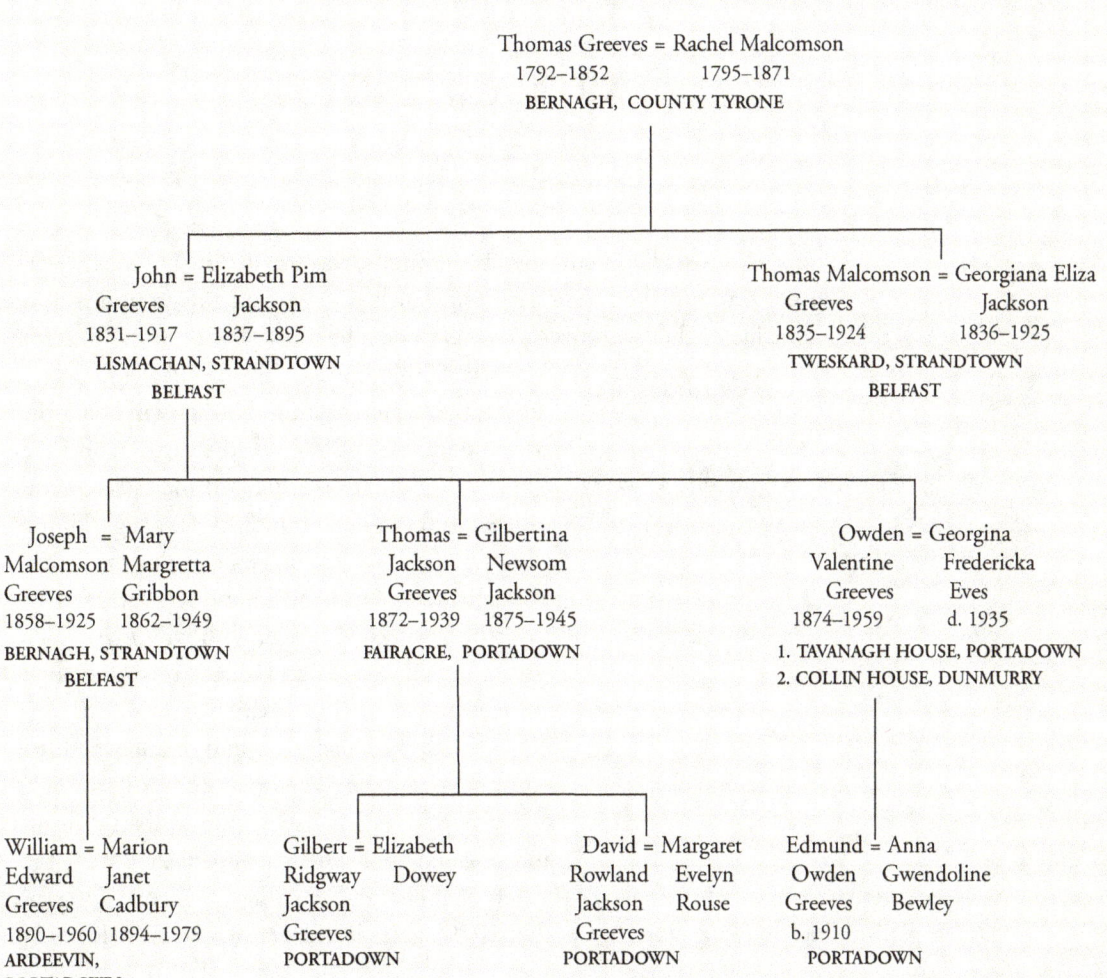

TAVANAGH HOUSE
PORTADOWN

Tavanagh House
JIM LYTTLE

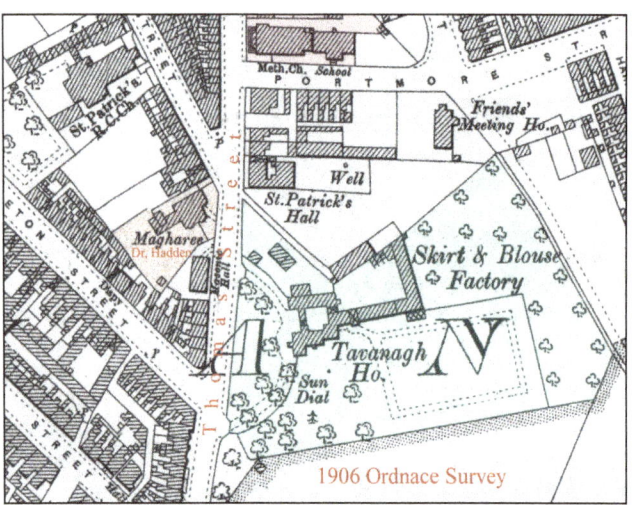

Map showing layout of Tavanagh
JIM LYTTLE

Tavanagh House, set in considerable grounds, was situated in Thomas Street, Portadown, but the house has been knocked down and the ground is now the present site of the swimming pool car park. The house was built in 1828 for Thomas Shillington, (1767–1830), who was a substantial businessman in Portadown, being the largest purchaser of grain in the district, and the owner of Shillington's Quay on the River Bann. Indeed, at the time of building, Tavanagh House was one of the largest houses close to the centre of Portadown. Tavanagh House was a three bay, two storey stuccoed house, with windows which were recessed, sashed and silled, retaining their glazing bars. The roof, which was slated, was hipped with moulded eaves and cornice, and the house was quoined. The door was set in a single storey porch, which had windows to the front, and a slated roof which stopped level with the string course. However, the Ulster Architectural Heritage Society listing of Buildings in Craigavon, November 1970, states in respect of Tavanagh House:

TAVANAGH HOUSE, PORTADOWN

Probably part 18th century, with many later additions, including an excellent stucco porch reflecting Egyptian tastes of the late regency c. 1820. Now Borough Surveyor's offices. Badly needs white-washing and tidying; could make a charming nucleus of redevelopment. Nice garden, trees, unsuitable wall.

Thomas Shillington was followed in Tavanagh House by his son, Thomas Averell Shillington, (1800–74), and eventually by his grandson, Thomas Primus Shillington, (1831–89), who had married Mary Jane Graham. After her husband's death, she lived on in the house, dying in 1915. The Shillington family were extremely important to the growth of trade in Portadown and they were also very devout Methodists, contributing also, very substantially, to the growth of Methodism in the town.

Owden Valentine Greeves, owner, with his brother Jackson, of the Portadown Weaving Co., Ltd., lived for a time in Rathowen, Carrickblacker Road, Portadown, a house which had previously been owned by John B. Bryson. In 1916 he, and his wife and family, moved to Tavanagh House, which he rented, after the death of Mrs Shillington, and remained there until 1929. Owden Greeves, who became chairman of the company, then bought Collin House, Dunmurry, which was closer to Belfast. Owden Valentine Greeves married Georgina Fredericka Eves in 1904, and they had a family of one son and three daughters. Edmund Owden Greeves, their son, eventually joined the business and, in time, became a director of the Portadown Weaving Company. Mrs Joan Fothergill, a daughter of the late Owden Greeves, has written about their time in Portadown,

Centre front row, Owden and Nina Greeves, at Collin House, Dunmurry
COURTESY GREEVES FAMILY

> My family lived at Rathowen before Tavanagh House and before I was born. My father rented Tavanagh from the Shillingtons and the only other "Tavanagh baby" was a Miss Shillington, who wished to end her days in the house, wherefore my family had to move! It was a lovely family house and garden and hag yard with extensive farm buildings. The latter were pulled down to make way for modern houses just before we left.

The Greeves left Tavanagh House in 1929 and Miss Shillington occupied the house until her death.

FAIRACRE
PORTADOWN

Fairacre Cottage, Seagoe, showing the River Bann in the distance

Fairacre is situated on the Seagoe Road to the north of Portadown. The house was built in 1906 by Thomas Jackson Greeves on one and a half acres of land which he had leased from the Duke of Manchester in 1903. Fairacre is essentially a two storey house with a smaller third storey and a steep roof which is gabled. The outside is stuccoed and string courses run level with the tops of the ground and first floor windows. The recessed front door is sheltered by a small single storey porch, and the windows are sashed and silled. Fairacre faces north but on the southern garden side of the house there are two conservatories, one on either side of a doorway leading to the garden.

Fairacre from the garden
JFR

T. Jackson Greeves was one of the founders of the Portadown Weaving Company and lived with his wife Gilbertina Newsom Greeves, and their family, at Fairacre until his death in

Fairacre from the front
JFR

1939. Their sons Gilbert R.J. Greeves, and David R.J. Greeves, both became directors of the Portadown Weaving Co. Mrs G.N. Greeves lived on at Fairacre until her death in 1945, when the house was sold.

Jackson Greeves at Fairacre, 1909

Ardeevin
JIM LYTTLE

ARDEEVIN
PORTADOWN

The house formerly known as Ardeevin, and now 'Skerry Hill', is situated at the junction of the Killycomain Road and the Gilford Road, leaving Portadown. This is a fine Victorian villa, which was probably designed by the Dromore architect, Henry Hobart, and built *c.* 1890. Ardeevin is a two plus attic storey house, built in red brick, now mellowed by age. The entrance is sheltered by a loggia style porch, which partially continues along the side of the house, and is surmounted by a tiled roof. The windows would appear to have originally been recessed, sashed and silled, but have now been replaced. A string course topped with dentils runs above the ground floor windows while another, dentilled underneath, runs level with, and incorporates the sills of the first storey windows. There are two bays on the front of the house which rise to two gables, having an attic window in each. Attractive gardens surround Ardeevin. David Graham Shillington and his wife Louisa Collen occupied Ardeevin after their

ARDEEVIN, PORTADOWN

marriage in 1895, and they continued to live there until 1924 when he became an MP in the Northern Ireland Parliament at Stormont and needed to live in Belfast.

Ardeevin then became the home of William Edward Greeves (1890–1960) and his wife Marion Janet Cadbury (1894–1979), a daughter of George Cadbury, who founded Bourneville Village, in England. They met in France in the First World War, she was a nurse and he was an ambulance driver, and she moved to Ulster after her marriage. William E. Greeves was younger than his cousins Owden V. Greeves and T. Jackson Greeves, whom he joined in the Portadown Weaving Company post-First World War, eventually becoming the Managing Director. W.E. Greeves and his wife had five children, three sons and two daughters, one of their daughters, Rosemary, becoming connected to another linen family, when she married Thomas A. Dickson, of Dicksons & Co. (Dungannon), Ltd. Their second son, George Malcomson Greeves, after completing a degree in Mechanical Engineering in Queen's University, Belfast, joined the company in 1948, and became Technical Director in 1953. However, with the decrease in demand for fine handkerchiefs, the Portadown Weaving Company closed down in 1959, and W.E. Greeves, DL, died in September 1960, aged seventy.

The Greeves built another house attached to the rear of the original building about 1960, and transferred the name Ardeevin to it, while the original house was re-named 'Skerry Hill' by the then owner Senator Greeves. After considerable service in the community particularly with Quakers, Marion J. Greeves was elected to the Northern Ireland Senate and was involved with a great deal of social work, being awarded an MBE in 1947. She was appointed Ulster Chief Commissioner of Girl Guides in 1951, and was also a member of Armagh County Council.

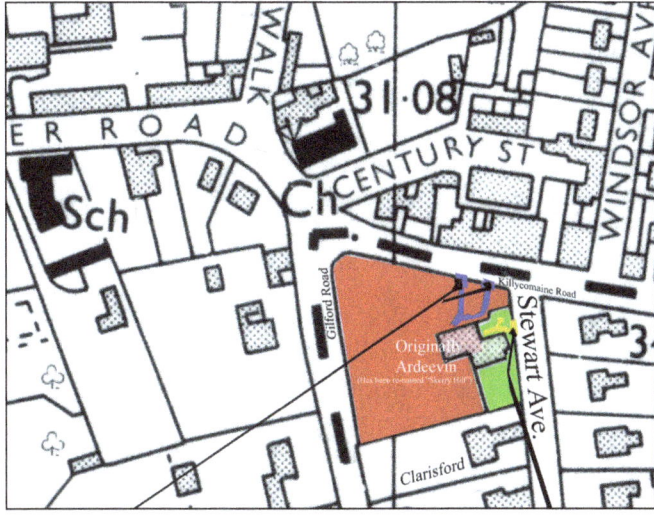

Back gates enter to Skerry Hill originally named Ardeevin. On moving to the new annex Senator Greeves brought the name Ardeevin with her.

JIM LYTTLE

ALTAVILLA
PORTADOWN

Altavilla
JIM LYTTLE

Altavilla was situated in Charles Street, Portadown and recorded by Griffith's Valuation as the seat, in 1864, of Averell Shillington. There is little now left of the original building, which is thought to have been erected in the 1830s, but had later additions, and is shown on the 1906 Ordnance Survey map to have been a house of considerable size. A new building known as Nazareth House, St Francis's Nursing Home, is joined to a small part of the original building, and now occupies the site. Altavilla had grounds of six acres and a gate lodge but this has been demolished.

Averell Shillington (1802–97) was the second son of Thomas Shillington (1767–1830) and Sarah Averell of Tavanagh House, Portadown. Averell Shillington appears to have originally been a linen merchant, selling linen produced by hand weavers in their homes. At that time Portadown was a centre for fine linen weaving, and as late as the 1860s there were some 4,000 hand loom weavers working in and around the town. However, Smith's *Linen Trade Handbook and Directory*, 1876, lists Castleisland Linen Co., power loom manufacturers and merchants, Portadown and Linen Hall, Belfast. Castleisland Linen Company, owned by Averell Shillington, was situated on the west side of the River Bann, and the Valuation Book of 1871 contains a statement that 'Castleisland Linen Co. complain that their weaving factory is overvalued 8 June 1870'. Therefore the Company was one of the very early power loom manufacturers of linen in Portadown. The fact that Castleisland have a listing as merchants in 1876 and are in the Linen Hall, Belfast, suggests the earlier history of merchanting before the power loom manufacture of linen. The Company is also mentioned in Bassett in 1888.

Averell Shillington was a very devout Methodist and was the Superintendent of the Methodist Sunday School in Portadown for 58 years from 1832 to 1890. He died aged 95 years in 1897.

Averell Shillington's son Thomas, who in time became The Rt. Hon. Thomas Shillington, PC (1835–1925), and inherited Altavilla, went on to run the Castleisland Linen Company, which was incorporated in 1908 with a share capital of £40,000. In turn his son, Thomas Averell Shillington ran the company but it was eventually liquidated in 1929. The premises were bought by Sam Lutton and the Brysons, but were subsequently sold to Raceview, and then to the Ulster Carpet Company who still occupy the site. Thomas Averell Shillington continued to live in Altavilla until his death in 1951, when he left instructions to his executors to sell the house.

Averill Shillington
JIM LYTTLE

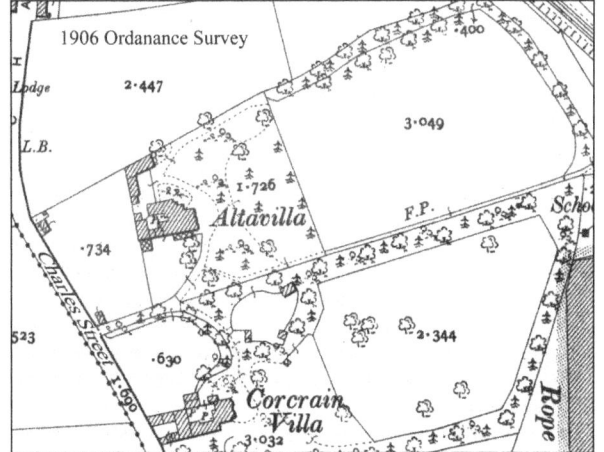

Map showing layout of Altavilla
JIM LYTTLE

9
TANDRAGEE AND ARMAGH

SHAW'S LAKE, GLENANNE

Photograph J.F. Rankin

MULLAVILLA HOUSE
TANDRAGEE

Mullavilla House was situated in County Armagh near to Mullavilly village on the road from Tandragee to Portadown. In 1837 the *Ordnance Survey Memoirs* record that Mr James Atkinson held the greater part of Mullavilly townland from the proprietor Count De Salis, and that Mullavilla House was occupied by J. Atkinson. William John Turtle bought Mullavilly lands and premises about 1848 from the Rev. David Babington for the sum of £600, but the farm was in a much neglected condition, being overgrown with trees and undrained. The house was partially thatched prior to rebuilding in 1866 when it was significantly enlarged. Mullavilla House was a five bay, two storey dwelling, which was quoined and had considerable outbuildings at the rear. The windows were sashed and silled, the roof was slated, and there was a conservatory on the left hand side of the house, which was added about 1893. Mullavilla House was sold by the Turtle family in 1944 and has since been demolished.

William John Turtle (1819–98) started a linen hand loom weaving business at Mullavilla in the 1850s, supplying yarn to domestic weavers from a yard at the house, and giving employment to between 1,200 and 1,400 hand loom weavers. In the early 1860s a factory to contain power looms was built in the grounds at Mullavilla, and James Irwin Annett of Newry was engaged as manager. At the same time a row of houses, called 'Turtle Row', was built to house some of the factory workers.

William John Turtle married Frances Haydock (1824–1908), and of their nine children, two sons, James Turtle (1856–1936) and William Haydock Turtle (1857–1936) inherited the family linen business. They later owned a warehouse and office in Belfast; James Turtle was in charge of the weaving factory at Mullavilla, while William Haydock Turtle was in charge of the linen sales. Two younger sons of William John Turtle, Henry Francis Turtle (1864–1935) and Herbert Samuel Turtle (1868–1917) 'served their time' as apprentices in the linen business, both in Dublin and in York Street Flax Spinning Co., in Belfast, and then they emigrated to America in the 1880s, setting up their own linen importing company, Turtle Brothers, Inc., in New York City. This consisted of a warehouse and finishing works, and some 'loom state' linen from Mullavilla

Mullavilla House *c.* 1896

BELFAST, 10 BRUNSWICK STREET
TELEPHONE: BELFAST 21356

CABLE ADDRESS: CRASH TANDRAGEE
TELEPHONE: TANDRAGEE 222

WILLIAM JOHN TURTLE
Linen Manufacturer

TANDRAGEE
CO. ARMAGH
NORTHERN IRELAND

The Turtle family *c.* 1895

Adults from left to right: Wm J. Turtle, his wife Frances H. Turtle, Jos. F. Turtle and Arabella Webb

COURTESY TURTLE FAMILY

was sent to the USA in bale form for dyeing and finishing as dress linen. Manufacturing at Mullavilla decreased during the 1929 Depression, and eventually the factory and Mullavilla House were sold in 1944, with the Irish branch of the firm being wound up by W. Herbert Turtle and Norman F. Turtle, sons of William Haydock Turtle. Norman F. Turtle lived at Mullavilla from 1939 to 1944. They then emigrated to New York, where the American office and warehouse were based at White Street, Lower Manhattan. The New York City business, Turtle Brothers, Inc., was carried on by W. Herbert Turtle and Norman F. Turtle until their retirement.

MANOR HOUSE
MILFORD

Milford House, Armagh
PRONI

Milford village, beside the River Callan, lies two miles south west of Armagh city on the main road to Middletown, and Milford House, more recently known as the Manor House, was situated on the outskirts of the village. The name Milford House appears on the Ordnance Survey map of 1835, and again in 1864, but in 1936 the name Manor House appears when the building became a girls boarding school. Mr William McCrum (1785–1879) built a mill at Milford for the dry spinning of flax in 1808, using water power, and it is claimed that the mill was the first in Ulster to use the dry spinning process for flax. As the spinning mill prospered William McCrum built houses for his workers and the village of Milford became established. The Ordnance Survey map of 1835 shows a flax mill beside his home, marked 'Milford House', and on the other side of the road a spinning mill and a flour mill are shown. William McCrum was eventually joined in the business by his son Robert Garmany McCrum (1829–1915), who had served an apprenticeship in the manufacture of linen in Lurgan. Bassett, 1888, records that in 1850 Robert Garmany McCrum, JP, changed the spinning mill into a factory for the weaving of

damasks, and latterly made substantial structural additions to the factory, which by 1888 employed about 450 people.

Milford House, Armagh
PRONI

In 1880 Robert Garmany McCrum employed the architects Young and Mackenzie of Belfast to renovate his existing home, Milford House, but known locally as 'the Cottage', and produce a mansion style structure. Joe McManus in his village history of Milford, 2002, has recorded a considerable description of the building:

> The house was a very early experimentation of mass concrete, and in fact does not contain a single brick. It is perhaps the only known building constructed with this type of material in Ireland. However, it seems that Robert Garmany McCrum's unusual choice of design may have been influenced by the work of Prince Albert (1819–61) at Osborne House. Osborne House, home of Queen Victoria, was the earliest experimentation by her husband, the Prince Consort, in the use of concrete on a large scale in construction.

Indeed the overall impression of the house was of great opulence with a total of thirty-six rooms, excluding attic bedrooms and basement quarters. The original house was extended to the rear and a south wing was added, containing the ballroom, which had a magnificent ceiling decorated by Rudolph Steiner in the manner of the Italian School of Art. A large conservatory, which was used to grow peaches, was added on the west side of the house.

William McCrum
PRONI D 2886/A/2/14/50 ALLISON COLLECTION

McManus, 2002, has given a detailed description of the interior commencing at the front door where he states there was a small entrance hall with, on the right, the telephone room; apparently Milford House was one of the first private residences in the area to have a telephone. McManus, 2002, continues:

> On the left double mahogany framed doors with glass panels led to a larger hallway, with plaster panelling on the upper walls and oak on the lower. A door to the rear gave access to the front staircase … A door to the right in the larger entrance hall led to the drawing room, its ceiling adorned with flower-shaped plasterwork. There were two doors on the left leading to the study and library. The study had a private telephone line to the factory, which Robert G. McCrum used when his health began deteriorating. A door connected the library and study. The next room was the ballroom – the largest. A corridor led to the billiard room with its stained glass window, the only window in this room. The dining room was at the back of the house. Its highly polished panelling was reminiscent of the French Second Empire style. Beside it were the Art Nouveau staircases to the basement and upper floor … An overall feature of the house was its connecting doors, so as one could pass from one room to the next without having to use the corridors. Upstairs there were seven bedrooms, complete with dressing rooms. Each bedroom had a fireplace and marble sink with brass taps in the form of lion's heads.

A new long avenue was created which led to the wide main street of Milford, this being noted for being one of the first in Ireland to be lit electrically. The entrance is described by Dean, 1994,

> The remarkably durable geometric pattern teak concave fence sweeps are flanked by High Victorian limestone pillars virtually identical to those at Clanwilliam, Co. Down differing only in being surmounted by ornamental metal fan-shaped electric light holders. The rugged square pillars rise from smooth bases, the body with engaged and banded polished colonettes at each corner.

Dean, 1994, also describes the gate lodge which was built at the new entrance:

> In contrasting hard red raw brick is the single storey T plan lodge, its three steeply pitched gables clad in diamond terracotta tile hanging and decorated with simple bargeboards with collar tie.

Gate lodge
JFR

According to McManus, 2002, Mr William Frazer Haldane was employed in 1880 to landscape the estate, and created formal gardens, which contained a two tier fountain, to the south side of the house.

Robert Garmany McCrum died in 1915 and the estate passed to his only son William. Unfortunately, by 1931, William McCrum had amassed considerable

Manor House 2007
JFR

debts, due to a decline in the linen industry, and the Wall Street Crash of 1929. The Northern Bank took over Milford House, which, in 1936, was leased and eventually bought by the 'Manor House School', a private boarding school for girls. This closed in 1966 when the property was bought by the Northern Ireland Hospital Authority for use as a special care home, but this has now closed, and the house is unoccupied.

The linen company at Milford was originally known as Messrs Robert McCrum & Co., but in 1886 the name of the business was changed to McCrum Watson & Mercer, with Mr Wesley Watson and Mr William Mercer becoming partners. Alongside the manufacture of linen damask, napkins, towels and sheetings were also woven at Milford. McCrum Watson & Mercer became a limited liability company in 1894 with members of the management becoming shareholders. The company owned a Belfast warehouse and also a linen factory in Armagh. Unfortunately, R.G. McCrum's only son William was not interested in the business and by the 1930s the factory was owned by the Northern Bank, but was kept going by the managers, Thomas Montgomery, Thomas Coote and Thomas Bennett. However, in 1949 the factory was sold to Captain Noel S. Smith, who already owned a factory, John Compton Ltd., at Glenanne. The name was changed to Callan Valley Mills Ltd., but the factory eventually shut in the early 1980s.

UMGOLA HOUSE
Armagh

Umgola House
JFR

Umgola House is situated about a mile from the centre of Armagh on the Monaghan Road and in the Callan valley. This is a very large red and yellow brick Victorian house, which was built about 1890 for John Compton, JP, who had bought the Umgola Weaving Factory in 1882 from the founder Thomas Wynne. Bassett, 1888, states:

> Umgola takes a front rank with the many charming places in the immediate vicinity of Armagh. Mr Compton's factory and premises occupy between nine and ten acres of the Callan valley.

According to Brett, 1999, the house is very elaborate as well as very large, with fine fretwork like bargeboards to its many gables. Umgola House had a substantial extension added in 1905, to the plans of J.J. Phillips, architect of Belfast, along with an iron framed conservatory. The house has an elegant interior with magnificent marble fireplaces and decorative plasterwork in the main ground floor reception rooms. There are two staircases in the house, the main staircase in the front hall, and a servants' staircase to the rear, but there is also a lift, which was installed for a later owner, Captain Noel S. Smith, when he was in a wheel chair.

UMGOLA HOUSE, ARMAGH

Umgola House is surrounded by mature trees and has a well maintained garden, containing a formal sunken garden and a rectangular pond. There is a glasshouse with vines and peaches.

Mr John Compton was succeeded in the house by his son, George, and after his death it passed to his married daughter, Jane Mary and her husband Captain Noel Smith. Following the death of his wife, Captain Noel Smith continued to live at Umgola House until his death in 1967. His nephew Alan Knighton Smith inherited the house but subsequently sold the property, when it changed hands several times before the present owners acquired it in 1979.

John Compton progressively improved the Umgola Weaving Factory during the late 1880s, more than doubling its original capacity, and weaving linens, drills and damasks using power looms. According to Bassett, 1888, the manufactured goods were sold in Belfast, Manchester, London and Northampton. Some workers' houses were built but the majority of the employees lived in Armagh and the neighbourhood. Captain Noel Smith, who had married a granddaughter of John Compton, inherited his weaving factory but this burned down in 1934 and the company moved to a factory at Glenanne. Captain Smith also bought the old McCrum Watson and Mercer factory at Milford, renaming it Callan Valley Mills. Comptons originally wove linen damask tablecloths at Umgola but, after the fire, the firm began to move into the upholstery, furnishing and ticking business, and over the years it increasingly concentrated on tickings until they accounted for ninety per cent of the output. When Mr Knighton Smith joined John Compton, Ltd., Glenanne, in the late 1960s they still produced a small amount of linen but the majority of their yarn was spun rayon which was used to weave tickings. Comptons had an important export business, supplying Australasia, Japan and Europe and at its peak had a combined workforce of 450. Both Glenanne and Milford were mill villages, Comptons owning a sizeable number of houses as well as some community amenities. Milford closed in 1983 and Glenanne in 1986.

An advertisement for the letting of Umgola House and Bleach Green, 1757

GLENANNE HOUSE
GLENANNE

Glenanne House
JFR

Glenanne House is close to the village of Glenanne, which is situated on the side of a hill overlooking the glen, and approximately four miles south of Markethill. In 1837 Lewis referred to Glenanne House, situated in the parish of Loughgilly:

> There are several substantial and some handsome houses, of which the principal are Glenaune, the elegant residence of W. Atkinson, Esq.

In his description of the house Brett, 1999, states that it is a mid-nineteenth century mill master's house, with the rear section of the main house possibly much older. There is a large mid-Victorian conservatory, and extensive outbuildings, walled garden, and very fine mature trees. Brett continues:

> The front, three-bay with three-light windows at each side of a wide porch: very wide oversailing eaves: Regency glazing-pattern: walls roughcast, with pebbles, painted ochre. The rear section has a shared gable with a Georgian-glazed window without reveals.

Bassett, 1888, explains the industrial background of the village of Glenanne,

GLENANNE HOUSE, GLENANNE

stating that bleach greens were established in the Glen at an early period, and about the year 1818, the late Mr William Atkinson settled at Glenanne, erecting extensive cotton spinning and weaving mills. Bassett continues:

> In 1841 Mr George Gray acquired possession of the mills and premises, and continued the cotton manufacture for fifteen years. He then remodelled the buildings to suit the manufacture of linen, and the mills have since been much enlarged.

These extensive mill buildings are illustrated in Bassett, 1888, with Glenanne House shown in the background of one of the illustrations. He states that power, keeping 316 looms at work, was obtained from Shaw's Lake, a body of water forty acres in extent, with a depth of about thirty feet. Indeed, this was a substantial linen manufacturing business of all grades from coarse to fine, with bleaching and beetling also being carried out within the grounds of 250 acres. The firm of Messrs George Gray & Sons consisted of Mr George Gray, JP, Mr Joseph Gray, JP, and Mr William B. Gray, with the first and last named shown as residing in Glenanne House in 1888.

However, the Umgola Weaving Factory on the Callan River burnt down in 1934 and Captain Noel Smith, who was the owner of John Compton, Ltd., bought the Glenanne mills from the Gray family continuing linen manufacture but also moving into the upholstery, furnishing and ticking business. Unfortunately, John Compton, Ltd., Glenanne, closed in 1986, due to overseas competition, although a small weaving unit still continues at Glenanne.

Hand bill reproduced from George Bassett, *County Down, 100 Years Ago*

Glenanne House was occupied by the Gray family until the Second World War, and continues to be occupied at present.

Upper Mills, Glenanne

TULLYDOWEY HOUSE
BLACKWATERTOWN

Tullydowey House
JFR

Tullydowey House is adjacent to Blackwatertown and lies south east of the road from there to Benburb, in County Tyrone. The house consists of two parts, the very old house which is seven bay, two storey, but with a lower roof line than the later Georgian building, which has harled walls and stone quoins. Bence-Jones, 1988, gives the following description of the house:

> A two storey gable-ended early or mid-18c house, with roof dormers, built near what is believed to be the remains of an old priory. Seven bay front; later gabled porch, with a fanlight in the form of a shallow segmental pointed arch above the door and sidelights.

Tullydowey House sits on an elevated site above the River Blackwater, with fine mature trees near the house, and a sloping lawn towards the River Blackwater, which is believed to have been an early bleach green. A lease was granted 2nd November 1776 by Francis Houston of the City of Armagh to Edward Eyre and Thomas Jackson, both of Maydown, linen drapers, of the farm and lands of

TULLYDOWEY HOUSE, BLACKWATERTOWN

Tullydowey, 139 acres, with the dwelling house, office houses, garden and orchard, now built, standing and growing thereon with the bleaching green now erecting. There is an early reference to Tullydowey in 1802 by McEvoy, when 'Jackson & Eyre' is listed as a bleach green in Blackwatertown, although the Eyre family appear to have lived in Maydown House. The initials 'T.J.' on a gate lodge and the date 1793 most likely refer to Thomas Jackson, who built Tullydowey House.

Belinda Jupp, 1992, lists for the house, a planted fort, a horse pond, a walled garden, and two gate lodges. Dean, 1994, gives considerable information concerning the two gate lodges:

> SOUTH LODGE 1793; architect not known. For the Province a lodge unique in its precocity being of a date when the newfangled Picturesque cottage style was still a novelty in England. That it should have bridged this quarter century time lag suggests that it may have been designed by a cross channel architect. A cute one and a half storey steeply gabled structure of unusual layout.

Dean, 1994, also mentions the two flue chimney stack which rises out of a gablet with ornamental bargeboards, and states, 'This houses a stone with the date and the monogram "T.J."'.

> NORTH LODGE 1843; architect not known. Another highly individual design in the English Picturesque cottage manner. Located outside the gates, one and a half storey with its gable facing the approach. This gable has the most unusually intricate carving to its bargeboard … Below is a window with the date 1843 on the head … Probably built for J. Eyre Jackson.

Hand bill reproduced from George Bassett, *County Down, 100 Years Ago*

Dean, 1994, gives a considerable description of the North Lodge, but unfortunately it has now been demolished.

The Jackson family appear to have made a considerable amount of money as linen drapers and bleachers, as James Eyre Jackson who died in 1862 left over £50,000. Relatives of the Jackson family continued to live at Tullydowey House until 1885, when the linen business at Milltown, and Tullydowey House were sold.

Milltown Mills, Benburb, County Tyrone, which was on the Armagh side of the River Blackwater, was purchased from the Jackson family by Joseph Orr & Sons, Cranagill, Loughgall, County Armagh in 1885. The works at Cranagill, for the manufacture of linen, had been set up by Joseph Orr about 1840, and after his death in 1877, the firm was run by his two sons, Jacob and

Tullydowey gate lodge
JFR

Mary Augusta McDonald, daughter of Joseph Orr

James Orr. Bassett, 1888, states:

> At Tullydoey, distant about a mile and a half from Milltown Mills, there is a handsome private residence belonging to this property. It is on the opposite side of the Blackwater, in Tyrone, and has attached to it 157 acres of land.

Cranagill, 1947

Joseph Orr & Sons were very successful power loom manufacturers of linens of different kinds, and their market was principally in the United Kingdom. The brothers Jacob and James Orr remained unmarried and lived at Cranagill, dying within weeks of each other in 1906. Two sisters of Jacob and James Orr, Mary Augusta McDonald and Frances Jenkinson Proctor, with their respective husbands, John R. McDonald and James E. Proctor, took over the firm. While the McDonalds lived at Cohannon House, near Moy, it seems the Proctor family moved from Limavady to live at Tullydowey House. In 1923 subscribers to the company included Frances J. Proctor, widow, Tullydowey, and her son Major George Norman Proctor, Indian Army, whose address was also Tullydowey, and who eventually became Chairman of Joseph Orr & Sons. Mary A. McDonald died in 1950, and with new directors the company struggled on but with diminishing sales it was finally liquidated in August 1968.

The late Tim Sinton of Thomas Sinton & Co., Ltd., Tandragee, in a 'Living Linen' recording, 1997, has told how his company became involved in 1969 with the company in Milltown, just beside Benburb – Joseph Orr.

TULLYDOWEY HOUSE, BLACKWATERTOWN

Joseph Orr's was an old established weaving interlining company which had been owned for many moons by the Proctor family, who lived in Blackwatertown. In 1969 Joseph Orr's was in liquidation, and we had been selling them tow yarn, and various yarns. At this point the office manager, who was a fellow called Errol Johnston, got us together with people called Milner & Butler, who supplied the bespoke tailors in the East End of London with all the things they needed. So then Milner & Butler and ourselves, we re-started Joseph Orr to produce linen interlinings, which is what they did. It was a wondrous wee factory. They took their water power off the Blackwater, they had turbines off the Blackwater, they had a wonderful 24 beetling mill which worked round the clock, and was driven direct off the turbines. They made their own electricity, again from the river through the turbines, but just prior to us taking over they had actually changed the weaving shed on to the grid because they found that they got surging in the electricity supply from the turbines. They made hollands, buckrams, ordinary canvases, stretch elastic canvases, shrunk ducks, paddings, all the whole range.

However, the bespoke tailoring trade became smaller and smaller, and bonded interlinings were being used by tailors, bringing about the end of the factory in 1984.

The river Blackwater
JFR

10
DUNGANNON

HINCKS PRINT PLATE VII
representing Winding, Warping and Weaving

WILLIAM HINCKS 1783

MILTOWN HOUSE
DUNGANNON

Miltown House, 1878
The Rt Hon Thomas Alexander Dickson and Mrs Dickson in their horse-drawn carriage

Miltown House is situated in well planted grounds on Wellington Road, which is on the southern outskirts of Dungannon. This is a two storey, three bay, Georgian dwelling to which two bay, single storey wings, were added possibly *c.* 1820, all on a semi basement, which is confirmed by the outline of the house shown on the 1834 Ordnance Survey map of Dungannon. Miltown House has been described as a good example of Palladian classical/revival style applied to a house of moderate size, which was originally an eighteenth century farmhouse, and is cement rendered with stucco surrounds. The doorcase has an elliptical fanlight, with glazed side panels, and is approached by a wide flight of steps. At the rear is a four bay, three storey nineteenth century extension, joined to the old house by a wide corridor and an elaborate double return staircase. The Ulster Architectural Heritage Society listing of 1970–71, on Dungannon, gives further details of Miltown House:

> Fan-finish window embrasures in all the rooms of c. 1820. In about 1880 french windows were inserted on the first floor at the rear giving access to an attractive ironwork balcony.

The Ulster Architectural Heritage Society also lists Miltown Mill stating:

> 2-storey good plain mill building of about 1870. Well maintained, the exterior ochre-washed.

However, none of the original factory buildings remain, the reference above is to a large building associated with the linen business and containing the lapping room.

Miltown House *JFR*

Miltown House is part of the industrial heritage of Dungannon, having belonged in 1841 to John Falls, owner of the distillery on the same site, in partnership with Arthur Vance. However, Nettleton, 1913, in his publication, *The Manufacture of Whisky and Plain Spirit*, lists John Falls as a distiller in Dungannon, as early as 1821, and this is confirmed by Pigot's *Directory* of 1824. Prior to the distillery there appears to have been a corn mill on the site, and it is possible that this continued alongside the distillery. On his death in 1844 John Falls bequeathed his interest in the distillery to Arthur Vance, who took on all the liabilities. William, the son of John Falls, succeeded his father as distillery manager, living in Miltown House until 1852. A family called McClelland bought the house and the distillery from Arthur Vance in 1852, but Robert McClelland died in 1857, and he was followed in Miltown House by Basil George Brooke, Lord Ranfurly's land agent.

Thomas Alexander Dickson, a son of James Dickson, purchased the distillery premises in 1863 and at once moved his corn milling business from the Manor corn mill to the distillery. The Manor corn mill had previously been operated by James Dickson and was near the back gate of

Rt Hon Thomas Alexander Dickson

COURTESY DICKSON FAMILY

Miltown House from the rear
JFR

Dungannon Park. However, in 1864, Thomas Alexander Dickson started linen weaving on the site of the old distillery, at the time of the American Civil War, when there was a boom in the linen industry due to the lack of cotton. The firm set up the first power looms working in the area, and in 1883 became known as Messrs Dickson, Tillie & Co., that style being retained until 1890, when the title Dicksons & Co. (Dungannon), Ltd., was assumed. The principals were Thomas Alexander Dickson, the founder, and his son, James Dickson. The company both produced and finished a wide range of goods embracing bleached linens, suitings, diapers, huckabacks, towels and tea towels. Prior to the First World War around two hundred and thirty people were employed at the works and factory in Dungannon.

Returning to the history of Miltown House, Basil George Brooke surrendered the lease to the property in 1867, and Thomas Alexander Dickson took over possession of the house. Thomas A. Dickson was Liberal MP for Dungannon from 1874 to 1880, being followed by his son, James, who was elected Liberal MP in 1880, and was the youngest of Mr Gladstone's supporters in the House of Commons. About 1886 Thomas A. Dickson moved to 'The Sycamores', Drogheda, setting up another successful linen business, which eventually became the Boyne Spinning and Weaving Co., Ltd. Meanwhile, James Dickson and his two sons carried on the business in Dungannon, although the wider manufacture of linen was curtailed in the First World War. Unfortunately his eldest son was killed in the conflict, but the company carried on under his second son, T.C. Harold Dickson, who also lived in Miltown House and died in 1972.

In the late nineteenth century, James Dickson's younger brother, Thomas, was also in the linen business, carrying on the Hazelbank Weaving Company, Lawrencetown, Banbridge, originally in partnership with his cousin William Walker, and living in Bellfield. After the First World War, Thomas Dickson retired to England and the business was carried on by his second son Norman, who also lived in Bellfield.

After Harold Dickson's death, Dicksons & Co. (Dungannon), Ltd., was managed by his second son, Thomas Alexander, who also inherited Miltown House. In 1946 he had married Rosemary Cadbury Greeves, a daughter of William Edward Greeves and his wife Marion Janet née Cadbury, bringing into the family another very strong linen connection, in this case to the Portadown Weaving Company. The Dickson family continued to manufacture a wide range of linens in Dungannon until in the 1950s the trade declined, and finally the company closed down in 1968. Miltown House continues in the ownership of the Dickson family.

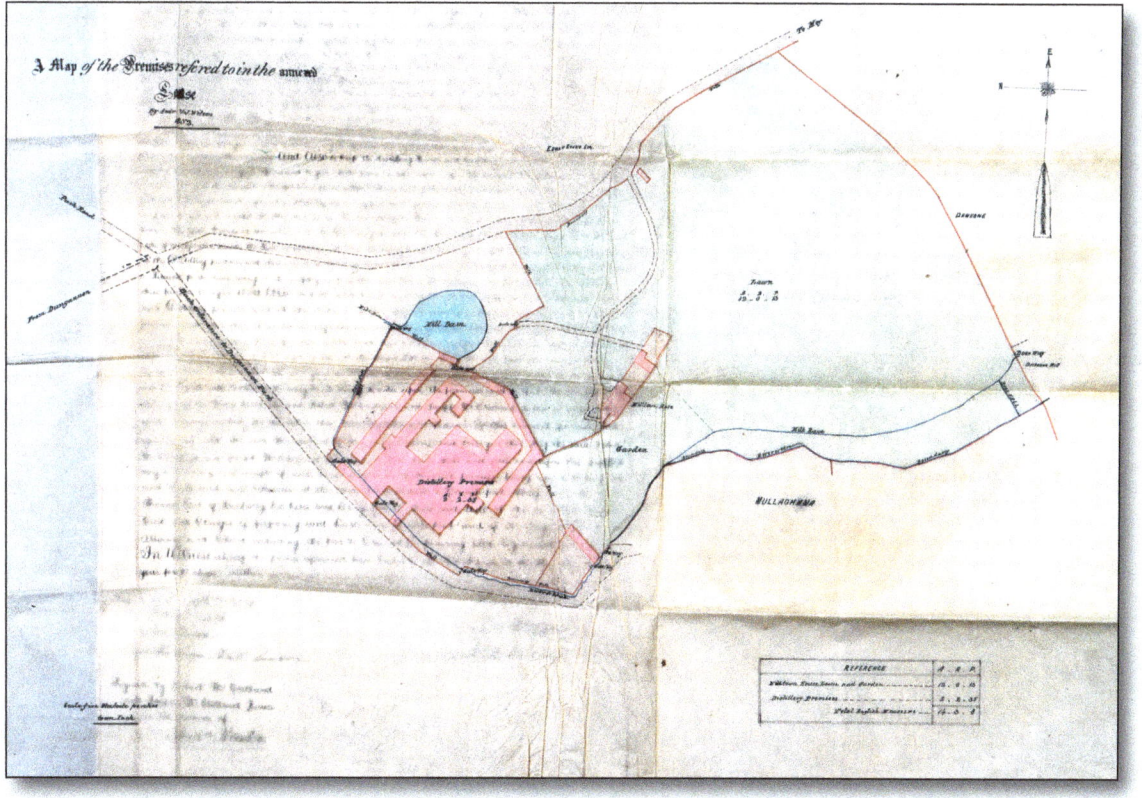

Map of Miltown Distillery and House, 1812
PRONI D/1932/8/183

DICKSON FAMILY TREE

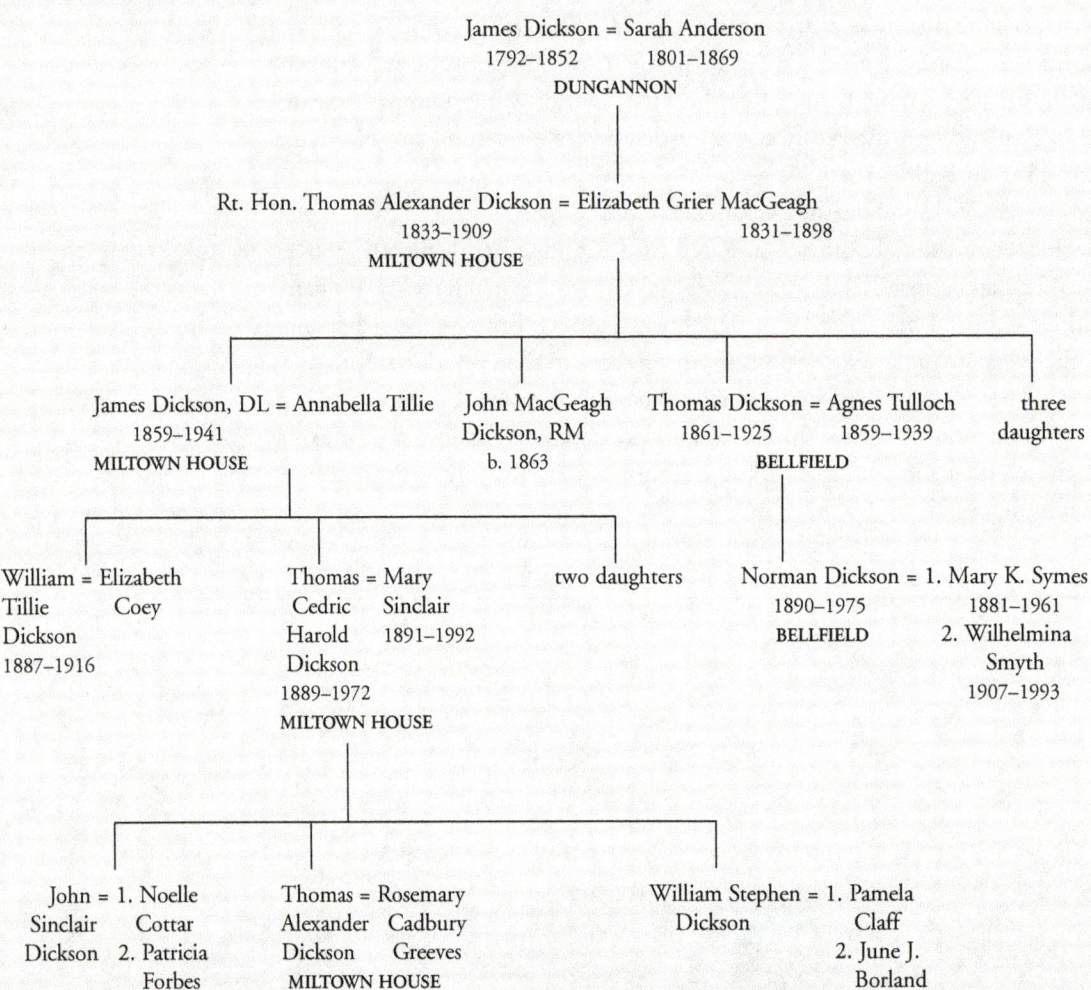

Aloha, now demolished
COURTESY MRS N. MILLIKEN

ALOHA
DUNGANNON

Aloha was situated off Cunningham's Lane, which was to the east of the Moy Road on the southern outskirts approaching Dungannon. The house was built in 1924 by Major Robert Stevenson, DL, and his Canadian wife, Laeta Ramage, who chose the name Aloha, meaning 'Welcome and Come Again'. Harry F. Stevenson, a nephew of Major Stevenson, has written of the house, in a private publication,

> It was an open plan house a few decades ahead of its time with a large landscaped and terraced garden adjoining part of the old Ranfurly Wood, which they had acquired.

Aloha was two storey, with attic dormer windows, and a hipped roof. In this open plan house all the ground floor reception rooms opened on to a terrace overlooking the garden, and the main entrance was on the side of the building. There were six bedrooms with front and rear staircases, and a playroom running the whole length of the attic floor. Major Stevenson's chauffeur had a bedroom over the garage, and set in fifteen acres, the property had both a front and back drive.

After the death of Major Stevenson in 1960, Mrs Stevenson eventually moved to England, and Aloha was sold to Dr and Mrs Milliken, who, after a period, sold the property to a builder. Aloha was demolished and a considerable number of houses built on the site.

The history of Stevenson & Son, Ltd., Dungannon, and subsequently Moygashel Ltd., commences in 1795, when two brothers, Robert and William Stevenson, registered as linen merchants in Newmills, near Dungannon. Hutchison, 1951, has stated that about 1800, 'Dungannon was quite surrounded by bleach greens', and continues:

> In 1795 there were in fact thirty important bleach greens in Tyrone (mostly centred round Dungannon which was the largest market town), compared with eighty in County Antrim, and thirty six in Armagh.

Major Robert Stevenson (1866–1960) Chairman, Stevenson and Son, Ltd., Dungannon

According to Harry Stevenson, Robert Stevenson, grandson of the original merchant, bought Bark Mill at Moygashel in 1875 from a Mr Boardman. A weaving shed was then added to the mill, with the cloth being bleached and dyed, selling as 'finished cloth'. Stevenson & Son was registered as a limited company in 1907, and Carter's *Linen Trades' Directory* of 1909 gives a figure of 200 looms for the factory. From 1907 to 1939 the company expanded gradually, but they began to exploit linen as a fabric for clothing, as well as for the traditional household uses, and before long they became the largest producers of dress linens in the United Kingdom. During the 1930s Major Stevenson recruited some young, up and coming managers who would play leading roles in Moygashel after the Second World War. These men included Max Eitel from Switzerland, who was an expert in textile chemistry, J.E. Finney, and James Lee. The company produced a considerable quantity of pure linen apparel fabric for both men and women, alongside plain household linens and canvas. Cloth was exported to over one hundred countries, and there were offices in London and New York, the latter being run by Hamilton Adams.

Stevenson & Son, Ltd., masterminded a large flax growing operation in the Second World War, most of which went to Braidwater Mill in Ballymena – Stevenson's major yarn supplier. They contributed to the war effort, manufacturing aero linens and hose pipes. Dungannon Park, comprising some six hundred acres, was purchased in 1943 from Mr Robert Brown of Donaghmore to allow expansion of the Moygashel factory, and the farming end of the business. In 1950, Stevensons, along with Smyth's Weaving Co., Ltd., of Banbridge, and Braidwater Spinning Company, formed a publicly quoted company, Moygashel Ltd., with Dungannon becoming the administrative headquarters. This allowed a very large expansion of the garment making division, the gents division being known as 'Steegan', and the ladies as 'Strelitz'. Moygashel furnishing fabrics for curtains and upholstery were renowned for quality, and, along with their clothes, became very successful and known world wide.

Moygashel Ltd., was taken over by the multinational company Courtaulds, Ltd., in 1969. However, with a decrease in the sales of linen, and facing competition from developing countries, the workforce dwindled from 2,000 to 760 in 1982. At this point, Courtaulds decided to close Brown & Adam, a division of the company, which dyed and finished the woven fabric at Moygashel, transferring that side of the work to a company in Rochdale, Lancashire. This was not successful, and Lamont Holdings purchased Moygashel later in the 1980s, using Ballievey, Banbridge to finish fabrics. Recently the company has been bought by Ulster Weavers, Ltd.

The Duchess of Kent visiting Moygashel in the 1950s.
Major Robert Stevenson stands in the centre wearing medals

THE GREER AND THE GREEVES FAMILY
OF COUNTY TYRONE

Joseph Malcomson Greeves
COURTESY GREEVES FAMILY

The Greer family, of which one branch changed their name to Greeves, is very extensive and originally came from Alnwick, Northumberland. Henry Greer came to Ireland in 1653, settling at Redford, near Grange, County Tyrone, and became an early member of the Society of Friends *c.* 1660. One of his sons, James Greer (1653–1718), married in 1678 into the Rea family of Lisacurran near Lurgan, and their four sons became very wealthy linen drapers. At this time a number of the Greer families lived in the area between Dungannon and Moy, and were highly esteemed linen merchants, so much so that the grandson of Henry, of Lurgan, John Greer, of The Grange, County Tyrone became Inspector General of the Linen Trade in Ulster. Neville H. Newhouse, Lisburn, 1967, has written an essay on 'Thomas Greer and the Society of Friends', in which he states:

> One branch of the family settled at Rhone Hill, Dungannon. Thomas Greer I lived there from 1724 to 1803, his son Thomas Greer II from 1761 to 1840, and his grandson Thomas Greer III (1791–1870) moved from Rhone Hill to Tullylagan. As it happens, a large number of the letters sent to Thomas Greer I, along with other family papers, have been preserved and are now in the Public Record Office in Belfast.

Thomas Greer, of Rhone Hill, Dungannon, son of John Greer of Grace Hall, has left a Market Book showing his business as a Dungannon linen draper between October 1758 and September 1759. Dr W.H. Crawford has carried out an analysis of this Market Book, in an article entitled, 'The Market Book of Thomas Greer, A Dungannon Linendraper, 1758–59', published in *Ulster Folklife*, Vol. 13, 1967. He states:

> That Greer was also a bleacher at this time is clear from his correspondence although the size of the undertaking was not mentioned. There is evidence, too, that he dealt directly with Quaker merchants in London, Warrington, and Manchester, and from their letters it appears probable that he acted as their agent in selling North American flax seed, in buying linen yarn for the English market and brown linens for bleachers, and in providing cargoes of finished cloth for sale overseas. He became one of the foremost drapers in County Tyrone.

Arthur Dobbs, in 1729, included Tyrone among the five Irish counties engaged in making linen, weaving tending to be concentrated in the eastern part of the county and spinning in the west. Exports of yarn from the Strabane area were taken up mostly by weavers in the Cookstown and Dungannon areas, where there were the greatest number of buyers and sellers, and the quality of Tyrone flax was high, equalling that in Down, Antrim and Armagh. Very few bleachers themselves manufactured linen, and indeed they were the aristocrats of the industry, being given universal respect as they attended markets. Large bleach greens were unknown in Tyrone in the early eighteenth century, and bleaching was confined to farms where there was ample room to spread the linen for bleaching. Later small bleaching concerns sprang up along the banks of rivers such as the Blackwater and the Rhone. According to McCall, 1865, in 1795 there were thirty important bleach greens in Tyrone, mostly centred round Dungannon, which was the largest market town. When John McEvoy visited Dungannon at the close of the eighteenth century he was given the names of the chief bleachers in the area, which included amongst them, William Grier, Thomas Grier, John Grier, all of Dungannon, and Robert Grier of Redford. In the Cookstown area Thomas Grier, Jr., of Tullylagan, then New Hambro, was recorded as a bleacher, again in McEvoy's *Statistical Survey of County Tyrone 1802*.

Mary Margretta Greeves
COURTESY GREEVES FAMILY

Meanwhile the weaving industry was expanding and in 1784, John Greer, of The Grange, Inspector General of the Linen Trade in Ulster, reported that the Cookstown market had a weekly turnover in sales of brown linen of £120, Stewartstown £800, and Dungannon of £1,500. During the first quarter of the nineteenth century Dungannon was a busy market town, with from 100 to 120 buyers attending sales on Thursdays, with many of these being Quakers, who had a reputation for fair dealing. However, by the middle of the nineteenth century the domestic system of both spinning and weaving had practically come to an end, when, in 1864, James Alexander Dickson introduced the first power looms in Dungannon, on the site of the old distillery works of John Falls. In 1875 the Stevenson family founded a power weaving concern at Moygashel, on the southern outskirts of Dungannon, which was to become Stevenson & Son, Ltd., Dungannon and later Moygashel Ltd.

Over a period of 100 years the members of the Greer family involved in the linen industry, and living in the area known as Grange, near Dungannon, became very numerous, and a grandson of Robert Greer (1660–1730) of Redford, William Greer (1719–76) adopted the name Greeves at the time of his marriage in 1744, to Mary Morton. It was descendants of this branch of the family who were to continue in the nineteenth century their involvement with the mechanised linen industry, when the brothers John and Thomas Malcomson Greeves set up J. & T.M. Greeves & Co., in 1862, later incorporated as J. & T.M. Greeves Ltd., 1899, flax spinners, Forth River Mills, Belfast. They became one of the major flax spinning companies in Belfast. Additionally, two sons of John Greeves (1831–1917), Thomas Jackson Greeves (1872–1939) and Owden Valentine Greeves (1874–1959) set up the Portadown Weaving Company, and were followed in the business by their nephew, William Edward Greeves, and also by their sons. With the considerable decrease in the linen industry post-Second World War both of these companies were forced to close in the late 1950s.

SOME MEMBERS OF THE GREER AND GREEVES FAMILIES

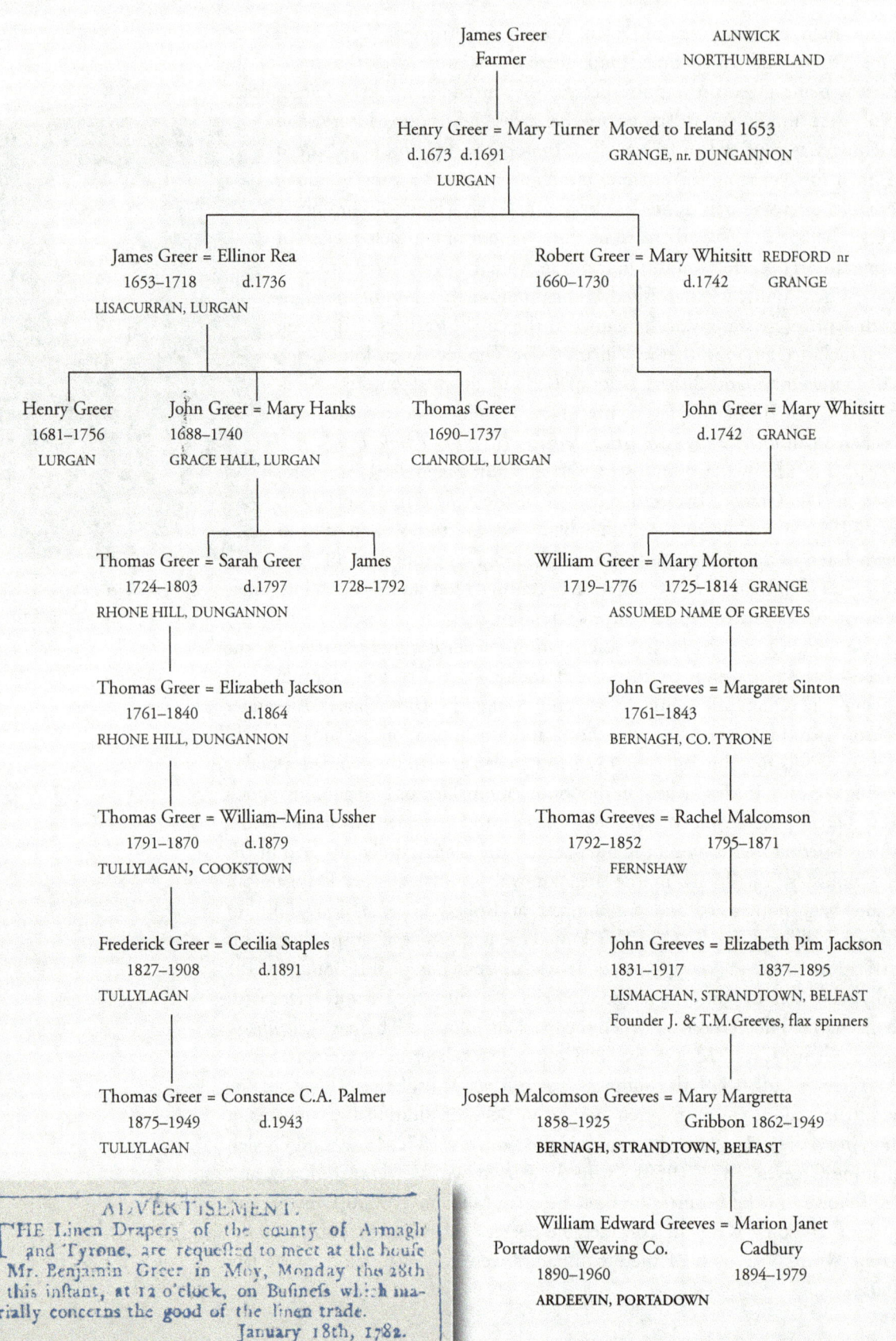

RHONE HILL
DUNGANNON

Rhone Hill is situated south east of Dungannon, near to the River Rhone, in the country mid-way between Moy and Dungannon, County Tyrone. This is a two storey, six bay, gable ended house with quoins, having an asymmetrical front with three bays to the left of the doorcase and two to the right. The house has simple classical Georgian features, and there is a miniature pediment with a round headed attic window vertically above the front door. Rhone Hill was built for the Greer family apparently about 1724 in grounds of around sixty acres. Rowan, 1979, states:

> The house itself has early features: it is of brick laid in Flemish bond, and the sash windows and boxes are almost flush with the front. Offices behind are dated 1729.

There is a two bay, two storey wing of stonework to the rear, which could be the original house or a later addition. Dean, 1994, states that the house had two gate lodges, both pre-1833, but now demolished, and the North Lodge was at the entrance to both the house and the beetling mill. Additionally, the Ordnance Survey map of 1833 shows Rhone Hill with a beetling mill and two gate lodges.

Rhone Hill
JFR

Thomas Greer (1724–1803) of Rhone Hill was a wealthy Quaker linen merchant and the owner of a number of bleach greens, but he was also the most influential Quaker in the north of Ireland. Newhouse, 1967, states that the minutes of the Grange Monthly Meeting show that for a long time he was a recorded Minister of the Society and made several journeys in Ireland and England on behalf of the Friends. A large number of the letters sent to Thomas Greer have been preserved, along with other family papers, and have been deposited in the Public Record Office of Northern Ireland. According to Hutchison, 1951, Thomas Greer was noted as litigious and combative, not being subject to the conciliatory influence of Friends. Indeed, this was a time when business success required a certain determination in that bleach greens needed good supplies of water, and there were a great many Quaker disputes about rivers and the right to divert them. In 1770 Thomas Greer I wrote to Thomas Knox, later to be Lord Ranfurly, at Molesworth Street, Dublin, requesting that he be granted a tenancy for his mills in preference to his brother James, of Stangmore, who was also a linen merchant and bleacher. Shrewdly cautious, Knox replied expressing concern at the differences between the brothers, acknowledging Thomas to be the most substantial tenant and suggesting a prudent and cautious conveyance which would make it impossible for anyone to injure any bleach green on his estate.

Thomas Greer married in 1746 his second cousin, Sarah, daughter of Thomas Greer of Redford. Their son, Thomas (1761–1840), joined his father in the linen business but also disagreed with him, and eventually became embroiled in arguments over access to bleach greens. Nevertheless, Thomas Greer (1) pursued his business interests vigorously, in 1776 buying the New Hamburgh Bleach Works, south of Cookstown, from the firm of Wakefield, Pratt & Meirs for £2,000, and soon after entering into partnership with Wakefield and Bell to run it. Additionally, in 1798, Thomas Greer of Rhone Hill leased one third of the New Hamburgh bleach green to his son Thomas, who was a linen draper.

Thomas Greer (2) followed his father in Rhone Hill, and his eldest son Thomas (3) lived at New Hamburgh (later known as Tullylagan), while his second son, William Jackson Greer (1797–1841) inherited Rhone Hill, as did his son Thomas Fergus Greer (1829–1901). In 1897 George Greer (1849–92), eldest son of Henry Greer of Lurgan, married secondly his cousin Lucy Matilda, eldest daughter of Thomas Fergus Greer of Rhone Hill, and moved to Rhone Hill from Bernagh after the death of his father-in-law in 1910. The Greers lived at Rhone Hill until 1936 when the house was sold. However, by the mid-nineteenth century they had given up the linen industry, and further generations of this family appear to have followed a career in the church or the army. In 1897, it is stated in the Valuation Book of Rhone Hill, in respect of the beetling mill, that the machines were away and the building in ruins, confirming the end of the processing of linen at this site.

TULLYLAGAN MANOR
COOKSTOWN

Tullylagan Manor, standing in sixty seven acres, is situated close to the River Claggan, about three miles south of Cookstown, on the main road from Dungannon to Cookstown, and was previously known as Tullylagan House, and formerly New Hamburgh. The house was built in 1824 by Thomas Greer (1791–1870), eldest son of Thomas Greer of Rhone Hill, on the occasion of his marriage to William-Mina Ussher, Camphire, County Waterford. Tullylagan Manor was originally built as two storeys over a basement, which was subsequently excavated, so that it became in effect a ground floor, and the house three storey. Bence-Jones, 1988, states:

Tullylagan Manor
JFR

> 3 bay front; 2 storey projecting porch, with coupled pilasters on both storeys and large window with entablature in upper storey. Eaved roof on bracket cornice. Wing at side, originally 1 storey over basement, which became a ground floor as in the main block.

In 1834 the *Ordnance Survey Memoirs* record for the Parish of Desertcreat,

'Thomas Grier Esquire, New Hamburgh near Dungannon', and it is also recorded that there are two bleach greens in the townland of Tullyleggan. Lewis, 1837, states in his description of the parish of Desertcreat in the 1830s:

Tullylagan Manor from the rear
JFR

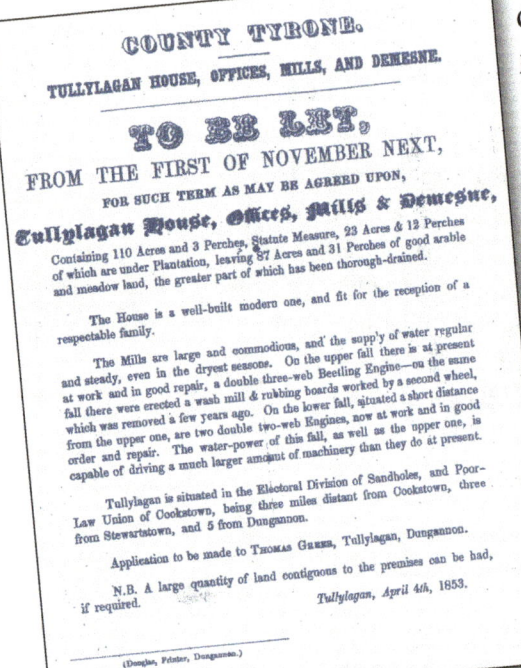

At Tullylagan are two extensive bleach-greens, and near Desertcreight is a smaller, which annually bleach and finish upwards of 30,000 pieces for the London market; and a great quantity is woven by the country people in their own houses, the occupation of weaving being followed generally by the inhabitants, in addition to agricultural pursuits.

However, in the first thirty years of the nineteenth century there was a great reduction in the number of small bleach greens. With the increasing industrialisation of the linen industry by the mid-nineteenth century more, and more, brown linens were sent to the great bleachers such as the Richardsons who used machinery for the finishing of cloth. In 1853 Tullylagan House, Offices, Mills and Demesne were advertised for letting by Thomas Greer, although he later appears to have thought of improving his house. Thomas Jackson, architect, wrote in 1869 to Thomas Greer, Tullylagan, enclosing plans, elevation and section of proposed addition to the house, which included a new front, but it is not clear that this work was carried out.

Thomas Greer died in June 1870, and the house was inherited by his son Frederick, who served in the Royal Navy. Tullylagan House and estate were leased to Washington Kinley in 1889, and he remained in the property until 1898. Frederick Greer died in 1908, but he had already leased Tullylagan House to his cousin Thomas MacGregor Greer, who is recorded in the house in 1906. However, at this time, the bleaching of linen appears to have totally ceased as, in 1913, the beetling mill is recorded at rest, and not likely to work again. Thomas MacGregor Greer, DL, County Tyrone, remained at Tullylagan Manor until his death in 1941. The house is now occupied by a prominent local businessman.

FERNSHAW
DUNGANNON

Fernshaw is situated about two miles south east of Dungannon on the Old Moy Road, in the townland of Bernagh. This is a two storey L-shaped house, having roughcast walls, with attic and slated roof, which is gabled. There is a return at the rear of the house which was later enlarged. The windows are Georgian-glazed sashes. This property was extensively restored in 1980 and 1981. John Greeves (1761–1843), linen bleacher and merchant, built the oldest part of the present house *c.* 1789, naming it 'Bernagh', or 'Little Bernagh' in order to distinguish it from the other house in the townland, 'Big Bernagh', now known as 'Bernagh'. This last house was built by Joseph Nicholson (1758–1817), John Greeves' cousin, and was only a field away from the other house, which is now known as Fernshaw.

Lieutenant Colonel J.R.H. Greeves, Chairman of J. & T.M. Greeves, Belfast, 1956–61, writing in 1967 about Fernshaw and his great-great-grandfather states:

> John Greeves married Margaret Sinton of Moyallon on 5th March 1789, and I expect that he had the house ready to receive his bride. It consisted, as far as I

Fernshaw, 1886

Joseph Malcomson Greeves and family, 1897
COURTESY GREEVES FAMILY

can tell, of the present dining room, hall and staircase, with two rooms over the dining room and two more above this. There was a chine closet off the dining room, which was later taken away, thus increasing the size of the dining room (then called the parlour). There was "a dairy under the stairs" and the kitchen appears to have been at the end of the hall – probably projecting as a short ground floor return.

In 1822 John and Margaret Greeves went to live with their younger son John in Armagh, where Margaret died in 1824. On 13th July 1825 the house was let to the Rev. James Stewart Blacker, Curate of Killyman and later Rector of Keady. He died in 1835, and his widow Eliza, who was a daughter of Cunningham Greg, of Ballymenoch, Holywood, surrendered the lease in 1836. During his term of residence he had made considerable additions consisting of the present back kitchen and garage, with three rooms over the return. He also threw the two rooms on the first floor into one and also the two garrets.

The house was again let to a Dr King who died in 1841, when Thomas Greeves, my great-grandfather, who lived in Perry Street, Dungannon where he had a drapery business at the corner of Northland Row, took it over and did some necessary repairs, afterwards letting it to "a clergyman of the established worship". In 1848 Thomas retired from business owing to ill health and went to live at Fernshaw where he proceeded to add the drawing room wing – i.e. Drawing room and back sitting room with the rooms over them; he also

FERNSHAW, DUNGANNON

enclosed the yard. I do not know when the porch was built, but it appears on all the photos of the house which I have seen.

Thomas died at Fernshaw on 31st August 1852 and his widow Rachel (née Malcomson) continued to live there until her death on 18th November 1871, when the house and land were sold.

This was the period of the diminution of the domestic linen industry with a great decrease in linen woven by farmers at their homes, and the movement to towns where mills and factories were set up for the industrial manufacture of linen. John and Thomas Malcomson Greeves, sons of Thomas and Rachel Greeves of Fernshaw, moved to Belfast and set up J. & T.M. Greeves & Co., 1862 (later incorporated as J. & T.M. Greeves Ltd., 1899), Flax Spinners, Forth River Mills, Belfast. This company was very successful in the spinning of linen yarn until the 1950s when, with a downturn in the manufacture of fine linens, it was eventually sold in 1959 to Herdmans, Ltd., Sion Mills, who ran the mill for a short time before closing in 1961.

Fernshaw
JFR

CASTLECAULFIELD HOUSE
CASTLECAULFIELD

Castlecaulfield House
JFR

Castlecaulfield House is situated in the village of Castlecaulfield, three miles west of Dungannon, and just north of the road from Dungannon to Omagh. This is a house that probably dates from *c.* 1750, but was constructed on the site of an older house, which, according to Burges, 1936, had been built in 1673 by Lord Charlemont. The Ulster Architectural Heritage Society listing for Castlecaulfield, 1971, gives the following description of Castlecaulfield House.

> Close to the church. Good unsophisticated low-built house, late-18th or early-19th century in appearance. 2-storey, 7-bay, single-storey projecting-cube porch in centre. Mature trees. A friendly unhurried type of house which Burges suggests is 17th century. It was formerly the Caulfield dower or jointure house.

Rowan, 1979, also gives a description of Castlecaulfield House.

> N of the church. A generous seven-bay, two-storey house with brick chimneys

and high curved flanking walls with battlemented tops. Mid c. 18. Harled wing in the middle of the back. Stables to the N dated 1785.

The Valuation Books in the Public Record Office Northern Ireland show David Acheson resident in Castlecaulfield House, with offices, weaving factory and land in 1872, and his descendants still live in the property, which had been purchased from the Charlemont Estate in 1870.

Lewis, 1837, states that Sir Toby Caulfield, later Lord Charlemont, in 1614, began building a mansion house in the Elizabethan style, which afterwards acquired the name of Castle-Caulfield, but unfortunately is now a ruin. The making of linen is referred to in an advertisement for the letting of this house and demesne of Castle-Caulfield near Dungannon, which was placed in the *Belfast News Letter*, 30th March 1761. Reference is also made in the advertisement to the mills of the manor of Castle-Caulfield:

Datestone in an outhouse
JFR

> as also the mills of the manor of Castle-Caulfield, new built last summer, and now in the most compleat order, on whose water a fall for a bleach-mill may be had of 25 feet, with continual water the driest summer with plenty of turf bog.

At the close of the eighteenth century when McEvoy, 1802, visited Dungannon he was given the names of the chief Dungannon and Cookstown bleachers by John Wilcocks, himself an eminent bleacher. Mention was made of bleachers near Dungannon and these included William Shaw of Castlecaulfield. Lewis, 1837, also states that in the 1830s the inhabitants of Castlecaulfield were mainly engaged in agriculture and the weaving of linen.

The linen firm of David Acheson, Ltd., (originally Acheson & Smith), was founded in 1874 by David Acheson and John Smith, setting up business at Castlecaulfield as power loom weavers. David Acheson (1841–1912) was the great-grandfather of the present owner of Castlecaulfield House, Peter N. Acheson. Additionally, David Acheson's father, Rev. Joseph Acheson, had been ordained to the congregation of Castlecaulfield Presbyterian Church in 1833, and remained there until his death in 1893. The linen factory was constructed on the site of an old corn mill, and although some of the buildings were retained, a new weaving shed with a glass roof was added. Achesons were linen manufacturers and finishers, latterly

David Acheson (1841–1912)
COURTESY PETER ACHESON

producing linen tea towels, embroidery linens and rayon tablecloths. Within the United Kingdom they had agents in London, Manchester, Glasgow, Newcastle and Bristol, but the company also had a sizeable export trade with Australia and New Zealand. In the late 1960s business decreased substantially due to Eastern European competition and the company was sold, later closing in 1978.

The Achesons of Portadown, who also ran a linen weaving factory, are second cousins of the Castlecaulfield Achesons, although there were no commercial links between the two companies. The Castlecaulfield Achesons are also related to the Browns of Donaghmore who owned a soap works, manufacturing the internationally renowned 'Colleen brand soap', but this was eventually closed about 1958.

Interior fanlight
JFR

BIBLIOGRAPHY

ARMSTRONG, D.L., *The Growth of Industry in Northern Ireland,* Oxford, 1999

ATKINSON, A., *Ireland Exhibited to England in a Political and Moral Survey of her Population,* 2 vols., London, 1823

ATKINSON, EDWARD DUPRÉ, *Dromore, An Ulster Diocese,* Dundalk, 1925

BANBRIDGE HERITAGE DEVELOPMENT LTD., *Linen Houses of Banbridge,* Banbridge, 1995

BASSETT, G.H., *County Armagh, 100 Years Ago,* Belfast, 1888

BASSETT, G.H., *County Down, 100 Years Ago,* Belfast, 1886

BENCE-JONES, MARK, *A Guide to Irish Country Houses,* London, 1988

Bessbrook, A record of industry in a Northern Ireland village community and of a social experiment, 1845–1945. Issued by The Bessbrook Spinning Co., Ltd., and J.N.Richardson, Sons & Owden, Ltd., Belfast, 1945

BLACKWOOD, R.W.T.H., MS, 'Genealogies', in Linen Hall Library, Belfast

BRADSHAW, *Directory for Lurgan,* 1819/1820

BRETT, C.E.B., *Banbridge,* U.A.H.S., Belfast, 1969

BRETT, C.E.B., *Buildings of County Armagh,* Belfast, 1999

BRETT, C.E.B., *Buildings of North Down,* Belfast, 2002

BRYSON, G. HERBERT, *Memories of a Long Life,* Dunmurry (privately published), 1982

BRYSON, ROSEMARY B., 'Harking Back', The British Library, National Sound Archive, 1985

BURGES, CAPTAIN YNYR A., *History of St. Michael's Church, Castlecaulfield,* Dungannon, 1936

BURKE, *Landed Gentry of Ireland,* 4th edition, London, 1958

CAMPBELL, M.P., 'Gilford and its Mills', *Banbridge and District Historical Society Journal,* Vol. II, Banbridge, 1990

CANSDALE, PETER D., *A Story of Progress, Spence Bryson & Co.,Ltd., 1880–1971,* (privately published), 1972

CARTER, H.R., *Linen, Hemp and Jute Trades' Directory,* Belfast, 1909

CARTER, WILLIAM, *A Short History of the Linen Trade,* Vol. ii, Belfast, 1952

CLARKE, R.S.J., *The Heart of Downe, Old Banbridge Families from Gravestone Inscriptions, Wills, and Biographical Notes,* Belfast, 1989

COHEN, MARILYN, *Linen, Family and Community in Tullylish, County Down,* Dublin, 1997

CRAWFORD, W.H., 'The Market Book of Thomas Greer, A Dungannon Linendraper, 1758–59', *Ulster Folklife,* Vol. 13, 1967

CRAWFORD, W.H., *The Hand Loom Weavers and the Ulster Linen Industry,* Belfast, 1994

CRAWFORD, W.H., *The Impact of the Domestic Linen Industry in Ulster,* Belfast, 2005

CROWE, W.H., *In Banbridge Town,* Belfast, 1964

CROWE, W.H., *Beyond the Hills, an Ulster Headmaster Remembers,* Dundalk, 1971

CROWE, W.H., *Bridges to Banbridge,* Dundalk, 1980

DAY, ANGÉLIQUE & McWILLIAMS, PATRICK (eds), *Ordnance Survey Memoirs of Ireland,*

    Vol. 1, *Parishes of County Armagh, 1835–8,* Belfast, 1990

    Vol. 3, *Parishes of County Down I, 1834–6,* Belfast, 1990

    Vol. 7, *Parishes of County Down II, 1832–4, 1837,* Belfast, 1991

    Vol. 12, *Parishes of County Down II, 1833–8,* Belfast, 1992

    Vol. 20, *Parishes of County Tyrone II, 1825, 1833–5, 1840,* Belfast 1993

DEAN, J.A.K., *The Gate Lodges of Ulster, A Gazetteer,* U.A.H.S., Belfast, 1994

DIXON, HUGH, 'Honouring Thomas Jackson (1807–1890) (architect)', *Proceedings and Reports of the Belfast Natural History and Philosophical Society,* 2nd series, Vol. 9, Sessions 1970/71–76/77

DOBBS, A., *Essay on the Trade and Improvement of Ireland,* Dublin, 1729

GILL, CONRAD, *The Rise of the Irish Linen Industry,* Oxford, 1923

GORDON, ERNEST, 'Edenderry Works, Banbridge', *Banbridge & District Historical Society Journal,* 1993

GREEN, E.R.R., *The Lagan Valley 1800–1850,* London, 1949

GREEN, E.R.R., *The Industrial Archaeology of County Down,* Belfast, 1963

GRIBBON, H.D., *The History of Water Power in Ulster,* Belfast, 1969

HARRIS, W., *Antient and Present State of the County of Down,* Dublin, 1744, reprint, 1977

HENDERSON, J.W., *Methodist College, Belfast, 1868–1938,* Vol. 1, Belfast, 1939

HORNER, J., *The Linen Trade of Europe during the Spinning Wheel Period,* Belfast, 1920

HUTCHISON, W.R., *Tyrone Precinct,* Belfast, 1951

JACKSON, BILL, *Ringing True, The Bells of Trummery and Beyond: 350 Years of an Irish Quaker Family,* York, 2005

JUPP, BELINDA, *Heritage Gardens Inventory 1992,* Belfast, 1992

LAWLOR, H.C., 'Rise of the Linen Merchants in the Eighteenth Century', *Irish and International Fibres and Fabrics Journal,* 1941–43

LEWIS, SAMUEL, *Topographical Dictionary of Ireland,* London, 1837

LINN, CAPTAIN RICHARD, *A History of Banbridge,* Banbridge, 1935

LITTLE, CANON G.N., *Historical Highlights, Parish of Aghaderg, Diocese of Dromore, Co. Down,* Banbridge, 1989

LOGAN, R.A., *A Window On The Past, A History of Gilford, County Down,* Banbridge, 2000

McCALL, HUGH, *Ireland and her Staple Manufactures,* 2nd edition, Belfast, 1865

McCANDLESS, PAUL, *Smyths of the Bann,* Banbridge, 2002

McCORRY, F.X., *Lurgan: An Irish Provincial Town, 1610–1970,* Lurgan, 1993

McCUTCHEON, W.A., *The Industrial Archaeology of Northern Ireland,* Belfast, 1980

McEVOY, JOHN, *County of Tyrone 1802, A Statistical Survey,* Dublin, 1802, reprint Belfast, 1991

McMANUS, JOE, *Milford, Red Bricks, and Golden Memories, A Village History,* Lurgan, 2002

MARSHALL, J.J., *History of Dungannon,* Dungannon, 1929

BIBLIOGRAPHY

NETTLETON, J.A., *The Manufacture of Whisky and Plain Spirit,* Aberdeen, 1913

NEWHOUSE, NEVILLE H., *Thomas Greer,* Lisburn (privately published), 1967

ORAM, R.W., *Craigavon,* U.A.H.S., Belfast, 1971

ORAM, R.W., & RANKIN, P.J., *Dungannon & Cookstown,* U.A.H.S., Belfast, 1971

PIERCE, RICHARD & COEY, ALASTAIR, *Taken for Granted,* Belfast, 1984

PIGOT, J. & Co., *City of Dublin and Hibernian Provincial Directory,* Manchester, 1824

RANKIN, P.J., *Rathfriland and Hilltown,* U.A.H.S., Belfast, 1979

RANKIN, P.J., *Mourne Area of South Down,* U.A.H.S., Belfast, 1975

RICHARDSON, JAMES N., *Six Generations of Friends in Ireland 1655–1890,* 3rd edition, London, 1895

RICHARDSON, JAMES N., *The Quakri at Lurgan and Grange,* Bessbrook, 1899

RICHARDSON, JAMES N., *Reminiscences of 'Friends' in Ulster,* Gloucester, 1911

ROWAN, ALISTAIR, *The Buildings of Ireland, North West Ulster,* Middlesex, 1979

SMITH, F.W., *The Irish Linen Trade Hand-Book and Directory,* Belfast, 1876

STEVENSON, J., *Two Centuries of Life in Down 1600–1800,* Belfast, 1920

VICTORIA COLLEGE, BELFAST, Centenary, 1859–1959, Belfast, 1959

WILLIAMS, JEREMY, *A Companion Guide to Architecture in Ireland 1837–1921,* Dublin, 1994

YOUNG, A., *Tour in Ireland 1776–1779,* (Hutton, A.W. ed.), London, 1892

YOUNG, R.M., *Belfast and the Province of Ulster in the twentieth century,* Belfast, 1909

PUBLIC RECORD OFFICE OF NORTHERN IRELAND,
REFERENCES

Millmount Survey D/1905/2/73A/15
Map of Miltown House & Distillery, Dungannon D/1932/8/183
Map of Bellevue (Bellfield) at Lenaderg, 1859 T/1107/26A
Linen drapers premises in Lurgan (water colour sketch) early nineteenth century D/1464/2
Survey Drummaran: Hugh Law 1831 for New Yarn Spinning Mill D/492/28
Woodbank, Gilford Survey lands A. Atkinson, 1800 D/1769/19/2C
    Including   Auction notice
                            Map of part of Ballymacanallen
                            Signature by James Dickson of Elmfield
Stramore House, Gilford Auction notice, 3 November, 1879 D/2714/6C (T/3684/1 photocopy)

PHOTOGRAPHS

J.W.Murland with horse 'Soothing Glass' D/3488/2
McMaster, Gilford, family photograph 1892 D/2714/6B
Stramore House D/2714/6B
McCrum, Milford D/2886/A/2/14/50 (Allison)
Ballyards Castle, Milford D/2886/A/2/6/29–42 (Allison)
Mrs Jane Richardson D/2362/5

PHOTOGRAPHS BY LAWRENCE

Callan Bridge, Armagh T/2418/3/12 5875WL
Milford House, Armagh T/2418/3/108 5868WL
Milford House, Armagh T/2418/3/121 8121WL
Woodhouse, Bessbrook T/2418/3/256 7275WL
Mount Caulfield, Bessbrook T/2418/3/266 7273WL

INDEX

NOTE: a reference ending with 'p' denotes a photograph/illustration.

Acheson & Co., J. & J., 188, 189
Acheson & Smith, 247
Acheson Ltd., David, 247–8
Acheson, David, 247
Acheson, John, 188
Acheson, Peter N., 247
Acheson, Rev. Joseph (father of David Acheson), 247
Adams, Hamilton, 234
Adamson, Alec, 132p
Aghaderg Glebe House, Loughbrickland, 67–8
Alexander, Norman (son of William Alexander), 93
Alexander, William, 93
Allen, Joseph, 177, 178
Allen, William James (son of Joseph Allen), 178
Aloha, Dungannnon, 233–5
Altavilla, Portadown, 208–9
American Civil War, 6, 71, 85, 126, 170, 194, 230
Anderson & Co., Messrs James, 28
Anderson, Catherine (wife of William Smyth), 51, 85, 89
Anderson, T.N., 28
'Andrew McCleland and Sons', 50
Annadale, Lurgan, 184–5
Annesley, Lord, 5
Annett, James Irwin, 212
Anne, Queen, 96
Annsborough Cottage, 6, 11
Annsborough House, 8–10
Annsborough, Castlewellan, 5, 6, 7, 11, 13, 14, 15, 16, 18
Ardeevin, Portadown (Skerry Hill), 206–7
Ardnabannon House, 11–13, 15
Ardnabannon Outdoor Education Centre, 13
Ards House, Donegal, 115
Ards Weaving Company, 36p, 37
Armstrong, Marianne (wife of Hugh Watson), 137
Armstrong, Thomas, 138p
Armstrong, Watson, 194
Armstrong, William (father of Marianne Armstrong), 137
Ashfield House, Dromore, 36, 39, 43–4
'Ashfield Village', 43
Atkinson, Abraham, 147–9
Atkinson, James, 212
Atkinson, Joseph, Jr., 81
Atkinson, Myra (wife of Maynard Sinton), 138, 143
Atkinson, William, 220, 221
Averell, Sarah (wife of Thomas Shillington), 208

Babington, Rev. David, 212
Baird & Co., Ltd., W.F.B., 181, 183, 195
Baird, Hugh (grandson of W.F.B. Baird), 179
Baird, James (grandson of W.F.B. Baird), 179
Baird, James (son of W.F.B. Baird), 178
Baird, W.F.B., 178
Baird, William (son of W.F.B. Baird), 178
Ballievey Bleaching Co., Ltd., 57, 68
Ballievey Bleaching Company, 24, 27

Ballievey House, Ballievey, 29–32, 31p, 71, 75
Ballyards Castle, Milford, 141–3
Ballydown House *see also* Roselawn, 28
Ballydown Weaving Company, 30, 41
Ballydown, Banbridge, 37, 45–6
Banbridge Academy, 30, 32, 58, 61, 62, 68, 80
Banbridge Agricultural and Farming Society, 89
Banbridge Bleaching Company, 28
Banbridge Reservoir Company, 64
Banbridge Weaving Factory, 50
Banford Bleach Works Co., 118, 122
Banford House, Tullylish, 118–20, 134, 144–5
Bann Reservoir Company, 23
Bann Vale House, Gilford, 105, 106, 111–12
Bannvale House *see also* Bann Vale House, 111, 112, 114, 116, 124, 147
Bannview House, Portadown, 188–9
Bannville Beetling Mills, 85
Bark Mill, 234
Barre, W.J., 142
Bassett, George, 4p, 19, 37, 81, 85, 92, 95, 103, 104, 118, 136, 138, 170, 176, 179, 188, 190, 214, 218, 219, 220, 221, 224
Beck, James A., 28
Beech Hill House, 141
Beechpark, Lurgan, 137–8
Belfast Academy, 56
Belfast and Northern Counties Railway Company, 117
Belfast Custom House, 36
Belfast News Letter, 95, 96, 109, 120p, 247
Belfast Ropeworks, 64
Bell & Co., Abraham, 117
Bell & Co., Thomas, 168p, 169, 170, 172, 173
Bell, Abraham (husband of Mary Christy), 117, 149, 169
Bell, Christy Walpole (né Edward Christopher Bell), 172
Bell, Edwin George, 174
Bell, Emily Jane (daughter of Samuel Alexander Bell), 172
Bell, Frederick W. (son of Samuel Alexander Bell), 170, 174
Bell, George, 169
Bell, George Philip (son of Edwin George Bell), 174
Bell, James Christy, 117
Bell, James Greer (husband of Anna Maria Uprichard), 106, 116–7
Bell, Richard, 169
Bell, Samuel (brother of Abraham Bell), 169
Bell, Samuel (son of Samuel Alexander Bell), 172
Bell, Samuel Alexander (father of Sara Bell), 165, 169, 170, 172, 173, 174
Bell, Sara ('Sissillia', daughter of Samuel Alexander Bell), 165, 172
Bell, Thomas, 169
Bell, Thomas (son of Abraham Bell), 169
Bell, William, 169, 173
Bellevue, Lurgan, 170, 171–2, 173
Bellfield, Lenaderg, 92–3, 231
Belmont House, Banbridge, 50–51, 85, 91, 123, 124
Bence-Jones, Mark, 164, 222, 241
Bennett, Thomas, 217
Bessbrook Spinning Company Limited, 153, 155, 165

Blacker, Eliza, 244
Blacker, Rev. James Stewart, 244
Blackstaff Flax Spinning & Weaving Co., Ltd., 170
Bleachers' Houses, 30,
    Ballievey House, 30
    Bishopscourt, Dromore, 30
    Newforge House, Magheralin, 30
    Sheepbridge, House, Newry, 30
Blood, Richard, 105, 111
Boultbee, Edith Cecilia Marianne (wife of Alexander Reginald Wakefield Richardson), 160
Boyne Spinning and Weaving Co., Ltd., 230
Boyne, River, 36
Bradshaw, Elizabeth (wife of George Crawford), 30
Braidwater Mill, 234
Braidwater Spinning Company, Ballymena, 85
Brett, Sir Charles, 81, 82, 164, 165, 175–6, 218, 220
British Library National Sound Archive, 145
Brooke, Basil George, 229, 230
Brookfield House, Banbridge, 50, 65, 84, 85, 88–9, 90, 91, 97
Brookfield Linen Weaving Factory, 88
Brookfield Spinning Co., Ltd., 178, 181, 194–5
Brown & Adam, 235
Brown, James J., 188
Brown, James Nicholson, 188–9
Brown, Robert, 234
Bryson, George Herbert (son of John Bell Bryson), 198–9
Bryson, James, 194
Bryson, John Bell, 149p, 194, 196, 198, 199p, 203
Bryson, Rosemary B. (née Sinton), 144
Bryson, Spence, 71

Cadbury, George (father of Marion Janet Cadbury), 207
Cadbury, Marion Janet (wife of William Edward Greeves), 207, 231
Callan Valley Mills Ltd., 217, 219
Campbell, Dr John, 26
Carswell, Nathaniel, 116
Carter, Arabella (wife of Thomas B. Johnston), 182, 183p, 184
Carter, William, 234
Castle Espie, 16
Castlecaulfield House, Castlecaulfield, 246–8
Castleisland Linen Co., 209
Caulfield, Sir Toby *see* Lord Charlemont
Charlemont, Lord, 153, 161, 246, 247
Christy, Alexander, 155, 156
Christy, Hannah (wife of Joseph Wakefield), 156
Christy, James, 130, 149
Christy, John, 109, 149
Christy, Joseph, 149
Christy, Margaret (mother of Margaret Dawson), 105
Christy, Mary (wife of Abraham Bell), 149
Christy, Thomas, 109, 121, 122, 134, 156
Churchill, Winston, 125
Clarke, R.S.J., 102
Clarke, Walter, 81
Cleaver, John, 53
Clendinning & Co., Ltd., James H., 179, 185
Clendinning, James, 179
Clibborn & Co., 52
Clibborn, Edward C., 52
Clibborn, James, 52
Clibborn, Thomas, 52–3

Clonaslee, Banbridge, 63–4
Cohannon House, 224
Collen, Louisa (wife of David Graham Shillington), 206
Compton Ltd., John, 217, 219, 221
Compton, George (son of John Compton), 219
Compton, Jane Mary (wife of Captain Noel Smith), 219
Compton, John, 218, 219
Conway, Sir Fulke, 152
Coose Vale *see* Glenbanna House
Coote, Thomas, 217
Corbet Lough, Tullyconnaught, 23
Corcrain House, Portadown, 190–91
Corcrain Villa, 188
Corry, Isaac, 161
Corry, James, 23
Corrywood *see also* Woodlawn, 16, 17
County Down Education Authority, 62
County Down Staghounds, 78, 107, 112
County Education Committee (Armagh), 82–3
Courtaulds Ltd., 235
Cowdy & Sons, Anthony, 107
Cowdy & Sons, Ltd., Anthony, 55, 73, 76, 78
Cowdy & Sons, William, 71, 194
Cowdy, Alfred, 73,
Cowdy, Anthony (son of Anthony Cowdy Sr.), 71, 73, 76
Cowdy, Anthony (son of John Cowdy), 71, 81, 82
Cowdy, Charlie, 73, 76
Cowdy, Edward, 73, 76, 81, 82, 83p
Cowdy, F. Charles, 76, 78
Cowdy, Hilda, 78p
Cowdy, Jack, 73, 76, 78, 80
Cowdy, John , 71
Cowdy, John B., 55
Cowdy, John R., 80
Cowdy, Lloyd, 76, 80
Cowdy, Tony, 73
Cowdy, William (son of Anthony Cowdy Sr.), 71
Cowdy, William Laird, 71
Craig, Mary (wife of James W. Murland), 5, 14
Craig, Samuel of Carricknabb (father of Margaret Craig), 14
Craigavad House, 39
Craigavon Development Commission, 110
'Crawford and Lindsay', 37, 41, 45
Crawford, Catherine (second daughter of George Crawford), 30, 36, 39, 41
Crawford, George (son of Gilbert Crawford), 30, 36
Crawford, Gilbert, 29
Crawford, Margaret (daughter of George Crawford), 30, 71, 75, 102
Crawford, Thomas, 30
Crawford, W.H., 168, 236
Crawford, Walter, 30
Cromwellian Grant , 71
Crowe, Dr. W. Haughton, 30, 32, 52, 58, 65
Crowe, Mrs W. Haughton, 31p, 32
Crozier, John (father of William Crozier), 134
Crozier, John (son of William Crozier), 134
Crozier, Samuel (son of William Crozier), 134
Crozier, William, 134
Crozier, William Jr. (son of William Crozier), 134

Daisy Hill Nurseries, 69
Darley, George, 121, 122

INDEX

Davies, Crossfield (son of J.H. Davies), 95
Davies, John Henry, 95
Dawson, Bobby, 107
Dawson, Margaret (wife of Henry Uprichard), 105, 110
Dawson, Thomas, 190p, 191
Dawson, Thomas (father of Margaret Dawson), 105
Dawson, William, 130, 131, 149
De Salis, Count, 212
Dean, J.A.K., 11, 17, 82, 104, 112, 116, 123, 142, 146, 154, 161–2, 172, 216, 223, 239
Demesne, The, Lurgan, 182–3, 184
Derry Lodge, Lurgan, 175–6
Dickson Ferguson & Co., 56, 126, 132
Dickson, Andrew John (father of Jessie Mary Dickson), 63, 130
Dickson, Anna (wife of William Smyth), 91, 94
Dickson, Benjamin, 56, 61, 95, 126, 129, 131–2
Dickson, James, 56, 61, 94–5, 97, 125, 126, 129, 131–2, 229, 230, 231
Dickson, James Alexander, 237
Dickson, Jessie Mary (wife of Norman Dickson Ferguson), 63, 64p
Dickson, Norman (son of Thomas Dickson), 231
Dickson, T.C. Harold (son of James Dickson), 231
Dickson, Thomas, 92, 103, 231
Dickson, Thomas A. (husband of Rosemary Greeves), 207, 229–30
Dickson, Thomas Alexander (son of T.C. Harold Dickson), 231
Dickson, Tillie & Co., Messrs, 230
Dicksons & Co. (Dungannon) Ltd., 207, 230, 231
Dixon, Hugh, 142
Dobbin, Clotworthy, 11
Dobbin, Jane (eldest daughter of Clotworthy Dobbin), 11, 19
Dobbs, Arthur, 236
Down County Council, 64
Down County Education Committee, 13
Druitt, Joseph, 190
Drumee House, 15
Drumlyn House, Moyallon, 159–60
Duff, William, 164
Dunbar McMaster & Co., Ltd., 97, 105, 111, 123, 125, 126, 129, 131
Dunbar Memorial School, Banbridge, 97
Dunbar, Dickson & Co., 56, 95, 98p, 125, 130
Dunbar, Hugh, 56, 96–7, 123, 125, 126, 168
Dunbar, Hugh (grandson of Hugh Dunbar), 96
Dunbar, Jane (sister of Hugh Dunbar), 97
Dunbar, Thompson & Co., 125
Dunbarton House, Gilford, 123–6, 149
Dundrum harbour, 6–7
Dungannon Park, 230, 234
Dunida House, Banbridge, 78, 79–80
Durham Street Weaving Company, 7
Dutton Hall, 19

East Downshire Steamship Company, 6–7
Eden Hall, Portadown, 138p
Edenderry House, Banbridge, 7, 61–2, 68
Edenderry House, Portadown, 192–3
Edenderry Linen Factory, 61
Edenderry Lodge, Banbridge, 77–8, 80
Edenderry Spinning Company, 195
Edenderry Works, Banbridge', 56, 64
Eitel, Max, 234
Elmfield Castle, Gilford, 61, 106, 107, 114, 130–32, 147, 149

Eves, Georgina Fredericka (wife of Owden Valentine Greeves), 203
Eyre, Edward, 222, 223

Fairacre, Portadown, 204–5
Fairview, Tannaghmore, Lurgan, 106, 110
Fallowfield, Lurgan, 180–82, 184
Falls, John, 229, 237
Falls, William (son of John Falls), 229
Fenell, Rachel (née Malcomson), 119
Fenton, Sarah (daughter of William Fenton), 19
Fenton, William, 19
Fenton's Bank, Rochdale, 19
Ferguson & Co., Ltd., Thomas, 56, 57, 59, 61, 64, 65, 68, 126
Ferguson, Geraldine (daughter of Thomas Ferguson), 66
Ferguson, Howard (son of Thomas Ferguson), 46p, 57, 58, 62, 64, 65, 68, 107p
Ferguson, James Dickson (son of Norman Ferguson), 57, 58, 62, 64, 68
Ferguson, Janie (daughter of Thomas Ferguson), 66
Ferguson, Jim, 68
Ferguson, John (father of Thomas Ferguson), 56
Ferguson, N.G.D., 58
Ferguson, Norman (son of Thomas Ferguson), 57, 58, 62, 63, 64, 65
Ferguson, S.M., 58
Ferguson, Sarah (daughter of Thomas Ferguson), 7, 10
Ferguson, Stanley, 57
Ferguson, Stanley (son of Stanley Ferguson), 57, 58
Ferguson, Stanley Carr, 69
Ferguson, Thomas, 56, 61, 64, 65, 66, 126, 132, 134
Ferguson, Thomas (son of Norman Ferguson), 57, 58, 64
Ferguson, Thomas, Esq. JP, 7, 12
Ferguson's Castle see Edenderry House
Ferguson's Irish Linen, 59, 71
Fernshaw, Dungannon, 243–5
Finney, J.E., 234
First World War, 12, 19, 73, 85, 86, 89, 107, 112, 124, 125, 192, 196, 207, 230, 231
Forster Green & Co., 106, 112
Forth River Mills, 237, 245,
Fothergill, Joan (daughter of Owden Valentine Greeves), 203
Franklin & Son (NI) Ltd., William, 59

Gallagher & Johnston Allen Ltd., 178
Gilford Castle, 61, 122, 128–9, 130, 131
Gilford Mill, 56, 149
Glass, Robert, 194
Glen, Isobel (second wife of Daniel Mulligan), 26
Glenanne House, Glenanne, 220–21
Glenbanna House (Coose Vale), Lawrencetown, 102, 104
Gleneden, Portadown, 196–7, 198
Glenmore Bleach Works, 153
Goffinet, Francois, 131
Gordon, Ernie, 64
Gordon, Jean (wife of Jim Ferguson), 68
Gordon, Malcolm (father of Jean Gordon), 68
Graham, Mary Jane (wife of Thomas Primus Shillington), 203
Gray & Sons, Messrs George, 221
Gray, George, 221
Gray, Joseph, 221
Gray, William B., 221

255

Great Exhibition, 52
Great Northern Railway Company, 117, 200
Great War *see* First World War
Green Vale, 6, 18
Green, Emily (wife of Henry Albert Uprichard), 106, 114, 132
Green, Forster, 106, 107, 114, 132
Green, Professor E.R.R., 31p, 41, 73, 168–9
Greenhall, Loughgall, 76, 82
Greenmount & Boyne Linen Company, 73
Greenvale House, Castlewellan, 18–19
Greer, Eliza, 116
Greer, Frederick (son of Thomas Greer of Tullylagan), 242
Greer, George (son of Henry Greer), 240
Greer, Henry, 236, 240
Greer, James (of Stangmore), 240
Greer, James (son of Henry Greer), 236
Greer, John, 45
Greer, John of The Grange (grandson of Henry Greer), 236, 237
Greer, John (of Grace Hall), 236
Greer, Lucy Matilda (wife of George Greer), 240
Greer, Sarah (wife of Thomas Greer of Rhone Hill), 240
Greer, Thomas (of Rhone Hill), 240
Greer, Thomas (son of John Greer), 236
Greer, Thomas 2 (son of Thomas Greer of Rhone Hill), 240, 241
Greer, Thomas 3 (son of Thomas Greer 2), 240, 241
Greer, Thomas Fergus (son of William Jackson Greer), 240
Greer, Thomas MacGregor, 242
Greer, William Jackson (son of Thomas Greer 2), 240
Greeves & Co., J. & T.M., 237, 243, 245
Greeves Ltd., J. & T.M., 200, 237, 245
Greeves, Bertha J., 200p
Greeves, David R.J. (son of Thomas Jackson Greeves), 201, 205
Greeves, Edmund Owden (son of Owden Valentine Greeves), 201, 203
Greeves, George Malcomson (son of William Edward Greeves), 201, 207
Greeves, Gilbert R.J. (son of Thomas Jackson Greeves), 200p, 201, 205
Greeves, Gilbertina Newsom (wife of Thomas Jackson Greeves), 200p, 204, 205
Greeves, John, 200, 243–4
Greeves, John (son of Thomas and Rachel Greeves), 245
Greeves, Joseph Malcomson, 200, 236p, 244p
Greeves, Lieutenant Colonel J.R.H., 243
Greeves, Owden Valentine (son of John Greeves), 200, 201, 203, 207, 237
Greeves, Rachel (née Malcomson), 245
Greeves, Rosemary Cadbury (daughter of William Edward Greeves), 207, 231
Greeves, Thomas (husband of Rachel Malcomson), 244–5
Greeves, Thomas Jackson (son of John Greeves), 200, 201, 204, 207, 237
Greeves, Thomas Malcomson, 200
Greeves, Thomas Malcomson (son of Thomas and Rachel Greeves), 245
Greeves, Wilfred J., 200p
Greeves, William (né Greer, grandson of Robert Greer), 237
Greeves, William Edward (son of Joseph Malcomson Greeves), 200, 201, 207, 231, 237
Greg, Cunningham, 244
Grier (Greer), John, 237
Grier (Greer), Robert (of Redford), 237, 240
Grier (Greer), Thomas Jr., 237

Grier (Greer), William, 237
Grier Greer), Thomas, 237, 242
Grubb, Anna (wife of James Nicholson Richardson 1), 152
Grubb, Helena (wife of John Grubb Richardson), 155p

Hadden, Prof David, 179p
Haldane, William Frazer, 216
Halliday, Mary (wife of John Bell Bryson), 198
Hamilton, H., 115
Hanna, James A., 180
Hatrick, H.C., 31p
Haughton & Co., Benjamin, 118
Haughton, Anna (wife of John Smyth Jr.), 91
Haughton, Benjamin, 118, 119, 130
Haughton, Thomas, 122
Hawthorne, Ann (wife of Robert Matier), 77, 78
Haydock, Frances (wife of William John Turtle), 212, 213p
Haydock, Jane (wife of Samuel Alexander Bell), 172
Hayes & Company, F.W., 79
Hayes & Sons, William, 71
Hayes, Elizabeth (daughter of Richard Hayes), 75
Hayes, Frederick William, 79
Hayes, Jane (wife of Samuel Law), 102
Hayes, Richard, 73, 75
Hayes, William (husband of Margaret Crawford), 30, 71, 73, 75, 79, 102
Hazelbank Weaving Company Ltd., 92, 103, 104, 231
Hazelbank, Lawrencetown, 102–3, 104
Herdmans Ltd., 193, 195, 245
Hincks, William, 1p, 21p, 22, 35p, 49p, 151p, 227
Hobart, Henry, 25, 65, 77, 79, 182, 206
Hogg Group, John, 7
Hogg, Ruth (wife of John Richardson), 152
Hogg, William (father of Ruth Hogg), 152
Horner, J., 165
Houston, Francis, 222
Hudson, William, 41, 45
Hughes, Robert, 141–2
Huntly Glen, 96, 97
Huntly House, Banbridge, 88, 96–7, 123, 124, 125, 168
Hutchinson, W.R., 234, 240
Hyndman, Emily (daughter of Robert Hyndman), 16
Hyndman, Robert of Holywood, 16

Irish Bleachers' Association Ltd., 95,
  Irish Bleachers' Association Redundancy Schemes 86
Irish Linen Board *see* Linen Board
Iveagh Harriers, 58, 78, 107, 112
Iveagh House, Banbridge, 65–6

Jackson, Bill, 116–17, 149, 169, 174
Jackson, James Eyre, 223
Jackson, Sarah (first wife of William Uprichard), 106
Jackson, Thomas, 222, 223
Jackson, Thomas (architect), 50, 88, 90, 91, 96, 123, 134, 135, 154, 161, 175, 242
Jaffé, Daniel, 118
Jennymount Mills, 7
Johnston & Co., Ltd., Philip, 7
Johnston & Co., Ltd., Arthur, 179
Johnston, Acheson (son of Thomas B. Johnston), 183

INDEX

Johnston, Allen & Co. Ltd., 177, 178, 180, 181, 183, 185, 194–5
Johnston, Arthur (son of James Johnston), 177p, 179, 184–5
Johnston, David, 179p
Johnston, Eleanor (daughter of Arthur Johnston), 184
Johnston, Errol, 225
Johnston, George, 179p
Johnston, Harry (son of Rev. Dr Johnston), 56
Johnston, J.J., 179p
Johnston, James, 177, 178, 179, 180, 185
Johnston, James E. (son of Sir John Johnston), 181
Johnston, Jim (son of James Johnston), 177p
Johnston, Joe (son of James Johnston), 177p, 183
Johnston, John (son of James Johnston), 178
Johnston, John (son of Thomas B. Johnston), 183
Johnston, Joseph (son of Arthur Johnston), 184
Johnston, Joseph Allen (son of Arthur Johnston), 149p, 179, 185
Johnston, Joseph Julian James (son of Thomas B. Johnston), 183
Johnston, Margaret (daughter of Arthur Johnston), 184
Johnston, Margaret (wife of W.F.B. Baird), 178
Johnston, Michael, 179p
Johnston, Rev. Dr, 56
Johnston, Sir John, 180, 181, 184
Johnston, Sir Richard, 121–2, 128
Johnston, Sir William, 128
Johnston, Thomas B. (son of James Johnston), 178, 180, 182, 183p, 184
Johnston, Thomas Carter (son Thomas B. Johnston), 183
Johnston, William (son of Rev. Dr Johnston), 56, 128
Jones, Mary Gregory (wife of Hugh Watson Jr.), 138
Joy, Robert (husband of Elizabeth Hayes), 75
Joy, Robert QC (father of Robert Joy), 75
Jupp, Belinda, 81–2, 223

Kane, Nancy (wife of Willie Uprichard), 107
Kay, James (of Preston), 5
Kendrew, John (Darlington), 4
Kennedy, Colonel Gilbert, 147
Kennedy, John (6th earl of Cassilis), 147
Kennedy, M. Allison (wife of George Philip Bell), 174
Kennedy, Rev. Gilbert (son of Colonel Gilbert Kennedy), 147
Kennedy, Thomas (son of Rev. Gilbert Kennedy), 147
Kigan, William, 82
Killycomain House, Portadown, 71
Kinley, Washington, 242
Kirkpatrick Brothers, Ballyclare, 107
Knox, Thomas *see* Lord Ranfurly

Lakeview, Lurgan, 135–6
Lamont & Sons Ltd., Samuel, 27, 57
Lamont Holdings, 235
Lamont, Edward, 27
Lanyon, Sir Charles, 39
Larmor, Graham Sir, 7, 12, 13, 15
Larmor, Peter, 15, 149p
Law, Hugh, 149
Law, John, 102
Law, Joseph, 104
Law, Samuel, 102, 103, 104, 168
Lawlor, H.C., 92, 96
Lawrence, Colonel Thomas Dawson, 113
Lawrence, Henry, 113

Lawrence, Rt. Hon. Henry, 113
Lawrencetown House, Gilford, 106, 107, 113–14, 132
Lee, James, 234
Lee, Kathleen Sweinton (née McMaster), 127p
Lefroy, Dean Jeffry, 67, 68
Lefroy, Rt. Hon. Thomas, 67
Lenaderg House, Lenaderg, 94–5
Lewis, Samuel, 8, 94, 115, 220, 242, 247
Liddell, Sir R., 46p
Lindsay, David, 36, 37, 39
Lindsay, David (son of David Lindsay), 36, 39, 43
Lindsay, David (son of Maurice Lindsay), 43
Lindsay, George Crawford (son of John Lindsay), 37, 41
Lindsay, J. Crawford, 37
Lindsay, John (husband of Catherine Crawford), 30, 36, 39, 41
Lindsay, John (son of David Lindsay), 36, 37, 39
Lindsay, Maurice (son of David Lindsay), 37
Lindsay, Maurice (son of Maurice Lindsay), 37, 43
Lindsay, Walter (of Tullyhenan House), 36, 46
Linen Board, 5, 102, 118, 165
  Linen Board Report, 23
Linen Hill, Katesbridge, 22
Linen Industry Research Association, 78, 189
Linen Thread Co., Ltd., 126
Linn, Richard, 23, 28
'Living Linen', 224
Logan, R.A., 113, 126
Loopbridge Weaving Company, 194, 195
Lough Island Reavy, 23
Lowry, Alexander, 22
Lurgan Weaving Company Ltd., 170, 172, 176
Lurgan, Lord, 138, 173, 175
Lutton, Jane Anne, 196
Lutton, Samuel C., 194, 198, 209
Lynn, W.H., 142

MacGeagh, H.G., 176
Macoun, James, 170
Macoun, William, 170
Magill, Sir John, 134, 146–7
Malcomson & Co., William, 28
Malcomson, Andrew, 117
Malcomson, Bell and Company, Messrs, 117
Malcomson, David, 117
Malcomson, John, 237
Malcomson, Joseph, 117
Malcomson, Sophia (wife of James Nicholson Richardson), 165
Malcomson, Thomas, 237
Malcomson, William (father of Sophia Malcomson), 165
Malone, Sarah Maria (second wife of William Uprichard), 106
Manchester, Duke of, 204
Manor House School, Armagh, 15, 217
Manor House, Milford (Milford House), 214–17
'Marketbook of Thomas Greer, The', 236
Marshall, John (of Leeds), 4
Martin, Andrew of Inch, 15
Martin, Anne (daughter of Andrew Martin), 14–15
Masaroon, W.R., 126
Matchett, Beatrice (wife of Arthur Johnston), 184
Matier & Co., Henry, 77, 194
Matier, Anna (daughter of Robert Matier), 77, 78
Matier, Henry, 56, 77

257

Matier, John (son of Robert Matier), 77, 78
Matier, Robert, 77
Matier, Robert (son of Robert Matier), 77, 78
Moyallon Vitriol Company, 149
McAuley, David, 116
McCall, Charles H., 79, 80
McCall, Hugh, 80
McClelland, Anna (daughter of Robert McClelland), 50, 85, 90, 91p
McClelland, Robert, 50, 90
McCormack, Rev. Joseph, 67
McCreight, Andrew, 147
McCrum & Co., Messrs, 217
McCrum Watson & Mercer, 217, 219
McCrum, Robert Garmany (son of William McCrum), 214, 215, 217
McCrum, William, 214, 215p
McCrum, William (son of Robert Garmany McCrum), 216, 217
McDonald, John R. (husband of Mary Augusta Orr), 224
McDonald, Mary Augusta (née Orr, daughter of Joseph Orr), 224
McEvoy, John, 223, 237, 247
McGarigan, Michael, 59p
McManus, Joe, 215–16
McMaster, Arthur Vaerstrate, 127p
McMaster, Florence (née Saxton), 127p
McMaster, Hilda, 127p
McMaster, Hugh, 127p
McMaster, Hugh Dunbar, 126, 127p, 149
McMaster, John George, 149
McMaster, John Walsh, 97, 125, 126, 131–2
McNeill, Katherine (wife of William Anderson 'Jumbo' Smyth), 50, 51p
McWilliam, James, 28, 73, 75
Meeke, William, 115
Mercer, William, 217
Mill House, 110
Mill Park House, 107
Millbank House, Tullyconnaught, 24–5, 26
Millmount House, Banbridge, 30, 75–6, 78, 102
Milltown Bleach & Weaving Works, 90, 94, 95
Milltown Bleaching Co., Ltd., 178, 181, 194
Milltown House, Lenaderg, 50, 85, 88, 90–91, 92, 94, 95, 123, 124
Milner & Butler, 225
Miltown House, Dungannon, 228–31
Montgomery, Elizabeth (wife of Hamilton Robb), 193p
Montgomery, Hugh Lyons, 113
Montgomery, Thomas, 217
Monuments and Buildings Record, Northern Ireland, 142, 165
Moorlands, Banbridge, 36, 39, 41–2
Morton, Mary (wife of William Greeves, né Greer), 237
Mount Caulfield House, Bessbrook, 163, 164–5, 172
Mount Pleasant, Tullylish, 121–2
Moyallon House, Gilford, 154–6, 157, 160, 162
Moygashel Ltd., 85, 179, 234–5, 237
Muckamore Works, 73
Mulholland, Andrew, 40
Mullavilla House, Tandragee, 212–13
Mullen, William, 193
Mulligan, Charles, 24
Mulligan, Daniel, 26
Mulligan, George, 23, 28
Mulligan, Gilbert (eldest son of John Mulligan), 26
Mulligan, James Charles (son of Charles Mulligan), 24

Mulligan, John, 23, 26, 28
Mulligan, John Francis, 26
Munro, General, 36, 39
Murland, Beatrice (wife of James Murland), 12p
Murland, Captain C. Warren, 19
Murland, Charles (youngest son of James Murland), 6, 7, 10, 11, 12, 14p, 16, 19
Murland, Clotworthy Warren (son of Charles Murland), 7, 10, 12
Murland, Henry (son of James Murland), 8, 15
Murland, Howard Ferguson, 3p
Murland, James, 4, 5, 6, 7, 8, 12, 15
Murland, James W. (son of James Murland), 5p, 13p
Murland, James Warren (son of Clotworthy Warren Murland), 12, 13p
Murland, Ltd., James, 7, 12, 15
Murland, Mary (daughter of Samuel Murland), 16
Murland, Mick (James Robert William, son of James Murland), 12p
Murland, Robert (son of Samuel Murland), 16
Murland, Samuel (eldest son of James Murland), 16, 17
Murland, William, 5, 8, 14–15
Murland, William (son of James Murland), 8
Murland, William Henry (third son of Charles Murland), 19
Murlands Solicitors, Downpatrick, 5p
Murphy, David, 22
Murphy, James, 22

Neil and Partners, John, 13
Nettleton, J.A., 229
New Hamburgh, 240, 241
New Hamburgh Bleach Works, 240
Newhouse, Neville H., 236
Nicholson & Sons, Joseph, 165
Nicholson, Alexander Jaffrey, 134
Nicholson, Elizabeth (wife of Jonathan Richardson 2), 152
Nicholson, General John, 134
Nicholson, John (father of Thomas Nicholson), 118, 144
Nicholson, John, of Donacloney, 26–7
Nicholson, John, of Stramore, 120, 134
Nicholson, Joseph, 165, 243
Nicholson, Martha (daughter of John Nicholson), 26
Nicholson, Rawdon Hautenville (son of John Nicholson), 134
Nicholson, Robert Jaffrey (son of Thomas Nicholson), 118, 120, 144
Nicholson, Sarah (wife of Jonathan Richardson 3), 152
Nicholson, Thomas, 118, 144
Nicolson, Jimsie, 132p
Northern Bank, 217
Northern Ireland Hospital Authority, 217
Northern Ireland Spinners, 195

Old Drumlyn House, Portadown, 157–8
Orange Order, 136,
  Uprichard Memorial Orange Hall, Major, 112, 122
Ordnance Survey, 11, 54, 71, 97, 157, 173, 175, 182, 208, 214, 228, 239,
Ordnance Survey Memoirs, 8, 22, 23, 25, 29, 45, 50, 52, 71, 75, 102, 109, 110, 111, 115, 122, 125, 212, 241
Orr & Sons, Joseph, 223, 224
Orr, Dean W.R.M., 147
Orr, Jacob (son of Joseph Orr), 223–4
Orr, James (son of Joseph Orr), 224

INDEX

Orr, Joseph, 223, 224–5
Owden, John, 152

Parkmount, Tullyconnaught, 25, 26–7
Parliamentary Committee (1825), 5
Phillips, J.J., 218
Pigot, J & Co., 104, 229
Portadown College, 193
Portadown Weaving Company, 200, 201, 203, 204, 207, 231, 237
Porthouse, Thomas (Darlington), 4
Preston, Sir John, 56, 92
Preston, Smyth & Co., Linen Merchants, 92
Pringle, Annie M. (wife of F. Charles Cowdy), 76
Proctor, Frances Jenkinson (née Orr, daughter of Joseph Orr), 224
Proctor, James E. (husband of Frances Jenkinson Orr), 224
Proctor, Major George Norman (son of James E. Proctor), 224
Public Record Office of Northern Ireland, 240, 247
Provincial Bank, 37

Ramage, Laeta (wife of Major Robert Stevenson), 233, 234
Ranfurly, Lord, 229, 240
Rankin, Peter, 14, 16
Rathown, Portadown, 198–9
Ravarnette Weaving Company, 71
Rebellion of 1798, 120
Rees, Fred B., 13p
Reilly Estate, Scarva, 61
Reilly, John Esq., 71, 75
Reilly, John Temple, 56
Rhone Hill, Dungannon, 239–40
Richard, William (son of James Nicholson Richardson 1), 153
Richardson & Nevin, Lambeg Weaving Factory, 157
Richardson, Alexander Airth, 155, 157
Richardson, Alexander Reginald Wakefield (son of R.H. Stephens Richardson), 158, 160
Richardson, Anne (daughter of Mrs J.G. Richardson), 162,
Richardson, Edith (daughter of John Grubb Richardson), 155
Richardson, Ethel Joanne (wife of R.H. Stephens Richardson), 157, 160
Richardson, Helena (daughter of John Grubb Richardson), 155
Richardson, Hilda (wife of Thomas Wakefield Richardson), 155
Richardson, James Nicholson 1 (son of Jonathan Richardson 3), 116, 118, 152, 157
Richardson, James Nicholson 2 (son of James Nicholson Richardson 1), 152
Richardson, James Nicholson 3 (son of John Grubb Richardson), 155, 162, 164p, 165, 172
Richardson, Jane Marion (née Wakefield), 156
Richardson, John (son of Jonathan Richardson 2), 152
Richardson, John (son of Jonathan Richardson 3), 152, 157
Richardson, John Grubb (son of James Nicholson Richardson 1), 152, 153, 154, 157, 160, 162, 165
Richardson, John Stephen Wakefield (son of R.H. Stephens Richardson), 158, 160
Richardson, Jonathan 1 (son of Zachary Richardson), 152
Richardson, Jonathan 2 (son of Jonathan Richardson 1), 152
Richardson, Jonathan 3 (son of John Richardson), 152
Richardson, Jonathan 5 (son of James Nicholson Richardson 1), 152
Richardson, Joseph (son of James Nicholson Richardson 1), 153, 156
Richardson, Joseph (son of Jonathan Richardson 3), 134, 152

Richardson, Joshua Pim (son of James Nicholson Richardson 1), 153
Richardson, Kathleen (wife of Samuel Bell), 172
Richardson, Mrs J.G., 162
Richardson, R.H. Stephens (husband of Ethel Richardson), 155, 157, 158, 159, 160
Richardson, Rev. John, 152
Richardson, Sons & Owden, Ltd., J.N., 152, 153, 155, 160, 194
Richardson, Thomas (son of James Nicholson Richardson 1), 153
Richardson, Thomas Wakefield (son of John Grubb Richardson), 155
Richardson, Zachary, 152
Robb & Co., Ltd., Hamilton, 193
Robb, Hamilton (grandson of John Robb), 192, 193, 194
Robb, Hamilton Jr. (son of Hamilton Robb), 192, 193p
Robb, Hannah (second wife of Thomas Dawson), 191p
Robb, Harford (son of Hamilton Robb), 192
Robb, John, 192
Robinson & Cleaver Ltd., 53, 54
Robinson, John, 53, 54
Robinson, William, 54
Rockville, Banbridge, 54–5
Rogers, G.M., 102
Roome, W.J.W., 159
Roselawn, Ballydown, 28
Rowan, Alistair, 239, 246–7
'Royal Irish Linen Threads', 79
Running, Lucinda (wife of Brice Smyth 4), 85

Saunders, Henry, 127p,
Saunders, Lucy (née Saxton), 127p
Scottish Provident Building, Belfast, 92
Second World War, 7, 57, 68, 73, 85, 95, 107, 125, 139, 153, 165, 179, 183, 221, 234, 237,
    flax production during, 7
Shaw, William, 247
Sherry, Charles, 141–2
Shillington, Averell (son of Thomas Shillington), 208, 209
Shillington, David Graham, 206–7
Shillington, Rt. Hon. Thomas (son of Averell Shillington), 209
Shillington, Thomas, 202, 208
Shillington, Thomas Averell (son of Rt. Hon. Thomas Shillington), 203, 209
Shillington, Thomas Primus (grandson of Thomas Shillington), 203
Simpson, Colonel Thomas, 141
Simpson, Janet Graham (wife of Frederick Maynard Simpson), 149
Simpson, Margaret (wife of Thomas Simpson), 141
Simpson, Thomas, 141
Sinton & Co., Ltd., Thomas, 139, 224
Sinton, Arthur (son of Thomas Sinton), 139
Sinton, Brigid (daughter of Maynard Sinton), 138, 143
Sinton, David H., 139, 194
Sinton, Diana, 132p
Sinton, Diana (daughter of Frederick Maynard Sinton), 149
Sinton, Frederick Buckby (son of Thomas Sinton), 118, 120, 138, 144, 145
Sinton, Frederick Maynard (son Frederick Buckby Sinton), 144, 149
Sinton, Margaret (née Christy), 149, 243–4
Sinton, Maynard (son of Thomas Sinton), 139, 142p
Sinton, Maynard Jr. (son of Maynard Sinton), 139, 142
Sinton, T.F.M., 149p
Sinton, Thomas (son of David Sinton), 139, 144

Sinton, Thomas (son of Thomas Sinton), 139
Sinton, Tim (son of Frederick Maynard Sinton), 132p, 149, 224
Slater's Directory of Ireland, 139, 169
Smith, Alan Knighton, 219
Smith, Captain Noel S., 217, 218, 219, 221
Smith, F.W., 209
Smith, John, 247
Smyth & Co., William, 84p, 85–6, 91, 95
Smyth & Sons, Brice, 84, 85, 88, 89, 90
Smyth Katherine (wife of Douglas Smyth), 91
Smyth, Andrew (son of Brice Smyth), 84
Smyth, Brice, 56, 77, 84
Smyth, Brice 2 (son of Brice Smyth), 84, 88, 92
Smyth, Brice 3 (son of Brice Smyth 2), 84, 88, 90, 92, 97
Smyth, Brice 4 (son of Brice Smyth 3), 84, 85, 88, 89, 90
Smyth, Brice 5 (son of Brice Smyth 4), 85
Smyth, Brice 6 (son of William Anderson Smyth), 85
Smyth, D. Wilson, 85
Smyth, D. Wilson, 46p, 97
Smyth, Douglas (grandson of John Smyth Sr.), 91
Smyth, Edward Fitzgerald 'Teddy' (son of D. Wilson Smyth), 85, 89p
Smyth, Evelyn ('Eva', daughter of William Smyth), 65
Smyth, Henry, 92
Smyth, James (son of Brice Smyth), 84
Smyth, James Davis (son of John Smyth and Anna McClelland), 85, 90
Smyth, John (son of Brice Smyth 3), 50, 84, 85, 88, 90, 91, 92, 94
Smyth, John Jr. (son of John Smyth and Anna McClelland), 85, 90, 91, 95
Smyth, Moira (daughter of D. Wilson Smyth), 97p
Smyth, Robert (son of Brice Smyth 3), 84, 88, 92
Smyth, Vera (daughter of D. Wilson Smyth), 97p
Smyth, Weir & Co., 92
Smyth, William (eldest son of William Smyth), 51, 65
Smyth, William (son of Brice Smyth 4), 85, 89
Smyth, William (son of D. Wilson Smyth), 85, 97p
Smyth, William (son of John Smyth and Anna McClelland), 85, 90, 91, 94, 95
Smyth, William Anderson (Jumbo), 50, 51p, 85
Smyth, William Anderson (son of William Smyth), 85, 89
Smyth's Weaving Co., Ltd., 85, 89, 234
Solitude House, Banbridge, 52–3
Solitude, Lurgan, 173–4
'Soothing Glass', 13p
South Eastern Education and Library Board, 13, 180
Southern Health and Social Care Trust, 111
Spence Bryson & Co., Ltd., 194, 195, 198, 199
Spence, Thomas Everard (son of Thomas Henry Spence), 199
Spence, Thomas Henry, 194, 196–7, 198, 199
Spence, William (Glasgow), 61, 129, 130, 131
Spotten, William, 126
Springvale Bleach Works, 105–6, 107, 110, 113, 132
Stauros Foundation, 143
Steele, James, 6, 8, 18
Steiner, Rudolph, 215
Stephenson, Harry F., 233, 234
Sterling, Agnes (wife of Brice Smyth 3), 84, 88
Stevenson & Sons Ltd. (Dungannon), 85, 234, 237
Stevenson, Major Robert, 233, 234, 235p
Stevenson, Robert, 234
Stevenson, Robert, (grandson of Robert Stevenson), 234
Stevenson, William, 234

Stewart, A.J.R., 114
Stewart, Alexander Robert, 115
Stewart, W.A., 125
Stewart-Liberty, Susan, 55
Stoney, Isaac, 122
Stormont Castle, 40
Stramore House, Gilford, 133–4, 137, 144
Stuart, George, 71
Summer Island, Loughgall, 81–3

Tamnamore House, County Armagh, 139
Tate, Dawson Jr., 188
Tavanagh House, Portadown, 202–03, 208
Taylor, Beatrice (second wife of Henry Albert Uprichard), 106
Temple, Lily (née Brooke), 127p
Thomspon, Robert, 125
Trench, Helena (daughter of Rev. Frederick Stewart Trench), 67
Trench, Lady Helena (wife of Rev. Frederick Stewart Trench), 67
Trench, Rev. Frederick Stewart (husband of Helena Trench), 67
Trinity College Dublin, 138
Tullydowey House, Blackwatertown, 222–5
Tullyhenan House, Banbridge, 37, 39–40
Tullylagan Manor, Cookstown, 241–2
Tullylish Cricket Ground, 120
Tullylish House, Gilford, 106, 115–17
Tullylish Presbyterian Church, 56, 58
Turner, Thomas, 11, 39–40
Turtle Brothers Inc., 212, 213
Turtle, Henry Francis (son of William John Turtle), 212
Turtle, Herbert Samuel (son of William John Turtle), 212
Turtle, James (son of William John Turtle), 212
Turtle, Joseph F., 213p
Turtle, Norman F. (son of William Haydock Turtle), 213
Turtle, W. Herbert (son of William Haydock Turtle), 213
Turtle, William Haydock, 212
Turtle, William John, 212, 213p

Ulster Architectural Heritage Society, 11, 14, 16, 51, 146, 157, 175, 202, 228, 246
Ulster Bank, 57
Ulster Carpet Company, 209
Ulster Volunteer Force, 112, 124
  Ulster Volunteer Force Nursing Corps, 124, 125p
Ulster Weavers (part of John Hogg Group), 7, 235
Ulster Weaving Co., Ltd., 7, 12, 15
Umgola House, Armagh, 218–19
Umgola Weaving Factory, 218, 219, 221
United Irishmen, 22
Uprichard, Albert, 132p
Uprichard, Anna Maria (daughter of William Uprichard), 106
Uprichard, Anna Maria (sister of William Uprichard), 106, 116
Uprichard, Beatrice Eileen (daughter of Henry Albert Uprichard), 106
Uprichard, Elizabeth (daughnter of William Uprichard), 106
Uprichard, Ellen Malone (daughter of William Uprichard), 106
Uprichard, Emile Llewellyn (son of Henry Albert Uprichard), 106
Uprichard, Forster (son of Henry Albert Uprichard), 106, 107, 114
Uprichard, Grace, 132p
Uprichard, Henry, 105, 106, 107, 110
Uprichard, Henry Albert (son of Henry Albert Uprichard), 106, 107, 111, 112, 132

INDEX

Uprichard, Henry Albert (son of William Uprichard), 106, 107, 114
Uprichard, Henry James (son of James Uprichard), 106, 110
Uprichard, J.T. & H., 105p, 105, 108p
Uprichard, James, 105, 106, 111, 130
Uprichard, James (son of William Uprichard), 106
Uprichard, Kane, 132p
Uprichard, Major Albert, 124
Uprichard, Penelope, 132p
Uprichard, Susanna (daughter of William Uprichard), 106
Uprichard, Thomas, 105, 106, 110, 111
Uprichard, William, 106, 111
Uprichard, 'Willie' (son of Henry Albert Uprichard), 106, 107, 132
Uprichard, Richard Rutledge Kane 'Rut', 107, 132
Ussher, William-Mina, 241

Valuation Books, 111, 131, 147, 175, 208, 203, 208, 209, 240, 247
Vance, Arthur, 229
Vernons College, 143
Victoria Steeplechase, Manchester, 13p
Victoria, College, Belfast, 77–8
Virginia Creeper, 28, 44

Waite, William, 176
Wakefield, Isabella (wife of John Nicholson), 134
Wakefield, Jane Marion (second wife of John Grubb Richardson), 155, 157
Wakefield, Joseph, 114, 156
Wakefield, Pratt & Meirs, 240
Wakefield, Thomas Christy (son of Joseph Wakefield), 156
Wakefield, Thomas Christy Jr. (son of Thomas Christy Wakefield), 156
Walker & Co., Messrs William, 53
Walker, William, 53, 103, 104, 231
Wall Street Crash, 217
Walpole, Hilda (wife of Edwin George Bell), 174
Warrain Country Club, Melbourne, 69
Warrain, Banbridge, 69–70
Warren, Jean Adair, 167p
Watson & Sons, Robert, 135, 136, 137
Watson (Lurgan) Ltd., Robert, 136
Watson, Armstrong & Co., 134, 137–8
Watson, C.S. Waller, 46p, 134
Watson, Francis (son of Robert Watson), 135–6

Watson, Harry P., 134
Watson, Hugh (son of Robert Watson), 134, 137, 138
Watson, Hugh Jr. (son of Hugh Watson), 138
Watson, Ivan V.W. (son of Waller Watson), 134
Watson, James, 138p
Watson, Joseph, 136
Watson, Robert, 117, 135–6
Watson, Robert (son of Hugh Watson), 138
Watson, Thomas (son of Francis Watson), 136
Watson, Wesley, 217
Watson, William, 136
Waugh, William, 53
Webb, Arabella, 213p
Weir, Henry, 92
Weir, Thomas, 94
Whyte, Charles, 96
Whyte, Robert (son of Charles Whyte), 96
Wilcocks, John, 247
William III, 36, 96
Williams, Edith (née Richardson, daughter of Mrs J.G. Richardson), 162
Wilson, Jane Robinson (second wife of William Anderson Smyth), 85, 89
Wilson, Joseph, 175, 176
Wilson, Margaret (wife of Joseph Wilson), 176
Wolfson, Isaac, 195
Wood Lodge, Castlewellan, 5–6, 8, 14–15, 16
Woodbank, Gilford, 131, 146–50
Woodhouse, The, Bessbrook, 161–3
Woodlawn, Castlewellan, 16–17, 19
Woods, Edith Uprichard (first wife of Frederick Buckby Sinton), 144
Woods, Frederick (husband of Anna Marie Uprichard), 106
Woods, Hanna Maria (second wife of Frederick Buckby Sinton), 144
Wright, James, 129
Wynne, Thomas, 218

York Street Flax Spinning Company, 73, 194, 212
Young & Mackenzie, 215

www.ingramcontent.com/pod-product-compliance
Lightning Source LLC
Chambersburg PA
CBHW081614100526
44590CB00021B/3437